Walking Tours of Historic Philadelphia

Also by John Francis Marion

Lucrezia Bori of the Metropolitan Opera
Philadelphia Medica
Famous and Curious Cemeteries
The Charleston Story
The Fine Old House
Within These Walls

Walking Tours
of
Historic
Philadelphia

John Francis Marion

 ISHI PUBLICATIONS
Institute for the Study of Human Issues
Philadelphia

Manufactured in the United States of America

Printing History

First published as *Bicentennial City: Walking Tours of Historic Philadelphia,* by the Pyne Press
First Printing, August 1974
Second Printing, April 1975
Third Printing, September 1975

Revised Edition as an ISHI Publications Paperback
First Printing, May 1984

Library of Congress Cataloging in Publication Data

Marion, John Francis.
  Walking tours of historic Philadelphia.

  (ISHI publications)
  Bibliography: p.
  Includes index.
  1. Philadelphia (Pa.)—Description—1981–   —Tours.
2. Philadelphia, (Pa.)—Buildings—Guide-books.   3. Historic buildings—Pennsylvania—Philadelphia—Guide-books.
4. Architecture—Pennsylvania—Philadelphia—Guide-books.
I. Title.   II. Series.
F158.18.M373   1984   917.48′110443   84-575
ISBN 0-89727-055-X

For information, write:

Director of Publications
ISHI
3401 Science Center
Philadelphia, PA 19104

Cover: garden of the Powel House
(photograph by Cortlandt V. D. Hubbard).

For Miriam Baum Milligan *con amore*

Sundial on Powel House

CONTENTS

City Hall from the Pennsylvania Academy of the Fine Arts

Acknowledgments

I am grateful to many Philadelphians for their help and encouragement with this book. The idea for it originated with Joseph and Madeline Fox, distinguished booksellers who love the city and its history. A chance remark of mine prompted Mary Capouya to see the possibilities and further convince me of them. Joseph E. and Ruth Branning Molloy, devoted Philadelphians, passionate historians, who are encyclopedic in their knowledge of books, people, customs and institutions, made valuable suggestions and answered innumerable questions. Every writer needs a confidant during the period of a book's gestation and its writing. I had Anne Einselen, novelist and for twenty years an editor on *The Ladies' Home Journal*. She read the manuscript in its various stages, commented wisely, and guided me.

Many on the staffs of Philadelphia institutions aided in various ways. Among them are: Whitfield J. Bell, Jr., Library of the American Philosophical Society; Victoria Byrne, Hill-Physick-Keith House; Margaret Collins, Atwater Kent Museum; Margaret K. Cortright, Philadelphia Museum of Art; David Crownover, University Museum; Clive E. Driver, Rosenbach Foundation; Margaret Gamble, University of Pennsylvania; Mary Lou Green, Philadelphia Convention and Visitors Bureau; Bessie L. Greenawalt, Philadelphia City Institute, Free Library of Philadelphia; Jerry Grundfest, Philadelphia '76, Inc.; Howell J. Heaney, Free Library of Philadelphia; Derry Hollingsworth, Franklin Institute; Sandra Horrocks, Philadelphia Museum of Art; John Kracker, Mütter Museum; Robert Looney, Free Library of Philadelphia; John Maass, City Representatives Office; Arthur T. Moore, Masonic Temple; Dorothy Palombi, The Philadelphia Contributionship; John D. R. Platt, National Park Service; Ann Preston, Drexel

x · *ACKNOWLEDGMENTS*

Museum Collection; Mary Nestler Reilly, St. Peter's Church; Richard Riddell, Free Library of Philadelphia; Murphy D. Smith, Library of the American Philosophical Society; Walter Smith, The Philadelphia Contributionship; Geraldine P. Staub, Drexel Museum Collection; Alois K. Strobl, Philadelphia City Planning Commission; Richard Talbot, Rosenbach Foundation; Margaret B. Tinkcom, Philadelphia Historical Commission; Lillian Tonkin, Library Company of Philadelphia; Neda M. Westlake, Van Pelt Library, University of Pennsylvania; Reeves Wetherill, John Wanamaker's; Dolores Ziff, Pennsylvania Hospital; and Doris Zimmermann, Library of the Federal Reserve Bank of Philadelphia.

Other private citizens answered puzzling questions or provided information not easily available elsewhere. I would like to thank: Léonie Bell, Mildred Dillon, Amelia Farr, Paul C. Harbeson, Earl R. James, Josephine G. Killhour, Eleanore Price Mather, Charles E. Peterson, Carolyn Pitts, Hannah Roach, David M. Robb, Frank E. Seymour, George Thomas, Mrs. Eastburn Thompson, Jr., and Eleanor Westcott.

"Mustang," Blackwell Court

Introduction

Philadelphia was called a "Green Countrie Towne" and also a "Holy Experiment" by William Penn. Since his time it has been called the "City of Brotherly Love," the "Quaker City" and the "Bicentennial City." It became three hundred years old in 1982. When the two-hundredth anniversary of Independence was celebrated in 1976, Philadelphia was the focus of attention throughout the United States and the world.

The events of 1776 were the most important in its history, but a part of Philadelphia's eternal charm and fascination is that a great deal of that history is unknown, forgotten or overlooked by the average wayfarer, though he may suspect it is there, waiting to be discovered.

One of the purposes of this book is to give the panorama of Philadelphia's history, the people who made it, where they lived and worked, and to exhibit the evidences of this historic past which linger despite the encroachments of the 20th century. Philadelphia is an anachronism, a city of contrasts. The modern commercial metropolis has grown and spread, yet the old remains.

Lewis Mumford pointed out that Philadelphia "contains more historic buildings than a similar acreage in any other American city, largely because so much history was made there between the meeting of the First Continental Congress and the removal of the capital to New York." Actually, long before the First Continental Congress (1774) and after the capital was removed to New York, then back to Philadelphia (1790), history was made here. The decade 1790 to 1800, one of the richest in our history, was a time of transition, of settling in. It was during these years that the Federal government and the infant Republic gained strength.

In 1809, while living with her friend Mrs. Swan at Mrs. Carson's at 351 Market Street, Sarah, Countess Rumford (1774–1852)—the New Hampshire lady who was the first American woman to be enobled by a foreign government—gave the highest praise to Philadelphia for its climate, the symmetry of its streets and the clean look of its buildings. In contrast she felt soot-begrimed London and St. Paul's looked as if they were made of black stone.

In addition to the 18th century buildings Lewis Mumford mentions, there are amenities about which Christopher Morley wrote: "Philadelphia, most liveable and lovable of large cities, makes a unique appeal to the meditative stroller." Those words were written more than a half-century ago. The same delights remain. Philadelphia is still a walker's paradise.

From the beginning Philadelphia was a planned city, one laid out on a gridiron, which accounts for the symmetry Countess Rumford admired. William Penn conceived it around a center square, with four other squares equidistant from the center, and the streets crossing at right angles. This may annoy some but it makes it simpler for the walker to find his way. The "Greene Countrie Towne" endures. It has tree-lined streets, green walks, private gardens, small squares, pocket parks and large public parks. The traveler in Philadelphia invariably remarks about the greenness of the city and its many trees.

Philadelphia has its own unique scale, which adds appeal. The tallest building is City Hall with the Alexander Milne Calder statue of William Penn on the tower. Because of sentiment, tradition and the dedication of the Art Commission, it is unlikely that any taller buildings will be erected. The concentration of skyscrapers is in Center City, but only a small section of it at that. The façades of the old city have a symmetry, a balance, a pattern, a rhythm. There may be a sameness at times, but even the sameness changes from section to section, area to area. In Germantown the houses are distinctly Germantown houses, recognizable as such; distinct, too, are those in Society Hill as opposed to those in University City or Rittenhouse Square.

When I undertook this book, Joseph Kury, a retired Philadelphia antiquarian bookseller, told me that I was embarking on "a voyage of discovery." He was correct. For even I, who have walked the city regularly for more than thirty-five years and investigated most of its nooks and crannies, rediscovered Philadelphia.

There is much that couldn't be included in a book of this size. Chestnut Hill, one of the most beautiful and distinctive sections of the city, was not left out purposely but because a walk in Chestnut Hill, as pleasurable as that is, is primarily an architectural walk. John Bartram's house and garden and the Edgar Allan Poe House are a goodly distance from the walks included. As fascinating as are the American-Swedish Historical Museum and Penn Treaty Park, where

Penn and the Indians met, they too are distant from sections of the city chosen for the walks.

Any book must have arbitrary guidelines. Here the considerations were history, architecture, myth, legend, folklore and anecdote. In these walks around Philadelphia I have tried to point out the historic houses and buildings, recount a little of the citizens who walked these streets before us and open the door to some of the glories of Philadelphia.

It is a wonderful city in which to live, as I have found from more than a quarter-century of residence. *Civilized*—with an appealing pattern of living, a city made up of a collection of small villages and towns where the past and the present meet as much as is possible in any large American city.

Ireland and Scotland share a Gaelic greeting—*Ceud Mille Fàilte* —which translated means "a hundred thousand welcomes." With these words, I hope you will enjoy the pleasures and treasures of the city while walking in Philadelphia.

John Francis Marion

Robert Horowitz

Independence Hall

The Most Historic Square Mile in the United States

The area around Independence Hall in Philadelphia has been called, rightly enough, the most historic square mile in the United States. Here are so many peerless buildings whose beauty has endured and grown with the years and whose historical associations recapitulate much of our early history and the founding of the Republic. In our own time historian Gerald W. Johnson has called Independence Hall "part and fabric of American history." It has always been an object of pilgrimage. Now it stands as a symbol of two hundred years of Independence.

The buildings on Independence Square itself have housed the Provincial Assembly, the Council, the Supreme Court, the Second Continental Congress, the Senate and the House of Representatives. Independence was declared here; the Articles of Confederation were drafted and ratified; the First Bank of the United States and the United States Mint were established; Vermont, Kentucky and Tennessee were admitted to the Union; Washington took the oath of office for his second term here and John Adams his as second president.

And not far away, Benjamin Franklin lived at Franklin Court; the American Philosophical Society, whose membership has been the most distinguished of any American institution, has held its meetings for almost two hundred years. The first and second Banks of the United States are nearby, as is Carpenters' Hall, the scene of the First Continental Congress.

When we consider that the Declaration of Independence and the Constitution—the documents upon which the United States is founded and which have inspired other democracies of the world—were written and adopted here, that our first five presidents were

1

involved in the life of Philadelphia and that of the infant republic while they lived here, and that the greatest American of the 18th century, Benjamin Franklin, was—when not abroad—engaged in every phase of Philadelphia activity, it is easy to understand why the area has been termed the most historic square mile in the nation.

The city of Philadelphia grew westward from the Delaware River, and when construction was started on Independence Hall in 1732, only fifty years after the founding of the city by William Penn, the area between 5th and 6th Streets was still on the edge of things. Some forty years later, when the events leading to 1776 were involving the citizenry, the city had grown west toward 8th Street. The streets were still unpaved in the thriving port city and at that time the square, or "State House Yard" as it was called in the 18th century, was not developed as we see it today. The city was unlighted, too, and except for an occasional lantern on a house or tavern, or one carried by the watch, all was in darkness after nightfall. On our walk throughout the gardens and greenwalks, the streets and alleys, in and out of the buildings of today's city we can sense what Philadelphia was like long ago and ultimately what the roots of American history are.

First Bank of the U. S.

For the best overall view of the area let us begin at the *First Bank of the United States,* 116 South 3rd Street, between Chestnut **1** and Walnut Streets.

This oldest bank in the United States was erected between 1795 and 1797 and was described not too many years ago as a "stately . . . building still standing in lonely grandeur." Since those words were written the National Park Service has begun to develop the area and the building's splendid setting we see today is the result. The building was occupied by the First Bank of the United States (founded 1791) until 1811 when its charter lapsed. Stephen Girard (1750–1831), a French immigrant who succeeded very rapidly in Philadelphia as merchant and shipowner and whom we remember as a philanthropist, bought it for his private bank in 1812 and the Girard National Bank occupied the building after his death, from 1832 until 1926.

A notable feature of the building is the pediment which is adorned with a beautifully carved American eagle, and the leafy Roman Corinthian capitals give it a special grace. The handsome gates, which flank the building and lead to the park, have been erected in recent years. The bank building was restored in time for the Bicentennial, and exhibits are frequently held here. The Visitors' Center across the street disseminates information about the area. The bell in the tower of the Center, cast at Whitechapel foundry, was a gift to the people of the United States in 1976 from Queen Elizabeth.

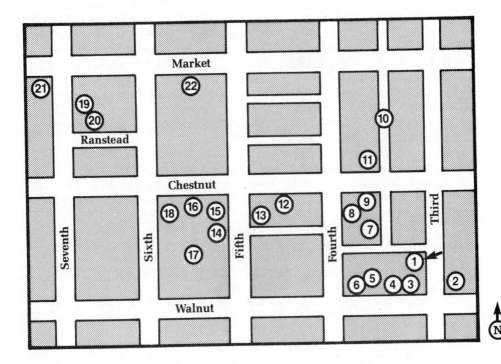

Walk south on 3rd Street to the corner of 3rd and Walnut Streets.
2 On the northeast corner is the *Philadelphia Exchange,* designed by
William Strickland, one of the foremost 19th century architects, and
built between 1832 and 1834. It was originally a gathering place where
merchants met to barter or sell their cargoes and merchandise. The
cornerstone was laid on the 100th anniversary of Washington's birth.
This masterpiece of elaborate Greek Revival has a Corinthian portico
on the west front and an unusual semicircular apse punctuated by
columns on the east, facing the river. The tower is not a conventional
cupola, but a free adaptation of the Choragic Monument of Lysicrates
in Athens. From here ships could be seen approaching up and down
the river. The small cobblestoned way, now Dock Street, on the north
side is the site of Dock Creek, one of the many small creeks which
originally flowed in from the river.

Turn right on Walnut Street and pass the small garden on the
3 corner; the first building is the *Bishop White House,* 302 Walnut
Street. (Tours are arranged at the Visitors' Center on 3rd Street, and
tickets can be procured there.) It was the home of William White
(1748–1836), rector of Christ Church and St. Peter's, who was also
Bishop of the Protestant Episcopal Church in Pennsylvania. The
Bishop's position in Philadelphia—he was Chaplain of the Continental Congress and later filled the same office for the United States
Senate—meant that the important men and women of his time came
here as guests. Washington dined here as a private citizen on November 19, 1798.

The first and second floors are open to the public and the furnishings are all of the period, fine examples of the time and an indication of the social standing of the Bishop and his family. There are two
Sir Godfrey Kneller portraits of the Bishop's grandparents which he
brought from England and also a portrait of White himself by Charles
Willson Peale. In the parlor there is a sofa which belonged to Robert
Morris (the Bishop's brother-in-law), and the dining room and kitchen
are exceptionally fine examples of the period. There is even an inside
"necessary," an unusual feature at a time when these conveniences
were in the back garden.

At the time of White's death, John Sartain, the Philadelphia
engraver, was commissioned to do an oil painting of the study. For
this reason we know today exactly what it looked like at the time.
The library fortunately was given intact to the Episcopal Academy,
and when the house was restored, the room (and its contents) was
returned to be re-installed. The house has great charm and it isn't at
all difficult to imagine the White family of five children (and much
later eleven grandchildren) living in these spacious rooms.

The houses along this row are either restorations or reconstructions. 311 and 313 are occupied by the Independence National
Park Service offices. 315 was built by Dr. William McIlvaine about

1793, and 317, 319, 321 and 325 are occupied by the *Pennsylvania* **4**
Horticultural Society, the oldest such organization in the nation. From
time to time there are displays for visitors, and at Christmas the
decorations are most unusual. The Society also has a justly famous
reference library, open to the public.

Adjoining the row is an authentically planted *18th century gar-* **5**
den, reproduced from one which was here in 1784. It is maintained
by the Horticultural Society, and the flowers and shrubs are set out
in the beds according to the season. It is spectacular in the spring
when the tulips and hyacinths are in bloom, and one may sit in the
summerhouse, a favorite retreat for walkers in this section, to enjoy
the prospect in any season.

Just opposite, on the other side of Walnut Street, is a small *park
and garden,* leading into St. Joseph's Church. This was the oldest
Roman Catholic parish in the city. However, the church is included
on Walk 3 through Society Hill, where the church is entered from
the Willings Alley side. On the other side of the 18th century garden,
339 and 341 Walnut are reconstructions of houses built in 1775; they
now serve as headquarters of the National Carl Schurz Association,
devoted to German-American history.

On the corner of 4th and Walnut Streets stands the *Todd House,* **6**
built in 1775 and occupied from 1791 to 1793 by John Todd, Jr., and
his wife, Dolley Payne (tickets at Visitors' Center). After Todd's
death in the yellow fever epidemic of 1793, she married James Madison, a young Virginia politician who was to become our fourth
president. Stephen Moylan, the Revolutionary War general, lived here
from 1796 to 1807.

Philadelphia Exchange (East Front)

Carpenters' Hall

The Todd House is smaller than the Bishop White House—the circumstances and finances of their tenants were very different—but it has been restored to the period of the Todds' tenancy. The kitchen is particularly inviting—as are all the kitchens on this tour—and the garden behind, with its pump, gives us some idea of what this house must have been like almost two hundred years ago.

Turn right from the Todd House and walk north along 4th Street. Halfway to Chestnut Street there are two entrances to the park, with **7** paths leading east to *Carpenters' Hall* (Tuesday–Sunday, 10:00–4:00; closed Monday). This famous building was erected between 1770 and 1773 by the Carpenters' Company, the oldest builders' organization in the United States (formed in 1724). Carpenters were architects as well as builders in those days, it should be remembered. The Company published a book of rules and prices for its members in 1786. *Articles and Rules* was also a pattern book, and its use was restricted to members of the Carpenters' Company who faced expulsion if they showed it to outsiders. There is an amusing story of Thomas Jefferson's writing for a copy of the book in 1817, but even the former president—an amateur architect—was denied access to the secrets of the Carpenters' Company.

Carpenters' Hall, although surrounded by unsightly buildings for years, has always stood out architecturally. Today, it is pristine in its beauty. Its proportions are perfect; it has a sense of balance, of time and place, and it was designed to endure. The Carpenters' Company still owns and maintains the buildings and holds meetings here. From September 5 to October 26, 1774, the First Continental Congress met in these rooms. Robert Smith, who designed the building for use as a guild hall (restored in 1857 and opened to the public), was a member of the Second Continental Congress in 1775, and Samuel Rhoads of the Carpenters' Company was a delegate to the First Continental Congress. The Continental Congress returned here briefly in 1783 because the State House was surrounded by an unruly mob of veterans.

The pedimented doorway with Doric detail wasn't finished until 1790 or so, and the interior columns were put into the hall about the same time. In 1791 the Bank of the United States took over the first and second floors, so the Company erected a building to house its own activities, on the west side of Carpenters' Court.

This building was *New Hall*. The present structure is in fact a **8** reconstruction of the one built in 1790 and used by the War Department in 1791 and 1792. It now houses the Marine Corps Memorial Museum, and there are flags, guns, swords, epaulets, uniforms and medals on display. The Continental Marine Corps was organized at Tun Tavern in Philadelphia in 1775, and after the Revolution the Marine Corps was established by the 5th Congress of the United States, meeting in Congress Hall, on July 11, 1798. On May 3 of that year the same Congress established the Department of the Navy.

The lovely gardens surrounding these buildings have been re-landscaped in recent years, and historic Carpenters' Court still retains its unique intimacy. It seems to the casual visitor as if the delegates to the first Continental Congress are still bustling in and out of the Court.

At the gates to Carpenters' Court on Chestnut Street is *Pember-* **9** *ton House*, which is today a museum entirely devoted to Army and Navy history from 1775 to 1805, and dedicated to the soldiers and sailors who served from Lexington and Concord to the Barbary Wars. The display is particularly instructive for children. There is, for instance, an exhibit of the major battles of the Revolution under the overall heading, "Steps to Victory." The locations of the attack on Trenton, December 26, 1776; the British surrender at Saratoga, October 17, 1777; the engagement of *Bonhomme Richard* and *Serapis,* September 23, 1779; and the battle of King's Mountain, October 7, 1780, are identified on a map when the appropriate button is pushed and a representation of the engagement lights up at the same time.

"Yorktown," showing the combined land and naval action which brought the Revolution to a close and the positions of the armies of the Continental forces, the British and the French and their navies as well, is equally fascinating to activate. Children and adults love "Try Your Hand at Maneuvering for a Sea Battle," which is part of the War at Sea, 1776–1805, exhibit. In this display the left switch controls the ship's rudder, the right trims the sails. Instructions tell us to "assume a southern wind . . . ," and, with success, a green light glows. It is a splendid way of making history come alive.

Opposite the Pemberton House and between the two bank buildings on Orianna Street is the entry to *Franklin Court*, the site **10** of Benjamin Franklin's last home. The house itself was not rebuilt, primarily because there is no extant picture of it. Instead a rough representation of part of it, by judicious use of stainless steel to indicate size, the angle of a roof or a stairway, was erected. There is surface garden planting—with the mulberry and plane trees that Franklin grew—providing some limited garden development. At the entrance is a plaque to Sarah Josepha Hale, the editor and writer.

The entire courtyard behind the five houses on the Market Street side has been excavated, and quotations from letters of Franklin and his wife Deborah appear on the flagstones. A subsurface installation has audiovisual devices to give the scope of Franklin's life and work.

Franklin began his house here in 1763; his wife Deborah moved into it in 1765, after he had left for England. The good Doctor didn't see it until a decade later, although he wrote his wife detailed letters as to what he wanted done. The final additions were made in 1788, two years before his death. Sarah (Sally) Bache, Franklin's daughter, died in this house in 1808, and in 1812 her heirs had the house demolished.

William Duane (1760–1835), the fiery editor of The Aurora who married the widow of Franklin's grandson, lived in another house in Franklin Court—that numbered 322 Market Street—from 1802 to 1809, as did James Wilson, an Irish immigrant who became editor of the paper. A century later his grandson, Woodrow Wilson, was elected president. Sarah Josepha Hale, editor of Godey's Lady's Book from 1837 to 1877, also worked here. Mrs. Hale was the first great women's magazine editor in the United States and the circulation of Godey's under her leadership reached more than 150,000.

Before continuing to Independence Hall, you should visit the
11 Philadelphia Maritime Museum, 321 Chestnut Street, on the right when leaving Franklin Court. (Monday through Saturday, 10:00–5:00; Sunday, 1:00–5:00. Adults, $1.00; children under 12, $.50. Group rates for ten or more.) Here man's great seagoing history is fully traced from the days of sailing ships to the age of steam, with the emphasis on the maritime heritage of Pennsylvania, New Jersey and Delaware. Exhibits of whaling harpoons, scrimshaw, ship models of every kind, figureheads, ceramics and silver, maps and manuscripts, paintings and prints abound.

Continue up Chestnut Street, crossing south at 4th Street, and
12 between 4th and 5th Streets, the splendor of the Second Bank of the United States, a superb example of the Greek Revival and one of Philadelphia's most handsome buildings, confronts us. The architect was the same William Strickland who designed the Philadelphia Exchange, and the bank was built between 1819 and 1824. Its façades are adaptations of the Parthenon with north and south Doric porticoes. Inside, the great banking room has a barrel-vault ceiling springing from Ionic colonnades. Bought by the Federal government in 1844, it was used as the Custom House until 1934 and is popularly known in Philadelphia as "the old Custom House." As a Bicentennial feature, the portrait gallery, containing over a hundred Revolutionary and Federal portraits, some from the Peale Museum—many painted

by Charles Willson Peale himself—which was once housed on the upper floor of Independence Hall, is open to the public (Daily 9:00-5:00).

Adjacent to the Second Bank and entered from the doors on Library Street facing south, rather than those on 5th Street, is *Library* **13** *Hall*, 105 South 5th Street. This reconstruction (1959) of the building which was originally built in 1789 and 1790 for the Library Company of Philadelphia is now occupied by the library of the American Philosophical Society. Founded by Benjamin Franklin in 1743, the Society's library contains an unrivaled collection of Franklin's books and papers as well as those of other great scientists from then until now. Washington, Jefferson, Adams, Hamilton, Thomas Paine, Caspar Wistar, David Rittenhouse, Baron von Steuben, the Marquis de Lafayette and James Wilson were members of the Society.

The portion of Library Hall facing 5th Street looks exactly like that shown in old prints of the original building, razed in 1884, even to the statue of Franklin over the doorway (the original statue, worn and weathered, is housed in the Library Company of Philadelphia, 1314 Locust Street).

Just opposite the 5th Street entrance to Library Hall and situated in Independence Square itself is *Philosophical Hall*, 104 South 5th **14** Street, also owned by the American Philosophical Society. Erected between 1785 and 1789, it contains the offices and meeting rooms of the Society and such furnishings as Franklin's clock and library chair and the chair Jefferson is said to have sat in while writing the Declaration of Independence. Not open to the public, the Hall may be visited by specially interested persons who apply by mail or telephone. The Society itself, the oldest learned association in the country, still carries on a full program of assistance to scholars engaged in research, holds frequent learned meetings attended by men of science and letters from over the world, and publishes scholarly papers and books.

Second Bank of the U. S.

15   Directly in front of Philosophical Hall and to the east of Independence Hall is the *Old City Hall.* The building, erected between 1789 and 1791, is in the process of being restored and renovated. It was first intended for use as City Hall, but from 1791 to 1800 it housed the United States Supreme Court, which was presided over by John Jay. Later it became City Hall and the seat of Philadelphia courts, until the present City Hall was built at Broad and Market Streets.

16   The dominant building on Independence Square is, of course, the State House or, as it is popularly known, *Independence Hall.* (Daily 9:00-5:00 in the winter; 8:00-8:00 from late spring until early autumn. Tours every fifteen minutes.) Begun in 1732 and considered finished by 1756 as the Pennsylvania State House, its architects are thought to have been Edmund Woolley and Andrew Hamilton. Until 1799 the building served as the meeting place of the provincial and state governments. The Second Continental Congress met here, and the stormy sessions of the Constitutional Convention, presided over by Washington, were also held here. The present spire which tops the tower proper was added by William Strickland in the restoration of 1828—a fact not generally known.

    Before entering the Hall, note two bronze markers in the flagstone pavement; one commemorates the flag raising here by Abraham Lincoln, February 22, 1861. The flag he raised had 34 stars, the last one for Kansas, which had just been admitted to the Union. The other marker is to John Fitzgerald Kennedy, who spoke on the spot July 4, 1962. In front of the entrance itself is a familiar statue of Washington erected in 1869. Philadelphia schoolchildren, beginning in 1860, gave their pennies to pay for it.

    To the left of the entrance hall is the *Pennsylvania Assembly Room.* Here the delegates from the thirteen colonies gathered and by July 4, 1776, had adopted the Declaration of Independence. The most important treasures in the room are the chair, with its *rising* sun carved on its back, and the silver inkstand designed by Philip Syng. The chair was Washington's during the Constitutional Convention and the inkstand was used for the signing of both the Declaration of Independence and the Constitution. The room has been restored to its appearance at the time of the Signing and the chairs, tables and writing equipment are of the period. The guide will point out where the Virginia delegation sat, a book printed by Franklin, and a cane used by Jefferson.

    Across the hall is the *Pennsylvania Supreme Court Chamber* with its handsome ochre-painted walls and the coat of arms of the Commonwealth above the bench. There are a prisoner's dock and jury boxes. All it needs are the principals to make it come alive.

    The visitor should ascend and descend the tower staircase slowly to savor the beauty, the simplicity and the elegance of the tower itself, with its Palladian window facing the old square and

Inkstand, Independence Hall

Rising Sun Chair,
Independence Hall

framing the statue of Commodore John Barry, "The father of the American Navy," standing among the ancient trees.

To the left on the second floor is the *Governor's Council Chamber*, its windows enhanced by blue shades and valances. The eight chairs and the armchair surrounding the table are complemented by eight silver candlesticks. This is the chamber where William Penn's sons and grandson, or their appointed representatives, presided over the Provincial Council, highest legislative body in the colony. Amid elegant surroundings the Royal Governor officially received members of the Pennsylvania Assembly, foreign dignitaries and Indian delegations. The events of 1776 brought an end to the Provincial Council, but similar authority was vested in a Supreme Executive Council over which Franklin presided from 1785 to 1788. The room has all the richness of the 18th century, but, with it, directness and simplicity, too. It was a working council room, with its grandfather's clock, telescope and two terrestrial globes.

The *Long Gallery*, which dominates the second floor, is flooded with north light from nine windows overlooking the three-block-long vista of Independence Mall. The chamber, when completed in 1745, was the largest public room in the Province of Pennsylvania. Suppers, balls and Grand Illuminations were held here to honor the great or mark public events. The greatest fête of the Proprietary period was a dinner for five-hundred guests on September 16, 1774, to honor members of the First Continental Congress.

In 1777 the British occupied the State House and converted these rooms into hospital wards for captured and wounded soldiers.

The other room on this floor is the Committee or *Assembly's Chamber*. From 1747 to 1752 it served as a combined committee room and library for the Pennsylvania Assembly. It was then given over to the militia of the City of Philadelphia for the storage of supplies and

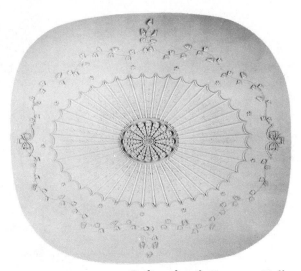

Ceiling detail, Congress Hall

small arms. In 1775 the Pennsylvania Assembly temporarily convened here, while the first floor chamber was occupied by the Continental Congress.

Independence Hall was used for levees in the 19th century, and among those so honored here were Lafayette, Henry Clay and Presidents Jackson, Van Buren, William Henry Harrison, Tyler, Polk, Fillmore, Pierce and Buchanan. Among those illustrious Americans who have lain in state here are Lincoln, the Arctic explorer Elisha Kent Kane, Henry Clay and John Quincy Adams.

Descending to the first floor, leave Independence Hall by the south door, which gives onto the square. In 1972 the National Park Service replaced the great outdoor clock, which was originally set into the west wall in 1752 and removed in 1828. A 14-foot carved replica of the remarkable clock head was installed on top of the 40-foot soapstone case structure. **17**

The hurried visitor may rush on, but linger if you can—saunter about the winding paving-stone paths and look at the Hall from the vantage point of the square. The proportions of the tower alone delight the eye, the symmetry of the building—in fact of the entire complex of buildings—is a tribute to the artisans and men who built

Fresco, Congress Hall

it. Here is the balance and order of the 18th century at its apogee.

And when we speak of these qualities, in some ways the epitome is yet to be seen. For, in *Congress Hall*, on the northwest corner of the square, is the distillation of all that was fine in the architecture of that remarkable time. It is small, self-contained, functional and beautiful.

18

Congress Hall, constructed in 1789 and 1790 as the Philadelphia County Court House, served as the meeting place of the Federal Congress from 1790 until 1800, when Philadelphia was the capital of the United States. Later in the 19th century it housed federal and local courts. Perhaps its most historic associations are Washington's inauguration here for his second term as president and John Adams' taking of his oath as president in 1797.

On the first floor is the *House of Representatives Chamber*. The valances of dark green above the windows enhance the mahogany of the desks and the studded leather chairs. In the south bay is an alcove where Representatives smoked and had a glass of sherry, port or madeira during the recess.

The staircases, right and left of the fanlighted door, are steep but they lead the visitor on to unexpected pleasures. The second-story landing, with the brass and glass lantern suspended above it, looks north as does the Long Gallery in Independence Hall. Here, however, the windows are larger and there is a sense of being airborne when looking from them. If the effect is too dizzying, there is a handsome settle on which to sit and look down the hall to the *Senate Chamber*. What the eye sees from this prospect is the small dais with its exquisite canopy in rich crimson. It is, in truth, a miniature throne. The chamber itself, with its matching valances framing the Venetian blinds, the deep red leather of the chairs and again the mahogany of the desks, is one of the most perfect rooms to be found anywhere. It was a stage setting for the Senate debates. And to add further esprit there is an 18th century fresco of an eagle, and the plaster beading on the ceiling—both elegant touches. An even smaller visitors' balcony than the one in the House of Representatives chamber overlooks the Senate.

On leaving Congress Hall by the front door, turn and study for a moment the perfectly proportioned windows, the door, its fanlight and the tiny iron balcony above.

Theoretically, the first walk should end here because the buildings, all of the 18th century or early 19th, have an architectural and historic unity. Their roles in our early, formative history were over, ironically, at the beginning of the 19th century, when the capital was moved to Washington, and Philadelphia was no longer the seat of national politics.

However, this has been Philadelphia history as well as United States history. As a final summation of Philadelphia history and an intimate look into the city's past, do not miss the *Atwater Kent Museum* at 15 South 7th Street. From Congress Hall, walk one block

19 west, cross Chestnut Street and continue one-half block north to the Museum.

Once the home of the Franklin Institute, the museum was designed by John Haviland and built between 1825 and 1827. This small but choice collection (daily 8:30–4:30) is devoted exclusively to Philadelphia history. There are games to delight a child's eye and ones to enchant children and adults alike. Dioramas picture various aspects of the city's history, and there is a musical clock once owned by John Jacob Michelet, who is said to have carried the Liberty Bell to safety in 1777. When the clock strikes the hour, soldiers march across the face and a band plays.

Here are the flags, uniforms, clothes, artifacts, games and household utensils of Philadelphia for two centuries and more. We see Franklin-type stoves, American folk art of all kinds and the Bank of America Room, created to represent the quarters of the first chartered bank in the New World. The museum is small and the collection a potpourri. The visitor can spend an hour, two hours or all day here.

On leaving the Atwater Kent Museum, go left to Ranstead Street

20 and along to the garden behind. Here is an original watch box of old Philadelphia. The "watch" who reported the hour "and all's well" kept an eye out for fires, thefts, attack by the enemy and any untoward events during the night. The watch box was his protection from rain, wind and cold between his rounds. The watch box stood at 8th and Walnut Streets until 1850, and then a farsighted Philadelphian, John Jay Smith, had it taken to his garden in Germantown. His grandson, equally farsighted, gave it to the Friends Meeting House at 4th and Arch Streets, where it stood until 1974, when it was presented to the Atwater Kent Museum.

Return to the main entrance of the Museum and walk to the corner of 7th and Market Streets. Here on the southwest corner is a small plot enclosed by a white fence (always a sign that the area is to be developed historically). This is the site of the *Jacob Graff*

21 *House*, where the Declaration of Independence was written. It was reconstructed for the Bicentennial celebration.

Jacob Graff, a bricklayer, built the house in 1775. It was a small brick dwelling, 16 by 50 feet, and it opened on 7th Street. There were two rooms on each floor and a center stairway between the rooms. In one of his rented rooms on the second floor Jefferson drafted the document—between June 10 and June 28, 1776—that was to change the world.

Through the years the house changed hands and suffered many vicissitudes. Simon and Hyman Gratz, brothers of Rebecca, whose grave will be visited on Walk 5, bought it in 1798 and added a fourth floor. Jefferson wrote to Dr. James Mease, a later occupant, on

September 16, 1825, less than a year before his death, and reminisced about his stay in the Graff House and the writing of the Declaration of Independence. By 1863 there was a printer's shop in the building, and it was razed in 1883.

Walk right to Market Street and right again to the pavilion between 5th and 6th Streets, which houses the Liberty Bell. In 1752 **22** the first bell, cast to mark the fiftieth anniversary of Penn's Charter of Privileges, arrived from England. On the bell's outside face were the words from Leviticus XXV:10, "Proclaim liberty throughout all the land, unto all the inhabitants thereof." The original bell cracked while being tested. Two Philadelphians, John Pass and John Stow, recast it and it was finally hung in April 1753. When the British entered Philadelphia in 1777, it was spirited away to safety near Allentown, Pennsylvania. The bell cracked again in 1835, when tolling for the funeral of Chief Justice John Marshall, and it has been stilled since. Its most famous ring was on July 8, 1776, when it summoned the citizens of Philadelphia to the State House Yard to hear the Declaration of Independence read by Colonel John Nixon.

"A Gentleman of Fashion,"
Atwater Kent Museum

Michelet Clock,
Atwater Kent Museum

North of Market Street

William Penn envisaged a beautiful waterfront for his city—something similar to the Embankment in London or the Potomac Basin in Washington, D.C.—but this was not to be. The area early became a scene of great commercial activity, and wharves, warehouses and taverns sprang up as they have for centuries in waterfront cities throughout the world. The district is thus one of the oldest and most historic in the city, for it was from the banks of the Delaware that Philadelphia grew westward toward the Schuylkill River.

There were dwellings here—Elfreth's Alley and Loxley Court attest to that—but they were modest homes in contrast to the larger ones to be seen in Society Hill on Walk 3. Perhaps this is the reason for the 19th century attitude toward those who were born or lived "north of Market." They were beyond the pale socially. However less socially acceptable and less affluent these residents were, they were still craftsmen and artisans, a solid, sturdy lot, the backbone of the young colony and the even younger republic.

Benjamin Franklin's home, although we pass its entrance here, was slightly south of Market Street, but, nevertheless, when he was in Philadelphia, he was a familiar sight on these streets, too. So were both Washington and Adams during their presidencies. Most of the notables of the time attended services at Christ Church, the largest edifice of its kind in the colonies when it was built. Later, there was an influx of Germans in the area around 4th and Race Streets and, of course, the Quakers were very much in evidence in this sector.

We must not forget that this area, too, contains one of William Penn's original squares—the northeast, which was renamed Franklin Square in 1825. Thomas Penn, son of the first Proprietor, issued a warrant for the establishment of a German congregation here in 1741 and for many years part of the square was a burial ground for that church. By 1835 the Supreme Court had ruled the Thomas Penn grant illegal. This forced the German Reform congregation to relinquish the property, and the graves and stones were covered over. During the Revolution the military authorities had erected a powder house, or magazine, here and an 1814 ordinance allowed the militia to drill or parade in the square.

Beyond the square to the north was that country area called the Northern Liberties, where Peggy Shippen, the Philadelphia belle who married Benedict Arnold, often rode with John André before her marriage. The term "Northern Liberties" actually referred to the land

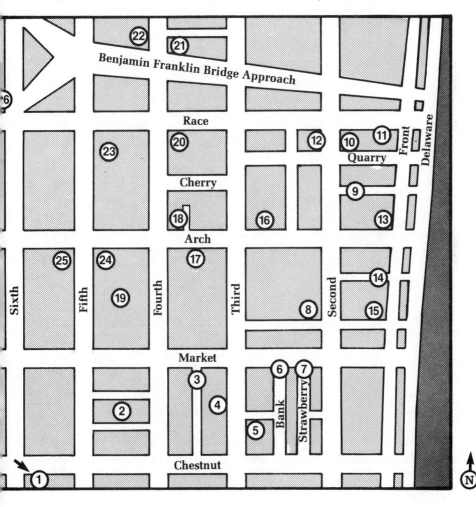

north of the city's boundaries—in the area of Vine, Callowhill and Spring Garden Streets today—which belonged to the original grant to Penn but wasn't part of the city as laid out in Thomas Holme's map of 1683. The city was first planned to cover 10,000 acres, but the original tract actually contained only 1,280. For every 500 acres of country land purchased from Penn, the buyer was to have received ten in the "great town," but with this reduction in its area no such arrangement could be carried out. Hence, the "Northern Liberties" and the "Western Liberties" were lands just outside the confines of the city where some purchasers received bonus grants.

However, around Franklin Square and in the area north of Market was lived much of the life we think of today as early American. The names of the men and women whose ghosts will be encountered are often familiar, sometimes unknown. Yet, along these streets walked our forefathers—those now called the Founding Fathers.

1 Using *Independence Hall* as a starting point—and it is a logical one—face north toward the Mall. On the right the center building of **2** the three on 5th Street, between Chestnut and Market, is the *Bourse* at 21 South 5th Street. Built in 1895 and modeled after the European bourses, it is the first example of a bourse in America. It once contained the offices of steamship lines, shipping brokers, wool and hemp merchants and similar businesses. A very imposing steel-frame building of red brick and brown sandstone, with a large interior court, or atrium, a gallery and skylights, it is strangely contemporary in feeling and blends in with the newer buildings adjoining and facing it. Today the Philadelphia Bourse is an elegant mall, featuring excellent restaurants, boutiques, snack bars, clothing and fine jewelry shops, a book store and a wine purveyor. Frequently musical and dance groups perform in the atrium to lend added warmth and color.

The Bourse, like so many Philadelphia landmarks, has undergone a facelifting recently. In addition to cleaning the façade facing the Mall, the owners have placed modern lamp standards—a cluster of white glass globes on each side, further evidence, if needed, that the contemporary and the old can be combined effectively.

Directly opposite the Bourse, on the west side of the Mall, is seen the handsome Rohm & Haas Building. The architects—George M. Ewing Company, with Pietro Belluschi as consulting architect—achieved a modern Italian look which again complements the 18th, 19th and 20th century buildings nearby. At night the stalactite-like prisms of the contemporary chandeliers are startling, yet blend beautifully with the surroundings. There is a small fountain on the open galleria behind—with a piece of sculpture jutting heavenward. All this overlooks the garden of the Atwater Kent Museum seen on Walk 1.

Walking from the Bourse, turn right and go to 5th and Market Street. Washington and his family lived in a brick house on High (Market) Street between 5th and 6th off and on between 1790 and 1797 while the seat of government was in Philadelphia.

At the studios of KYW-TV turn right again, walk to and cross over 4th Street, remaining on the south side of Market Street. Between 4th and 3rd, there is a row of 18th century houses which **3** have been restored. Number 314 was built in 1797, 316 and 318 in 1787, 320 in 1753 and 322 in 1788. The row is as Benjamin Franklin completed it, leaving the archway as a passage to his own home in Franklin Court (it is this foundation that we saw from Chestnut Street on Walk 1).

The modern-day storefronts along Market Street clash with the beauty and simplicity of these 18th century façades, but there is always a symbol of the period before us—the spire of Christ Church.

Just below the corner of Market Street on the west side of 3rd is another of the elegant, yet simple Hellenic façades of William Strickland: the *Norwegian Seamen's Church*, 22 South 3rd, which **4** was the Mechanics Bank in the 19th century. Built in 1837, it is another fine example of the Greek Revival style. In 1931 it was dedicated as a church, and on the second floor are recreational facilities for the seamen.

On the other side of the street, at 37-39 South 3rd, just below Elbow Lane, is the *Leland Building*, a commercial structure of 1855. **5** On the street floor is the Little Bourse restaurant and below stairs a rathskeller. "The continuous granite piers and recessed spandrels provide an early architectural solution for the tall, narrow commercial building," the historian tells us. Its windows graduate from larger to smaller from the ground up, which creates an illusion of greater height.

It is generally accepted that Louis Sullivan, who preceded Frank Lloyd Wright as America's greatest architect, was influenced by the Leland Building when he designed some of the country's first tall buildings. Lewis Mumford says, "Sullivan thought of the skyscraper as a 'proud and soaring thing' whose character could be established by stressing the vertical lines. . . ."

Before arriving at the corner of 2nd Street, it would be wise to stop and wander for a moment down two small streets to the right— Bank and Strawberry Streets. *Bank Street* has the distinction of **6** having several good restaurants for either luncheon or dinner. There is also an art gallery in addition to a number of attractive loft apartments. Bank Street was originally named White Horse Alley.

Both little streets have old loft buildings, typical of the 19th century, and they retain the character of another age. *Strawberry* **7** *Street* is an amalgam. There are old warehouses, a rather posh art gallery, fascinating façades, and Number 37 has been restored in an interesting manner. Others are also being restored; what is most pleasant about Strawberry Street is that it is lost in the labyrinth between Chestnut and Market Streets, but, raising your eyes, you can still see the spire of Christ Church ahead. Actually, the spire has been visible from the turn onto Market at 5th Street. One of the most interesting views of this ancient tower is that from the Benjamin Franklin Bridge, which links Philadelphia and Camden. Downriver, the Walt Whitman Bridge similarly connects South Philadelphia with southern New Jersey. The Benjamin Franklin Bridge is recommended to bridge-walkers for spectacularly lovely views of the city and its river. Pedestrians are not permitted on the Walt Whitman Bridge.

At 2nd and Market Streets, where there was an 18th century market house in the middle of the street, the church appears in all its beauty. The buildings on the north side of Market, which had hidden it from view, have been razed and a small garden on the corner provides benches and an oasis for the sightseer. *Christ* **8** *Church,* like most of the city's older churches, has long had benches in the churchyard for this purpose.

The church is one of America's most historic shrines and as such Philadelphians have always revered it. Organized in 1695, during the reign of William and Mary, it was built between 1727 and 1754 when George II was king. There was a bas relief of His late Majesty on the church in the 18th century, but we are told that it was removed in the 1790s in a wave of either anti-British or pro-republican sentiment. A similar medallion is back on the church now above the Palladian window on 2nd Street. Philadelphia, very pro-British and fond of royalty and the trappings of kings, could not hold a grudge for long. From time to time laymen speak at the Lenten noontime services here, and H.R.H. Princess Ileana of Rumania, daughter of King Ferdinand and Queen Marie and great-great-great-great-great granddaughter of George II, has spoken on several occasions.

Washington, Jefferson, Franklin and Betsy Ross worshiped here and, perhaps, its most important single feature is the font at which William Penn was baptized. It was sent to Christ Church in 1797 from London by All Hallow's Church, Barking-by-the-Tower. Two Signers of the Declaration of Independence, Robert Morris (1734–1806) and James Wilson (1742–98) are buried in the churchyard, as is Pierce Butler (1744–1826), who signed the Constitution and was a member of the Constitutional Convention. Five other Signers are buried in Christ Church Burial Ground, which will be seen later in this walk.

Flags of the Magna Carta barons often hang from the gallery inside, memorial tablets line the walls, slabs marking family vaults are beneath our feet. The chandelier brought from England in 1744 is still in use as is the "wineglass" pulpit, made in Philadelphia by John Folwell in 1770. The pews of Washington and Betsy Ross are

Christ Church

Christ Church

marked by small brass plates, and, generally, the feeling of history abides in this church as much as in any American shrine.

A stroll around the *churchyard* is in order, especially if you are fortunate enough to be there when the eleven bells in the tower are rung. The bells of Christ Church rang all day on July 4, 1788, when ten out of thirteen states agreed to ratify the Constitution. Here lies Major-General Charles Lee (1731–82), usually called a traitor but here named "Knight Errant of Liberty" by his biographer, Samuel White Patterson. Lee had been courtmartialed in 1778 for his retreat at the Battle of Monmouth Court House and disrespect shown to his Commander-in-Chief. Robert Morris, the financier of the Revolution, lies on the other side of the tower near Butler. Near the tower door itself is a black, weathered and ancient slate, which records that "Here lies the body of James Bingham, 30 December 1714, aged 46."

On leaving the churchyard, notice the well-worn stepping-stone by the curb. It is a bit of vanishing Americana that we see throughout Philadelphia, a city that is seldom far removed from its past.

No visit to Philadelphia would be complete without a stop at **9** *Elfreth's Alley,* often referred to as the oldest street in America with dwellings on both sides. It was opened shortly before 1702 by Arthur Wells, a blacksmith, and John Gilbert, a bolter, and is only a stone's throw away from Christ Church, in the shadow of the Benjamin Franklin Bridge. Just cross 2nd Street and walk north one-and-one-half blocks toward the bridge. Here among storehouses, wholesalers and the jobbers of commerce is a single street that provides a glimpse into the 18th century. It is named for Jeremiah Elfreth and was the home of carpenters, printers and craftsmen of all sorts. Benjamin Franklin once lived here although no one is sure in just which house. Betsy Ross visited the alley, for, although at the time of the Revolution Philadelphia was the second largest city under British rule (London was larger), the city itself was small by today's standards and most people in the city were known to one another.

In June, usually on the first Saturday, Elfreth's Alley residents open their homes and gardens to the public. The oldest houses are thought to be 122 and 124, which were built between 1725 and 1727. At other times, the Mantua Maker's House (1762) at 126, which is maintained by the Elfreth's Alley Association, is open to the public (usually during the summer months only). A mantua was a capelike cloak quite popular with our 18th century ancestors. Halfway down toward Front Street and the Delaware River, there is a small cobble-stoned way to the left, Bladen's Court. There are only three houses that actually open on Bladen's Court, but two others have rear or side doors onto it. The last house has a spinning balcony, a tiny porch on the second story the width of the house itself, where, in earlier times, the lady of the house set her spinning wheel on pleasant days.

Retracing our steps along Elfreth's Alley to 2nd Street, it is wise to turn right and walk the few steps to Quarry Street (Drinker's Alley). The Prince de Talleyrand boarded on the southeast corner in 1793. *Fireman's Hall Museum* is housed on the northeast corner **10** of Quarry Street (Tuesday–Saturday, 10:00–4:00; closed Sunday and Monday).

Benjamin Franklin, who organized the first fire department—the Union Fire Company on December 7, 1736—would be proud

indeed of this unique museum, for there is nothing connected with fire departments, fire fighting and firemen that is not here. There are fire engines from 1799, 1802, 1830, 1896, 1903 and 1907, with beautiful old brass fixtures. The first ones were hand drawn, hand operated by the men themselves and before our modern ones, of course, there was the horse-drawn fire engine.

Here are the leather buckets for water, miniature engines, nozzles, horses, firemarks from old houses, parade hats—those wonderful stiff hats that look as if they were made of tin—early fire insurance policies, medals and even a brass pole which goes from the third to the first floor, typical of those that firemen slid down for generations.

Perhaps the art of the fire engine was carried to its apogee in the "Spider Hose Reel," made in 1804. The wood, the carving, the brass bells, the wrought iron lantern in front and the mirrors on each side of the reel make this a work of art. It is elegant.

The building itself was erected in 1902 as headquarters of Engine Company 8, the oldest continuously active fire company in the United States and a direct lineal descendant of Ben Franklin's Union Fire Company.

11   Walk right to Race Street and pause at number 136. This 19th century house, its door extremely rare, is certainly different from others seen in the area. It is funereal in appearance and the double panels, with the molding which looks like shirred crepe, are unique. The houses at 140 and 142 have been restored but 140 has a stoop (*stoep*, as the Dutch called it) of a later vintage. Stoops served as front porches—since these houses had none—in the pleasant weather for generations of Philadelphians. They are remembered for their whiteness—scrubbing one's stoop to glittering brightness was done with a sense of pride by the goodwives of the past. The brick is old in these houses, almost a faded rose in color, and there is an arched walkway between the houses leading to an old garden in the back. Non-Philadelphians don't expect to find houses and gardens in this old, rundown, commercial area, but Philadelphia's peculiar charm is always the unexpected just around the corner.

The house at 144 *Race* is a 19th century one, like 136 of the "crepe door," but even more unusual. The first floor façade is of stained wood, superimposed over the brick—almost a cabinet-work effect—and is very rare. Most old Philadelphia houses are entirely of either stone or brick. Stone is native to Pennsylvania and in the 18th century brick was brought from Europe as ship's ballast. The English who built in the late 17th and during the 18th century had reason to remember the horrors of the fire of London (1666) and wanted no recurrence in Philadelphia.

12   Retracing our steps to 2nd and Race Streets, cross over and turn left. Opposite the Fireman's Hall Museum, at 150 North 2nd Street, is a charming 18th century wooden, two-story dwelling, which has fortunately been saved from both fire and oblivion. Next to it one really should note the brick front of number 148. It is a true horror—bastardization everywhere—but the lines, the structure and the brick of the old building are there. This, too, will probably survive to be someone's home, or a shop, once more.

Returning to 2nd and Arch Streets, turn left on Arch and walk again toward the river. On the northwest corner at 101–111 Arch, there is a series of fine iron-front buildings constructed between 1855 and 1857. The group typifies the buildings the Victorians gave us, **13** which today are appreciated for their beauty and functionalism.

Opposite at 102–106 are several houses from the middle of the 18th century. During the 19th century they were used as stores. Number 102 has a dormer at the roof, and these houses will undoubtedly be restored.

Warehouses, commercial buildings and lofts don't have the allure for the layman that grand town houses or even small, intimate ones have. Man likes to see the lares and penates of his ancestors— the antiques—in their proper surroundings. However, nothing reveals the character of a town or city like the buildings near its rivers and wharves. Here was the lifeblood of Philadelphia.

Stroll along Front Street to see some marvelous 19th century buildings and an occasional 18th century one, such as that at 46 North Front Street, at the northwest corner of Cuthbert Street, formerly Coomb's Alley. Built in 1785 as a home and store for John Clifford, it became a store and warehouse from 1821, when Samuel Wetherill acquired the property and it remained a Wetherill store and warehouse—Samuel was a druggest and paint manufacturer—until 1919. During Wetherill's ownership the granite piers were added.

It cannot be stated too often that we must remember and constantly be aware of the small islands of architectural beauty floating amidst the terminals of commerce in Philadelphia. Even Philadelphians are often unaware of them. On our historical-architectural quest we should never fail to examine the lowliest alley, the darkest byway, the most decrepit entry, for beyond may lie a real find.

And that is exactly what we are about to do. Cuthbert Street is nondescript, uninviting, shabby. Yet, if we turn right here and walk halfway back, at 112–116 we find three houses built about 1760 by Henry Harrison, a merchant, as rental properties. Coomb's Alley, to **14** call it by its old name, was once similar to Elfreth's Alley in character, and these three houses and the one adjoining are being restored. Here—as on Strawberry Street—one is within the sound of the bells of Christ Church and the sight of its spire, and yet removed from the noise and the tempest of the city.

There is a space next to the houses where several others once stood and then a house that has been restored. Next to this is a splendid four-story loft, with a door on each landing (rather unusual).

There is the inevitable hook at the top, for raising and lowering goods, and old "S" irons which lend support to the ancient structure.

Opposite at 121 is a red brick and stone building that has a Frank Furness cast to it. Not so elaborate or so bizarre as some of Furness' buildings, it is still of his era. Note the fleur-de-lis on the decorative molding and the marvelous frieze above the second-story windows.

If you are fortunate, while walking over the cobbles toward Front Street you may see a freighter or steamship passing, its funnels or decks visible over the wall that protects the subway tracks from the river. This may still be a commercial district, but there are pleasures here no suburbanite can savor—the sound of a ship's horn at night, the sight of the vessels themselves or the wind that breathes in and out of these alleys, around these corners.

On Front Street again, walk one short block south to Church Street, which was Jones Alley about 1700 and by 1762 had been given the grander and more romantic name of Pewter Platter Alley. Before turning into Church Street, examine 14 North Front, which is on the southwest corner of Audubon Place. Built sometime between 1830 and 1865 this granite stone front has Celtic-like decorations. It is a rather humorous accent among the plain fronts along this way.

15 Turn into Church Street now toward the *Stephen Girard warehouses* at 103–111. They were built between 1847 and 1848, well after Girard's death in 1831, but belong to the Girard Estate, which is still being administered in Philadelphia. One look at these handsome, balanced fronts suggests that someday they will be turned into apartment flats.

Christ Church is just a few steps away, a quick transition from the commercial to the historical and the beautiful. Walk toward it, **16** turn right and walk again to 2nd and Arch Streets. Another turn to the left brings us, less than a block away, to the *Betsy Ross House*, 239 Arch Street (daily 9:00–5:00).

Elizabeth Griscom Ross Ashbourn Claypool (1752–1836)—she married three times—made the first American flag, or at least tradition tells us she did. We do not know if she lived in this particular, charming house—some say it was a door or two away—but she did live in one of these similar houses. The one you visit was built about 1760 and thousands of persons visit it each year—its popularity is second only to the Liberty Bell. The cellar and its kitchen, furnished in the period, and the sitting room, bedrooms and children's playroom are typical of the time, and few leave the premises disappointed.

Continue west on Arch Street to 3rd, cross to the other side, and midway between 3rd and 4th we come to the *Friends Meeting* **17** *House*, the main part erected in 1804, the west wing in 1811 (daily 10:00–4:00). The oldest Friends Meeting House still in use in Philadelphia and the largest in the world, it is the site of the Philadelphia Yearly Meeting, held every spring, of Friends living in Philadelphia, the

far left:
Girard House,
Water Street

left:
Betsy Ross House

southern half of New Jersey, Delaware and parts of Maryland.

Inside are dioramas depicting the main events of William Penn's life and his contributions, showing that Penn's inheritance belongs not only to Pennsylvania but to the nation. Shown are Penn the Peacemaker, laying down his sword (1668); Penn the Defender of Liberties, in prison (1670); Penn the Builder of Democracy, writing his "Frame of Government" (1682); Penn the Friend of the Indians, completing a treaty with them (1682); Penn the City Planner, with his surveyor Thomas Holme, studying Holme's map (1683); and Penn the Founder of Schools (1699).

The ground around the Meeting House was first used for burial purposes under a patent issued by William Penn in 1701, and many victims of the yellow fever epidemic of 1793 are buried here. The epidemic produced the fearful street cry—"Bring out your dead!"— as the carts bearing bodies rumbled over the Philadelphia cobbles. Burials continued until 1803, and the Meeting House was erected the following year. Charles Brockden Brown (1771–1810), the first American novelist *(Wieland)*, is buried here. Strangely enough, James Logan, certainly one of the three greatest Philadelphians of the Colonial period—with William Penn and Benjamin Franklin—lies here in an unmarked grave. It is ironic but perhaps fitting that this great Quaker who so loved Philadelphia lies—as does Mozart in Vienna— in an unknown grave. His spirit still lives in his adopted city and we find much to remind us of him in these walks.

Just in front of the entrance is a memento of another age, a horse trough. The legend in the stone says it was a project of the Philadelphia Fountain Society, Instituted A.D. 1869 and was "Presented by a Lady." It also tells us to heed the horses' plea, "Give Us Water That We May Drink." Horses are seldom seen on Philadelphia streets today, except for the mounted police, but a number of such fountains have survived.

Cross directly opposite, and between 321 and 323 Arch is *Loxley*

Court. Through the iron gates can be seen the beautifully restored houses, a private and quiet corner in the heart of downtown Philadelphia. Not many years ago these entrancing houses were shabby and rundown. This restoration by Earl James, a Philadelphia builder who has restored many houses, was done as a unit and every effort was made to restore the houses authentically.

18

Benjamin Loxley, a carpenter who worked on Independence Hall and Carpenters' Hall, was the court's first resident in 1744. The Methodists took over a tavern or "pot house" at Number 8 as their second meeting house in 1768. They held prayer meetings on the first floor and the minister preached out of the second-floor window to the congregation gathered in the courtyard below. Loxley himself lived in Number 2, and it was the key from the front door of this house that Benjamin Franklin used in his kite flying experiment with lightning. The houses are 18th century dwellings, the earliest of the ten built about 1770.

Adjacent to Loxley Court is a firehouse and in the garden that separates them is a rather flagrant representation of Benjamin Franklin, made of thousands of copper pennies. It was erected in honor of the 100th anniversary of Philadelphia's Paid Fire Department.

At this point, walk south along 4th Street, and, after you pass the entrance of the Holiday Inn, notice the two interesting plaques affixed to the wall of the building. One reminds us that on this very site stood the "New Building," erected in 1740 for George Whitefield and also for use as a charity school. For some time, in fact until about 1802, the "New Building" was used by "the School, Academy, College, and University of Pennsylvania successively."

The other memorial serves to commemorate the historic organization of the American Unitarian church. In one of the buildings of the University of Pennsylvania, "The First Society of Unitarian Christians in Philadelphia," which was actually the first church in America to adopt the official Unitarian name, was formally organized at ceremonies here on June twelfth, 1796, under the very noteworthy influence of Dr. Joseph Priestley (1733–1804), the celebrated theologian and philosopher, the discoverer of oxygen and the founder of modern chemistry, as well as the inflexible defender of human rights. Dr. Priestley later left the Philadelphia area to settle in Northumberland, Pennsylvania.

19

A few steps farther and we are at the lovely greenwalk that leads to the *National Museum of American Jewish History.* (Sunday, 12:00–5:00; Monday through Thursday, 10:00–5:00; Friday, 10:00–3:00; closed Saturdays. Adults, $1.50; students and senior citizens, $1.25; children under 12, $1.00; children under five free.)

National Museum of American Jewish History

The museum, a symbol since its founding in 1976 of the contributions of the Jewish people to the growth and development of the United States, is the only such institution exclusively dedicated to a comprehensive narration of the Jewish experience in this country and to a documentation of the full range of Jewish participation in the social, cultural, political and economic evolution of the nation.

There are permanent exhibitions of portraits, photographs, furniture and a variety of religious ceremonial objects, as well as changing ones which concentrate on contemporary arts and crafts. Of interest, too, is a complete and faithfully restored room of furniture belonging to Rebecca Gratz and her family, who are discussed in greater detail on Walk 5. Now return to 4th and Arch Streets and the fire house there.

At 4th and Arch Streets, instead of going to 5th and to the entrance of the United States Mint, it is really preferable to turn right, go beyond the fire house and pause at 4th and Cherry Streets. Behind us are the roofs of Loxley Court and before us is a group of charming houses, restored for commercial purposes. At *327 Cherry Street* is a flower shop in a building graced by a loft on the second story. The original building of 1761 was once a German Lutheran School. Most of the front burned in 1878; from the side of the building the new brick can be distinguished from the old.

The old bricks and the mustard-colored trim bring this small part of the old city alive. The owner has created a charming courtyard-patio to one side, with bushes and plants in tubs along the wall. It is on the next corner, at 4th and Race, however, that one of the most exciting restorations stands.

It is the *Old First Reformed Church* of the United Church of **20** Christ (originally the German Reformed Church). The present building is the third church on the site and was dedicated in 1837 (the church was founded in 1727). In 1882 the congregation moved to another location—this had originally been a German-speaking neighborhood—and then this lovely old building was used as part of a paint factory; between 1882 and 1966 some unsightly appendages were incorporated. When the congregation returned to its original location, these eyesores were removed, the old brick cleaned and restored. The factory owner had built a brick wall in front of the old reredos—the ornamental screen behind the altar. When the brick wall was removed during the restoration, the original wallpaper reredos could be seen and copied back. This exciting enclave behind the Mint is evidence of how a city can be renewed, and this project has encouraged others to take up the challenge in other areas. Philadelphia is unique in that a house or group of houses can be restored in the most unlikely places. The restorations need not be in an area like Society Hill, which is entirely residential, but like these houses or those on Cuthbert Street, or Elfreth's Alley, may be in the midst of a commercial area.

21 If we walk north on Fourth Street and go under the bridge, we come to *Old St. George's Methodist Church,* 235 North 4th Street (daily 10:00-4:00, except Christmas). Called "The Cradle of American Methodism," it is the oldest Methodist church in the world, in continuous use for more than two hundred years.

The church was the site of the first three conferences, 1773, 1774 and 1775, of American Methodism and the first visited by many of the early British itinerant preachers like Francis Asbury. It was also the site of the first Methodist Book Concern, an early publisher in the city.

Climb the stairs to the church which is on a second-floor level—the street has been lowered here and the center window on the second floor was once the entrance door.

The building was started for a German Reformed Congregation which had split. The roof and the walls were erected, but because of a lack of funds the congregation couldn't complete it and the trustees were jailed. A young man purchased it for £700, much to the dismay of his father who was furious over his son's extravagance. The father then sold it to the Methodists, who moved into it on November 24, 1769.

When George Washington was in desperate straits at Valley Forge, he asked Robert Morris, the Philadelphia banker and merchant, for $50,000 for the needs of his starving army. On January 1, 1777, Morris raised his friends from their beds and secured the money, but the long night before he had held his own personal vigil in St. George's, praying for guidance in securing the money.

The British then occupied Philadelphia, using Old St. George's for a cavalry school—it still had a dirt floor and its front door opened directly onto the street.

In 1784, Richard Allen, the first Negro licensed to preach by the

Methodists in America, was licensed by St. George's and the following year Absolom [sic] Jones, the second Negro, was licensed.

The church has fragile, black, lacy chandeliers of iron that contrast beautifully with the white interior. The gallery, erected in 1792, is graced with wooden candlesticks and contributes to the church's simplicity and charm. There is a fine portrait of the first official pastor, Reverend Joseph Pilmoor, done by John Neagle in 1822. Neagle portraits are found in countless homes and museums throughout the city and are much valued.

There is a charming *garden* between the church, museum and library (8,000 volumes), and stones mark the graves of John Dickens (1746–98), the pastor who organized the Methodist Book Concern in 1789, and among others that of a child whose name is indecipherable, who died January 5, 1793, aged eight months. That was the year of the yellow fever when 4,000 died of the fever and 20,000 fled the city.

The *Methodist Historical Society* museum has a collection of furniture, church silver, even a cobbler's bench, the saddlebags which were used by itinerant preachers, and cases full of memorabilia of all sorts, even tickets for a Love Feast of 1770!

When the Benjamin Franklin Bridge was being planned in 1921, St. George's was threatened. Through the efforts of Bishop Thomas B. Neely the bridge plans were changed to miss the church by 14 feet, although the street had to be lowered, too.

Leaving Old St. George's we pause briefly at *St. Augustine's* **22** *Catholic Church* opposite. This is not the original, which was founded in 1798 and destroyed in the anti-Catholic riots of 1844 when many Catholic churches were burned. The city was in a state of near-anarchy then and even the governor was intimidated by the mob. Rebuilt in 1847, the church is of interest because the Irish friars of the Order of St. Augustine, who established the parish in 1796, also founded St. Augustine's Academy at this location in 1811—the forerunner of Villanova University, the oldest Catholic institution of higher education in Pennsylvania.

Returning to 4th and Race Streets, go around the corner to the 5th Street entrance of the *United States Mint*. (Daily, 9:00–4:30; **23** closed Sunday.)

The first Mint was erected in 1792, and the first coins were silver half-dimes made by hand from silver plate belonging to President Washington himself. The following year copper cents and half-cents were manufactured for public use.

The Mint tour is self-guided and fascinating to take. Walk along a gallery, with windows on one side and look down at the various operations taking place. Well-lettered signs identify the process— Bonding Mill, Blanking Presses, Annealing Furnaces, Coining Presses —and by pressing buttons along the way recorded information on what is going on below is available.

These facts alone would impress any visitor: the larger presses stamp out 600 coins per minute, the smaller 300, and one blow of the press strikes the obverse and reverse designs plus any design on the edge.

The *museum area* contains cases of medals and coins (United States and foreign) and the first coining press of 1792 on which the coins were laboriously struck by a screw press. A Pyx is also on display. A locked box with one or more slots on top, the Pyx was for coiners who were required to place randomly selected coins in it as they were produced. The Pyx was then opened only in the presence of the committee to test the coinage. This particular 18th century Pyx was donated by the Master of the Netherlands Mint.

Don't leave without seeing *Peter, the Mint Eagle*. Early in the 19th century he adopted the Mint as his home. He became a pet and the mascot of the men in the Mint and of the neighborhood at large. Everyone loved Peter; he was never molested. Even young boys— notorious tormentors and teases—respected him.

One day Peter was perched on a flywheel when it suddenly started and his wing was caught and broken. He was tenderly cared for by his Mint mates, but in spite of their efforts Peter died within a few days. Peter was mounted and is still with us today—the spirit of the past in the modern Mint. It is thought that Peter was the model for the eagle on the United States silver dollars (1836–39) and for the Flying Eagle cents (1856–58). Speaking of eagles, the two which flank the front entrance as we descend to the street were brought here from the third Mint at 16th and Spring Garden Streets—perhaps also inspired by Peter.

24 Just opposite the Mint is *Christ Church Burial Ground*. Here Benjamin and Deborah Franklin's graves can be seen from the street through the grating. Next to them lie John Read, Deborah's father; their daughter and son-in-law, Sarah and Richard Bache (and generations of later Baches); and a small marker is for Francis Franklin, Benjamin and Deborah's son who died in 1736 at the age of "4 years, 1 month, and 4 days." The infant mortality rate was extremely high in the 18th century.

At Franklin's death some 20,000 Philadelphians followed his cortege to his grave here, as his death in 1790 severed the tie to Colonial Philadelphia. William Smith, Provost of the University of Pennsylvania and his old enemy, gave the eulogy in Christ Church, and the Comte de Mirabeau did the same before the French National Assembly in Paris. Franklin was as well loved by the French as by the Americans and as honored by them, too. One of the least likely people to be a descendant of Franklin was Nancy Cunard (1896– 1965), the British poet, rebel, bohemian, heiress to the Cunard shipping fortune and espouser of rights for the Negro. Franklin would have been proud of Nancy's zeal if not her methods.

Just beyond Franklin's grave is the raised tomb of David Hall (1714–72), Franklin's partner in their printing business from 1748 to 1766. Children throw pennies on Franklin's grave for good luck, and each year in January, on the anniversary of his birth, which falls during Printing Week, ceremonies are held here and wreaths placed upon the graves of Franklin and Hall.

Also buried here are Benjamin Rush (1745–1813), the father of American psychiatry who was also a Signer; Philip Syng Physick (1768–1837), father of American surgery; and Edwin J. De Haven (1816–65), Lt., U.S.N., who commanded the first Grinnell expedition to the Arctic in search of Sir John Franklin.

In addition to Benjamin Rush and Franklin, three other Signers lie here: George Ross (1730–79), who was also a member of the Provincial Assembly and the Continental Congress; Joseph Hewes (1730–79), a Quaker merchant who left the Meeting and never returned after he signed the Declaration but devoted the rest of his short life to the arduous work of the Congress; and Francis Hopkinson (1737–91), whose name we come across in so many places throughout the city. He was a composer of note, a wit, and involved in countless activities in the city including designing the first flag. He represented New Jersey as a member of the Continental Congress. The burial ground is a reminder of the scope of the lives of these men, how much they did for the new nation.

Opposite the burial ground and the only building on Independence Mall is the *Free Quaker Meeting House,* built in 1783, the last **25** year of the Revolution. (Memorial Day to Labor Day: Tuesday–Saturday, 10:00-4:00, Sunday, 12:00-4:00. Closed Monday. Other times of the year by appointment.)

"The Fighting Quakers," or the Free Quakers as they are some-

Christ Church Burial Ground

*Free Quaker
Meeting House*

times called, were a splinter group who broke with the main body during the Revolution. They took the oath of allegiance and bore arms. There were about two hundred of them in the beginning and from 1783 until 1834 they met here. Betsy Ross, as Mrs. Claypoole, worshipped here, and Betsy was, if anything, ecumenical before it was fashionable. We have seen her pew in Christ Church and she was married to Joseph Ashbourn at Old Swedes'.

Of particular interest is Betsy Ross's tissue pattern for the star, given to Samuel Wetherill, one of the founders of the Free Quakers, by Betsy. Tradition has it she told Washington she could fold a piece of cloth and with one snip of the scissors make a perfect five-point star. Wetherill put the pattern in a safe which was, in true Philadelphia fashion, not opened for one hundred and fifty years. In 1922, when the safe was opened by A. P. Wetherill, it was in the custody of the White Lead Works of Wetherill & Brother, successor to Samuel Wetherill, who founded the first manufacturing company for white lead in the United States in 1762.

The building was used as a school under William Marriott from 1800 to 1836, later as a library and, finally, as a warehouse. Even

Flea Market, Independence Mall

after the Free Quakers ceased to function as a separate Meeting, the group continued as an outlet for charitable work. The money gained from renting the building out was used for that purpose and when it was sold to the federal government the proceeds were put to charitable uses.

In 1961, after years of being rented out to commercial interests, the meeting house was moved 33 feet westward when 5th Street was widened. The interior was stripped to the brick walls, additions and alterations were removed and careful restoration was done according to the designs of the founder, Samuel Wetherill (1736–1816). A portrait of his son, Samuel, Jr. (1764–1829) by Thomas Sully hangs here and two of the original benches have been returned. Even a number of goose quill pens and excuse notes from the days of William Marriott's school were found beneath the floor boards.

Leaving the Meeting House, look north past the first park with the fountains to *Franklin Square,* one of William Penn's five original **26** squares. It is still one of the greenest spots in Philadelphia, for the trees are old and large. Once surrounded by fine houses and churches, the square fell on difficult times as the city changed. In spite of being at the entrance to the Benjamin Franklin Bridge and in the not-too-distant past a part of the tenderloin, Franklin Square retained its own beauty. The city swirled around it, but it remained quiet, a place of repose for many footsore dwellers. Walt Whitman was one of its better known bench-sitters as was Christopher Morley.

Turn now and face Independence Mall to retrace our way to the starting point. Walk past the colonnades (thirteen arches in each), which flank this segment of the Mall, and proceed to Independence Hall. Look for activity here. On Sundays from late spring until early fall there is a Flea Market in operation and, from time to time, other displays and celebrations—speeches, pageants—during the week.

This was an area of commercial and industrial buildings, rundown and seedy, less than twenty years ago. The Cradle of Liberty was crowded in on all sides, hardly visible unless one was upon it. Between 1953, when the state began razing the old buildings, until 1966 when it was officially finished, the Mall—under the supervision of the General State Authority—took shape.

Independence Hall emerged from the shadow of the structures that hemmed it in and were never meant to be there when the building was erected. Standing at the fountain—dedicated in 1955 to Judge Edwin O. Lewis, one of the idealists who had vision enough to see and work toward this goal as early as World War II—we can admire our historic shrines in one of the most magnificently revitalized areas in the world. City planners and architects come from Europe, Asia and South America to see the "Philadelphia Story," an ongoing and continuous saga.

A Glimpse of Society Hill

Society Hill is neither an elevation nor the site and badge of social position. The "notable eminence" one ancient chronicler records there has eroded with time, and the "Society" for which it was named no longer exists. However, Society Hill is notable again today as the very model of urban renewal and urban amenity in an historic setting.

It was the Free Society of Traders, to whom William Penn made liberal concessions of land and privileges, that gave its name to Society Hill. This strip of land, running from river to river and bounded by what are today Spruce and Pine Streets, seen from the decks of *Welcome,* the ship that bore Penn to his adopted city, was virgin territory with woodlands stretching westward to the Schuylkill. There were, of course, Dutch and Swedes living to the south in Southwark (Wicaco).

The Society, whose land formed a manor of some 20,000 acres, was authorized to appoint and remove its officers and was given the right of transportation of its goods free from any but necessary state and local taxes, while it could levy needful taxes within its limits for its own support.

In 1683 its assets included a sawmill, a glasshouse and a tannery in Philadelphia, but forty years later the Society came to an end with "an Act of Assembly then having put its property into the hands of trustees for sale to pay its debts."

Near the Delaware, where the greatest activity centered in the early years, was higher ground which soon became known popularly as Society Hill. In 1726 there was a flagstaff on the hill, which was then the town common, and the British ensign was raised there on Sundays and holidays. By 1740 the friends of George Whitefield, the

36

Calvinist Methodist preacher who led the "Great Awakening" and electrified Philadelphians, erected a stage for him on Society Hill where he exhorted some 25,000 persons at two meetings in a single day. (David Garrick, the great English actor of the 18th century, said Whitefield could make people weep or tremble by the various ways he uttered the word "Mesopotamia!")

In time the name spread to an even greater area than the original charter provided for, and today it is used loosely to include the land from the Delaware River to Washington Square and from Walnut to Lombard Street. The term itself had fallen into disuse as the section became a less desirable residential one in the 19th century, until the rebirth of Society Hill in the 1950's, under the auspices of the Redevelopment Authority, the Historical Commission, the City Planning Commission and other governmental, civic and private agencies. The renaissance of Society Hill was the beginning of the renewal of Philadelphia.

The charm of Society Hill is that its homes are not museums, but are lived in by Philadelphians who delight in 18th and 19th century houses. It is not a Williamsburg or an Old Sturbridge, but a vital part of the city.

In the 18th century Society Hill was removed from the avenues of commerce and had the residential character it has today. Men and women of history, whose names are still familiar, all walked these streets, were entertained in these homes, worshiped in these churches, sat by these firesides.

We can see what Society Hill was like in the 18th century, for literally thousands of houses from that time remain and many have been restored to their past glory. This part of the city bears out Lafayette's charming Gallic tribute to Philadelphia when he returned there in 1824 and 1825. He called it "the great and beautiful town of Philadelphia."

Enter this "town" at 4th and Walnut Streets. There stands the *Todd House,* visited on Walk 1, and across the street on the southeast **1** corner is a small park. This garden leads to Old St. Joseph's Church, but we shall enter the church through Willings Alley. The garden itself is one of the many to be seen throughout this part of the city and is one of a series of such gardens, green walks and courtyards which have helped recreate the leisureliness of the 18th century city.

South on 4th Street, on the other side at 212 South 4th Street, is *The Philadelphia Contributionship* for the Insurance of Houses **2** from Loss by Fire. Few walkers in Philadelphia realize there is an insurance company housed in such a distinguished building or furnished with such splendor. Perhaps "quiet splendor" would be even more fitting a description. Here is the headquarters of the oldest fire insurance company in America, founded by Benjamin Franklin and his friends in 1752. (By appointment, 627-1752.) According to Nicholas Wainwright in *A Philadelphia Story,* the Company is basically "a mutual insurance corporation which writes perpetual fire insurance and extended coverage on brick and stone dwellings in Philadelphia and adjacent counties." The building itself was erected in 1836.

Those who sign the guest book with a quill pen are given one in return as a souvenir. Take the elevator to the fourth floor and work your way down to the museum on the first.

Here at the top of the house, before 1900, lived the treasurer. Now one room is fitted as an office with an old partners' desk (flat-topped with drawers on each side), a roll-top desk, a fine leather chair with a swinging reading stand, an old tin water container (not a cooler!). In short, here are the accoutrements of an insurance office of times past.

The second floor is spectacularly elegant. The board room and the adjoining dining room are lighted by superb crystal chandeliers. Perhaps the pièces de resistance are the chairs: fourteen matching side chairs in the board room and sixteen matching arm chairs in the dining room—blond mahogany with cane seats—which were ordered when the building was opened and have served the directors ever

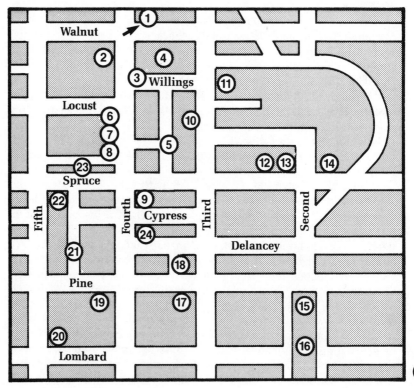

since. A seating plan on the wall gives the holders of the twelve seats on the board since the Contributionship's inception. Our old friend, Benjamin Franklin, is listed as the first incumbent of seat number one.

Across the hall is a room which might be called a double parlor, in which the company holds its annual meetings. Two especially fine marble fireplaces with gilt mirrors frame one wall. There are beautiful crystal candelabra on each, flanked by charming old cachepots. One pair bears portraits of Napoleon and Josephine. From the walls of all these rooms, fine portraits of the officers watch us from another time, another age.

Descend to the museum on the first floor, be sure to touch the ivory amity button on the newel post for good luck and then walk back and see the beautifully planned and executed garden behind. Set among the flowers and bushes is an old milestone—a kind of relic which is fast disappearing from sight. The Contributionship once paid for such markers to be placed on the road from Philadelphia to Trenton.

The museum presents a fascinating collection of memorabilia in its cases. There are firemarks, firemen's hats, miniature engines and lanterns, as one would expect in a fire insurance company museum. And even Hester Bateman, one of the great 18th century silversmiths, made a handsome Waterman's Arm Badge in 1776, which we admire with its crown and No. 21 on the face. When the Contributionship was founded, Philadelphia was ruled by a king not a president.

The Articles of Association, which is also known as The Deed of Settlement, containing 1,774 signatures, is displayed with pride. The lieutenant-governor of the Province of Pennsylvania was the first to subscribe, but the first private citizen to sign his name here was the ubiquitous Benjamin Franklin.

Beneath this are drawers containing a selection of the most valuable papers in this well-documented company. There is a survey of Carpenters' Hall made in 1773—incidentally, the Hall is still insured by the Contributionship. We can also examine surveys of John Penn's and Franklin's houses. Ben's shoe buckles are here and the seal designed by Philip Syng, one of the original directors and a distinguished silversmith, who also designed the inkstand used by the Signers in Independence Hall.

Recross 4th Street to the corner of *Willings Alley*. It was this **3** small street, between 3rd and 4th, that Rudyard Kipling remembered so fondly and asked about when writing to a Philadelphian years later. Turn left and walk the few steps to *Old St. Joseph's Church*, the **4** seat of the oldest Roman Catholic parish in Philadelphia, founded in 1733. The narrow archway, with its iron gates, recalls the legend that Benjamin Franklin advised the Catholic congregation to design the narrow entryway so that, if religious toleration in Philadelphia ever ran a little thin, the church would not be so open to attack. The first church was built in 1733, enlarged in 1821 and rebuilt (the present building in 1838). It survived a period of church-burning during the anti-Catholic riots of 1844. The archway occasioned Agnes Repplier's description of Old St. Joseph's as "a church as carefully hidden away as a martyr's tomb in the catacombs," and it probably appeared that way to Philadelphians long ago.

The archway leads to an inner courtyard, with the rectory and its beautifully balanced façade on the right. A quiet spot, it provides a fitting entry into the church. On the north wall there is a commemorative plaque paying tribute to William Penn, who brought religious toleration and understanding to the Colony, with this inscription:

When in 1733
St. Joseph's Roman Catholic Church
was founded and
Dedicated to the Guardian of the Holy Family
it was the only place
in the entire English speaking world
where public celebration of
the Holy sacrifice of the Mass
was permitted by law.

The church interior has been restored in recent years. There is a particularly impressive painting of the crucifixion behind the main altar and a graceful curving balcony, a rarity in Catholic churches. Lafayette, the Comte de Rochambeau and Admiral de Grasse—Frenchmen all who came to the young republic's assistance in the Revolution—were worshipers here.

Leave Willings Alley; to the left is a parking lot adjacent to the rectory. Until recent years two small rows of alms houses faced each other on this property. A small plaque on the wall once informed the walker that it was on this spot that Evangeline, the heroine of Longfellow's poem, found her fellow-Acadian, Gabriel. The marker is no longer there. Looking toward the river, the front of St. Paul's Episcopal Church, which will be visited later, is visible.

We retrace our steps toward 4th Street, and on the left just off
5 the Alley there is another charming courtyard. *Bingham Court* is modern in concept. In the center is a man-made copse of evergreens. A contemporary sculpture erected in 1970, "Unity" by Richard Lieberman, provides a further accent to the open space.

On 4th Street there is a row of restored houses on the right as we approach Locust Street. The small *garden* on the northwest corner is on the spot where Louis Philippe lived in exile before his ascension to the throne of France in 1830. It is now maintained by the Mutual Assurance Company, and the gardener there once confessed that he had planted poisonous plants near the fence to keep people from picking

Society Hill Towers

the flowers that grow in profusion there spring, summer and autumn. This area was once the home of other French exiles including the Prince de Talleyrand.

Locust Street between 4th and 5th Street is worth a quiet stroll. There are only six dwellings in this one block, gardens predominating. On the north side a greenwalk leads to the Greek Revival porch of the Second Bank of the United States. Midway in the walk is a rose garden planted by the Daughters of the American Revolution and dedicated to the Signers.

On the south side of Locust Street between 410 and the school of the sisters of Notre Dame is the *Magnolia Tribute Garden*. There is no more quiet or restful spot in Philadelphia than this beautifully balanced park. A single gentle stream of water reaches skyward from the fountain. Benches for the elderly, for readers seeking quiet or for a mother with a sleeping child flank the paths. Over the wall can be seen the roofs of houses or an occasional headstone from St. Mary's churchyard beyond. And the sound of birds is heard continually in this lively garden, contributed by the Garden Club of America in honor of the "founders of our nation."

Returning to the corner of 4th and Locust Streets, we are at the entrance of the *Mutual Assurance Company* for Insuring Houses from Loss by Fire. The building is not open to the public, but it has a fascinating history and equally fascinating contents, as does the adjoining house which also makes up the company's offices.

This company—the second oldest fire insurance company in America—was founded in 1784. The Contributionship down the street, in 1781 made a rule that "no house having a Tree or Trees planted before them shall be Insured or Re-Insured" or, "if any person in future having a House Insured shall plant a Tree or Trees before it in the Street, if not removed in three Months from the time of planting he shall forfeit the benefit of Insurance." When the Mutual Assurance Company was founded, a tree was taken for its symbol on the firemark, and the Mutual Assurance Company has since been popularly known as the "Green Tree."

The Company occupies two equally historic houses. The *Shippen- 6 Wistar House* on the corner of 4th and Locust, with the garden and fountain adjoining, was built about 1750 by Dr. William Shippen (1712–1801), a prominent physician who served in the Continental Congress in 1778 and 1779. It was then occupied by Dr. William Shippen, Jr. (1736–1808), who gave medical lectures here for a time to students who couldn't go abroad to study medicine at the great medical centers and was professor of Anatomy and Surgery at the College of Philadelphia in 1765. He was one of the first to use bodies for dissection and had to defend himself in the press against the accusations of "body snatching."

The house was a center of social activity for the great families—the Willings, the Powels and others being entertained here—and through the marriage of Dr. Shippen, Jr., to Alice Lee of Stratford Hall, Virginia, Richard Henry Lee and Francis Lightfoot Lee were among the visitors. John Adams reported that he had breakfasted here and, of course, Washington slept here. Dr. Shippen faithfully served the Army as chief of the medical department during the Revolution, and when the British occupied the city the family left the house.

In 1798 the house was sold to Dr. Caspar Wistar (1761–1818), who lived here until his death. Another of Philadelphia's famed physicians, he was associated with the University of Pennsylvania and Pennsylvania Hospital and was one of the early exponents of vaccination. Baron von Humboldt, the naturalist whose portrait hangs in the library of the American Philosophical Society, was one of the many distinguished scientists to visit Dr. Wistar here. Wistar's open houses for fellow members of the American Philosophical Society and their guests, transient dignitaries of the learned, scientific and artistic world, started the long tradition of "Wistar Parties" which continued after the doctor's death. The Wistaria vine was named for this Wistar, too.

Adjoining the Shippen-Wistar House at 240 South 4th Street, and abutting the burial ground of St. Mary's Church is the *Cad- 7 walader House,* also owned by the Green Tree. Built in 1826 by Joseph Parker Norris in what had been a garden of the Shippen-Wistar House, this four-story house (plus dormered attic) has particularly graceful fanlights over both doors that face 4th Street. It was bought in 1837 by Judge John Cadwalader (1805–79) and is referred to locally as the Cadwalader House. The house went to his son, Dr. Charles, until the Mutual Assurance Company acquired it and the Shippen-Wistar House as well. The insurance company furnished both with superb examples of furniture of the period, and has hung a portrait of Washington by Rembrandt Peale, one of S. Weir Mitchell by John Singer Sargent, a Thomas Eakins of General George Cadwalader and a Duplessis portrait of Franklin painted from life in Paris.

8   Next we come to *Old St. Mary's Church,* founded in 1763. It was the first Roman Catholic cathedral of the Diocese of Philadelphia (1810–38) and was enlarged in 1810 and renovated in 1963. Although St. Joseph's Church was founded first, the present building of St. Mary's is older than that of St. Joseph's. Washington, who certainly showed no favoritism when it came to attending services, worshiped here as well as at Christ Church and St. Peter's.

Along the north wall of its *burial ground* are found the graves of the early Bouviers. Jacqueline Kennedy Onassis' great-great grandfather, Michel Bouvier (1792–1874), the first of the family to come from France, and his descendants all lie beneath the vault which is enclosed with a brass railing. Thomas FitzSimons, signer of the Constitution, member of the Continental Congress and Representative in the 1st, 2nd and 3rd Congresses of the United States; Stephen Moylan, a general officer in tne Revolution and aide-de-camp to Washington; and George Meade, grandfather of George Gordon Meade (1815–72), the Civil War general who was the hero of the Battle of Gettysburg, all lie in this old and historic burial ground. Here, too, is the grave of Commodore John Barry (1745–1803), "Father of the American Navy." The newest bridge across the Delaware at Chester has been named for him. A statue of Barry can be seen in Independence Square, and one of FitzSimons stands before the Cathedral of SS. Peter and Paul on the Parkway.

We now walk toward Spruce Street and turn left. At *338 Spruce,* on the south side of the street, is the house where Joseph Hopkinson, jurist and son of the Signer of the Declaration of Independence, lived when, on April 22, 1798, he composed "Hail, Columbia!"

9   Adjoining it at 336 is the *Wharton House.* It and the others stand on what was once known as "Old Almshouse Square" (3rd to 4th, Spruce to Pine). The present house was built in 1790 by Samuel Pancoast, a builder and one of the founders of the Carpenters' Company. In 1800 the house was occupied by Anthony Morris who, in 1813, represented the United States at the Court of Spain and conducted the diplomatic negotiations which resulted in the purchase of Florida from Spain. At his death in 1860, aged ninety-five, he was the last survivor of the wedding party of President James Madison and Dolley Payne Todd. Later residents were William and Deborah Wharton, whose son Joseph (1826–1909) founded the Wharton School of Finance at the University of Pennsylvania, one of the most important of its kind in the world. The Wharton House is now the rectory of Christ Church.

The other houses on this side, 326 to 334 Spruce Street, were built by Stephen Girard and are of a later vintage, but one of their charms is the original amethyst glass in a number of the windows. Just a half-block east is St. Joseph's Way on the north side of the street. This leads back into Bingham Court, which we just saw opposite St. Joseph's Church. A few steps farther along the Way is a vestpocket court, the four charming houses of *Bell's Court*, 1813–15 A.D. (as the cornerstone indicates). The houses have three stories—called "Father, Son and Holy Ghost" in Philadelphia—and the iron-fenced garden is a surprise when come upon for the first time.

Backtracking, we can see the spire of St. Peter's Church as we re-enter Spruce Street. Turn left toward 3rd Street. The next stop is one of the finest Georgian houses in the United States, the *Powel House* at 244 South 3rd Street. (Open 10:00-5:00 daily, except in winter when the hours are 10:00–4:00. Closed Monday and certain holidays. $2.00.) Built in 1765 by Charles Stedman, it was purchased in 1768 by Samuel Powel, who was the last Colonial mayor of Philadelphia and the first mayor after the Revolution. Samuel's wife Elizabeth was a sister of Thomas Willing, who with his partner Robert Morris helped finance the Revolution. Powel, with so many other Philadelphians, died of yellow fever in 1793, but the family lived in the house for over forty years. **10**

The story of how the Powel House was saved for future generations is a dramatic one. In 1930 it was discovered that the house, occupied by commercial interests, was to be demolished in six weeks time. Miss Frances Anne Wister, the redoubtable granddaughter of Fanny Kemble, appealed to her friends and interested individuals to help preserve the mansion. It was through the remarkable efforts of this strong-minded woman with a deep sense of history that the Powel House stands today. Before Miss Wister acted the Philadelphia Museum of Art had already removed the woodwork—and fireplaces—in the ballroom on the second floor, and the Metropolitan Museum of Art in New York had acquired the woodwork in the supper room. These rooms can still be viewed at the museums. However, the ceiling in the ballroom is the original—for some reason the museum didn't take that—and once the house was saved, experts copied back the woodwork in these two rooms. This, of course, like the Hill-Physick-Keith House, is restoration on a grand scale, which we see throughout the city. The other side of the coin is the individual restoration done by homeowners in the area. Although more modest, it is authentic in detail.

On the first floor, the living room or parlor, the dining room and the magnificent entrance hall are open to the public. In the parlor is a signed Gilbert Stuart of Anne Pennington (1805), now considered one of the house's most valuable furnishings, and the knife boxes in the dining room actually belonged to the Powels. The marvelous tea chest, which requires two people to lift when full, the Nanking china

The Powel House

given by George and Martha Washington, the portraits by John Hesselius, the handsome furniture, among the most beautiful to be seen in Philadelphia, make walking through these rooms an unforgettable experience. In the newel post of the staircase of Santo Domingo mahogany is the ivory amity button, which the guide always points to as the repository of the contract for the house, or mortgage, when paid. The papers were put in the newel post and sealed with the amity button for safe keeping. With this 18th century version of a safe-deposit box, everyone knew where the deed or mortgage was. (However, getting the papers out was another matter, and the history books do not tell us how this was done.)

On the second floor the ballroom dominates, and it was here that Washington, Adams, Franklin, Lafayette and other worthies were entertained by Mrs. Powel, one of the most brilliant hostesses of her time. John Adams wrote: ". . . a most sinful feast again! Everything which could delight the eye or allure the taste; curds and creams, jellies, sweetmeats of various sorts, twenty sorts of tarts, fools, trifles, floating islands, whipped sillibub, &c., &c., Parmesan cheese, punch, wine, porter, beer, etc." The ballroom with its magnificent Waterford chandelier, circa 1790, contains a pianoforte from 1795 in addition to a French harp and an arm harp. The splendid gilt-framed mirrors reflecting the chandelier enable us to envision the balls that were held here.

In the bedroom are displayed a wig stand, a bootjack and a sewing cabinet given to Mrs. Powel by Martha Washington. One endearing story has it that, when the house was thought to be doomed, a workman took all the old Delft tiles from the bedroom fireplace. However, when word went abroad that the house was saved, he brought the tiles back and installed them again himself. Most of the firebacks in the house were discovered in the basement, fortunately discarded there rather than into the alley behind. The Powel House has one of the loveliest gardens in Society Hill, and a walk through it convinces us that it must have been a haven in the 18th century, too.

Immediately next to the Powel House is *242 South 3rd Street,* a home that is not open to the public. On this site, however, was the home (1766–1771) of John Penn (1729–95), the last Colonial governor of Pennsylvania, a son of Richard Penn and grandson of William Penn. It was also the home from 1771 to 1810 of Benjamin Chew (1722–1810), the last Colonial Chief Justice of Pennsylvania, whose great house Cliveden is to be visited on Walk 11. During the years 1778 to 1780 it was the home of Juan de Miralles (1715–80), the first Spanish diplomatic representative to the United States. He died while visiting Washington at his Morristown, New Jersey, headquarters. The house then became the residence of his successor, Francisco Rondón, who lent it to Washington during the winter of 1781–82. So, at one time the Washingtons and the Powels were next-door neighbors. No wonder they became such fast friends in later life.

Farther along toward Willings Alley are two handsome houses with spectacular ironwork along the small balconies on front. One should never pass any Philadelphia ironwork without stopping, and these are among the most striking examples in the city. The *Bishop Stevens House* at 232 South 3rd Street was formerly used as an office of the Episcopal Community Services.

11   Just opposite is *St. Paul's Episcopal Church*, built in 1761. It is no longer used as a church but as headquarters for the Episcopal Community Services of the Diocese of Pennsylvania. However, the interior of the building has not been changed radically and sometime in the future it will probably be used as a church again. When it was built it was the third Protestant Episcopal Church in the city of Philadelphia and the largest in the province. Stephen Girard and Mary Lum were married here in June, 1777. In the burial ground is the grave of Edwin Forrest (1806–72), the great tragedian known for his "Spartacus" and other dramatic roles. His feud with William Macready, the English actor, caused the Astor Place Riot in New York (1849), in which 30 people were killed and another 36 wounded. The Forrest Theatre on Walnut Street is named for him, and he endowed the Edwin Forrest Home for retired actors which is still providing a home for aged thespians a century after his death.

Drama of another sort occurred in this area in the last decade of the 18th century. Alexander Hamilton, the first Secretary of the Treasury, lived on Walnut Street near 3rd, just around the corner. It was while living here in 1791 that he had a liaison with a Mrs. Mary Reynolds, only to be blackmailed later by her husband James. The two Reynolds disappeared from the stage of history, as well they should, but in 1797 Hamilton published a book about the affair in order to set the record straight and protect himself from his enemies —one of whom was James Monroe.

Return to Spruce Street, note the fine old *brownstones* opposite and, at 3rd and Spruce, pay particular attention to the property on the southeast corner—the house built in 1764—with its handsome walled garden and summerhouse. A former owner instructed visitors to the garden that the *summerhouse* should always be referred to as a "belvedere." There is a small gate on the 3rd Street side to peer through into the formal garden.

Turning left, we proceed along Spruce Street and find at 217 the **12** *Davis-Lenox House*. The sign on front tells us:

> *Built in 1759 by James Davis*
> *house carpenter & officer*
> *of the Carpenters' Company.*
> *Added to in 1784 by Major*

David Lenox, Continental
soldier, 44th member First
City Troop, President of the
Bank of the U.S., U.S. Marshal for
the District of Pennsylvania,
Representative of the U.S. to
the Court of St. James's.

It is now a private residence, as are all the others in this area. This block is one of the loveliest in Society Hill for it has a mixture of sizes and styles of houses. Some like the Davis-Lenox House and its neighbors on each side were homes of the wealthy establishment (as was the Powel House). Others, such as those opposite, which are smaller and more modest, were owned by men and women of substance if not great means.

Near the entrance to the three skyscraper apartment buildings designed by I. M. Pei, the Society Hill Towers, are two magnificent town houses that have been restored. With the contemporary fountains and sculpture of the modern complex serving as a backdrop, these two residences typify the old versus the new which stand juxtaposed throughout Society Hill. One of them, the Abercrombie House of 1758, at 270 South 2nd Street, is now the *Perelman Antique* **13** *Toy Museum.* (Open every day 9:30-5:00. Adults, $1.00, children under fourteen, $.55.) The museum asks us to walk into America's childhood and that is exactly what we do.

There are roller skates, mechanical toys, whistles from 1850 to 1890, and what could be more appropriate than to look at them and recall B. Franklin's essay, "The Whistle." We find clockwork toys, perambulating toys, Humpty Dumptys, Jacks-in-the-box and jacks. The latter were used as far back as 1814, and we find examples here from 1850 and 1885. There are stereopticons and even a circa-1830 Phenakistiscope (when a series of action pictures are set spinning the effect is that of a motion picture), a zoetrope from 1867 which is the earliest optical toy in America. In cases, a little high for the smallest children, there are dolls, teddy bears, marbles, mechanical toy penny banks, trains, Mickey Mouse and Donald Duck toys, card games, blocks and soldiers. This excursion into another time with toys makes it all great fun.

Just across 2nd Street from the toy museum, the building next to the swimming pool of Society Hill Towers is *"A Man Full of Trouble,"* **14** 125–27 Spruce Street. (By appointment, 743-4225. Adults, $1.00; children, $.50.) This restoration, slightly askew because of time's passage, is the only tavern remaining from Colonial Philadelphia. It was built about 1759 on the banks of Little Dock Creek, which has been filled in and lost to view, in an area in which mariners, cordwainers and dockhands swarmed—and patronized this inn. The tavern was in actuality the building nearest the river, for at that time its neighbor, the Paschall House, did not have connecting doors to the tavern.

Because it was a tavern and has the intimacy and scale of an inn, "A Man Full of Trouble" has a different appeal from the grand houses we have visited. The rooms are low ceilinged and the tavern room itself, for eating and drinking, is warm and inviting. Here are a dresserful of superb English Delft china, old pewter, a set of Windsor chairs owned by John Jay, the first Chief Justice of the United States. An "Honesty Box"—which the guide will tell us about with pleasure—demanded a penny and then the honesty of the pipe smoker who would take only one pipeful of tobacco. We see those other playthings of riotous nights in the taverns—puzzle jugs. The drinker would have to be clever to siphon the ale through the handle and not let any spill out of the latticework in the porcelain.

The cellar, which contained the kitchen, has been excavated; the archeologists found glass, china and other artifacts which have been pieced together and are on exhibit. The maids and the hired men slept on cots down here—very 18th century communal. There are musket slots on the landings between the first and second floors for defending the tavern against attack, and in the attic a room where men off the ships often slept four in a bed. It may be difficult to imagine how it was done, but sailors were smaller in stature then or, maybe, just less demanding.

From the tavern the Head House and the old market at Pine Street can be seen. Before reaching Pine Street, however, turn right on Delancey and stroll the long block to 3rd Street, passing *Philip Street* and *American Street* on the north side. Take one side of the street going and the other side returning. Small houses with the appealing overhang above the first floor, a formal Japanese garden adjacent to an 18th century house, and *Drinker's Court* (1765)—a tiny and charming hideaway—are to be seen on this one street. Return to 2nd Street.

15   *The Head House,* Georgian in design and built in 1803 for meetings of the commissioners, fire companies and citizens, dominates the market arcades behind. Sometime in the middle of the 18th century a pair of market houses was built in the center of 2nd Street. They were later enlarged and had grown to some 440 feet by 1811. These were probably the oldest public market houses in the country before they were torn down and the market itself, used by craftsmen today to display their wares, can probably claim the distinction of being the oldest market still in continual use.

Lewis Mumford spoke of the Head House as "a building that should be treated tenderly and remain undisturbed." It is an island around which traffic moves slowly and the life of this part of Society Hill swirls. The only other building so felicitously situated—that comes immediately to mind—is the Old State House in Boston.

From *Head House Square*—beautifully restored with shops, res- **16** taurants, an ice cream parlor, an apothecary shop, antique shops, all contributing to its 18th century feeling—walk west on Pine Street toward 3rd. Of particular interest are the charming backs of the buildings which face the square. They look onto Stamper-Blackwell Walk lined with gaslights.

"A Man Full of Trouble" Tavern

New Market, South 2nd Street

St. Peter's Way

17   At 3rd and Pine Streets stands *St. Peter's Church,* one of the landmarks of Society Hill. Before entering the churchyard, note the house on the northwest corner. This was for a time the home of Thaddeus Kosciusko (1746–1817), the Polish patriot who fought for the American cause during the Revolution. One of his first duties was helping fortify the city against the British fleet's expected attack. The house has a double history for it was also the birthplace of Colonel John Nixon (1733–1808), who first read the Declaration of Independence publicly in the State House Yard on July 8, 1776. An ancestor of President Nixon, he was a soldier in both the French and Indian War and the Revolution as well as a sheriff in Philadelphia.

St. Peter's Church, one of the oldest still standing in Philadelphia, is also one of the most beautiful. The interior, which was first used for services in 1761, is plainer and simpler than that of Christ Church, but its double-ended style with the altar at the east end and the pulpit at the west is unusual. The land for the church was given by Thomas and Richard Penn, proprietors of the Colony, no longer Quakers but Episcopalians.

The land St. Peter's and the burying ground cover is the largest open tract in this part of the city, and it provides a beautiful vista for the houses opposite. Toward the 4th Street end the largest monument in the cemetery is one to the naval hero Stephen Decatur (1779–1820), who was killed in a duel. Here are also the graves of Benjamin Chew, jurist and owner of Cliveden in Germantown; Nicholas Biddle, the banker whose home you will see on Walk 5; Charles Willson Peale, the portrait painter and father of a family of distinguished painters; Dr. William Shippen, whose home was noted on this walk; and seven Indian chiefs carried off by smallpox in 1793.

During the Revolution, when everything of value was being hidden (and fortunately much has survived), the two bells given St. Peter's by Christ Church were taken, along with the Liberty Bell, to Allentown for safekeeping during the British occupation of the city.

St. Peter's, like so many Philadelphia institutions, is slow to change, but it may give us pause to learn that electricity was not installed until 1926. Things sometimes move more slowly in Philadelphia than elsewhere.

St. Peter's Way, opposite the gates to St. Peter's, is a greenwalk **18** leading to Delancey Street and a delightful playground-park for children. The park, which is modern in concept with sculpture for children to climb over as well as the standard swings and jungle-jims, was dedicated in 1966 in memory of the Reverend William De Lancey (1797–1865), rector of St. Peter's parish and provost of the University of Pennsylvania, whose family gave its name to Delancey Street and Place. The park will be seen later when we visit the Hill-Physick-Keith House, which is just in front of it.

Society Hill is blessed in the number of old churches which have survived, and at 4th and Pine there is another, the Third Presbyterian Church, more familiarly known as *Old Pine*. Although built in 1768, **19** the church was altered twice (in 1837 and 1857) and a Greek Revival front was added. However, its handsome Corinthian columns give an air of elegance to the old neighborhood. Old Pine has as many historical connotations as any building in the city. Sixty men from the congregation, 35 of whom were commissioned officers, were members of the Continental Army. General John Steele, a parishioner, was personal aide-de-camp to Washington and served as a field officer at Yorktown on the day Cornwallis surrendered. During the Revolution the British used the church as a hospital and later, when they had used the last of the pews and woodwork for firewood, the church was commandeered as a stable by the dragoons.

One hundred Hessians are buried in a common grave along the east wall of the church. William Hurry (1721–81) is buried here.

William's fame rests on the fact that he rang the Liberty Bell at the first public reading of the Declaration of Independence. There is a small stone in the lot of Thomas Brainerd, the sixth pastor, to "Our Charley," another reminder of personal loss.

20 We can see the *Presbyterian Historical Society*, 425 Lombard Street, at the south side of the burying ground. Walk to 5th and Pine Streets, turn left and walk one block to reach the entrance. (Monday-Friday, 9:00-5:00. Closed on legal holidays.) Founded in 1852, the Society contains a library of over 100,000 published volumes and archives of several million manuscripts, including 13,000 bound church records.

Inside the museum are paintings by such well-known painters as Rembrandt Peale, James Peale, Jacob Eichholtz, Bass Otis, John Neagle and Samuel Finley Breese Morse, primitives, portrait busts, letters, pewter plate and a tall clock which belonged to John Witherspoon (1723–94), the only minister to sign the Declaration of Independence. He was also the president of the College of New Jersey (later Princeton) from 1768 to 1794. His statement during the debate over whether or not the time was propitious for Independence at the Second Continental Congress has come ringing down through the years. John Dickinson, who was advocating moderation until the time was ripe, provoked Witherspoon to shout: "In my judgment, sir, we are not only ripe but rotting."

In the *garden* outside are six larger than life-size figures, statues by Alexander Stirling Calder, of American Presbyterian personalities who played a significant role in the history of the church—Francis Makemie (c. 1658–1708), John McMillan (1752–1833), Samuel Davies (1723–61), James Caldwell (1734–81), Marcus Whitman (1802–47) and Witherspoon. At one time the statues were mounted on the Witherspoon Building, Walnut and Juniper Streets, but they were removed in 1961 and placed in this garden in 1967. Return now to Old Pine.

21 Opposite Old Pine we enter *Lawrence Street*, which contains old and new houses and leads, naturally enough, to Lawrence Court. Leaving Lawrence Court, we pass by the steel sculpture of the kangaroos—a comic touch and just right here—and proceed to the *Society*
22 *Hill Synagogue*, built in 1829 as the Spruce Street First Baptist Church. For a time it was a Rumanian Synagogue, but is now a Conservative one. It has the distinction of having been designed by Thomas U. Walter, who was the architect responsible for the dome and the Senate and House wings of the national capitol. The exterior has already been restored, and the interior is undergoing restoration. The synagogue's situation on Spruce and Lawrence Streets, its side and back to Lawrence Court, is beneficial, for the building is a massive one and the opening to one side and behind lessens this bulk. A drawing for the building by Walter is in The Philadelphia Contributionship, which was visited at the beginning of this walk.

Just opposite the synagogue at *429 Spruce Street*—the house **23** with the stepping stone by the curb—is the three-story dwelling where Congressman James Madison brought his wife Dolley Payne Todd in 1795 when Philadelphia was the capital of the nation. The widowed Dolley Todd lived at her mother's boarding house and among the guests at the boarding house was Senator Aaron Burr. It was he who introduced Dolley to James Madison of Virginia. That meeting not only led Dolley to the altar a second time but also to the White House and a secure place in history. It is thought Dolley was named for Dorothea Dandridge, Patrick Henry's second wife, a neighbor of her family.

Return to Lawrence Street beside the synagogue and walk into *Lawrence Court*, taking a left at the statue of the kangaroos, and proceed along Cypress Street to 4th Street. Note the amazing roofs, staircases, outdoor terraces and sculpture which are collected here. It is a European or North African scene in outline—incongruous, yet fitting.

When we reach 4th Street, we can see on an angle the *Hill-Physick-Keith House* between Cypress and Delancey. At 321 South **24** 4th Street is one of the most magnificent houses in America, and it is fortunately open to the public (Tuesday–Saturday, 10:00–4:00; Sunday, 1:00–4:00. $2.00). There are a number of houses open to the public in Society Hill, but none is quite like the Hill-Physick-Keith House. For one thing it is the only free-standing house in Society Hill and for another it is the only Federal house in Philadelphia that has been restored with Federal furniture. From the moment we enter and hear the custodian's friendly, "Welcome to Dr. Physick's house," we are spellbound.

This splendid house was built in 1786 by Henry Hill, an eminent merchant and executor of Benjamin Franklin's will. He lived here until his death in 1790, when the house was purchased by Miss Abigail Physick, who gave it to her brother, Philip Syng Physick (1768–1837). The good doctor—whose grave we saw in Christ Church Burial Ground—lived in the house from 1815 until his death, and his descendants lived here until 1941.

The house reflects an age of grace, balance, symmetry and proportion. There is a feeling of space everywhere, an airy quality. We are about to see some of the finest Federal and Empire furniture in Philadelphia. Napoleon's influence is everywhere, in the magenta of the Aubusson rug in the study (it was the Emperor's favorite color), the Napoleonic swan motif in the yellow wallpaper in the entrance hall (all the wallpapers and the fabrics used for upholstery or draperies were made especially for the house), in the golden bee woven into the upholstery.

The fanlight in the entrance hall is one of the largest in Philadelphia and is the original one installed in 1786, except for seven panels that have required replacement. The black and white marble floor was ordered by the doctor himself.

The study, often called the green room, has an unique mirror over the fireplace. The motif of Cleopatra's head, feet and the asp entwined between them, the French eternal flame and the American eagle are all incorporated in it. The gilt George Washington clock (one of nine known) bears a slightly different version of the motto we all know today: "First in War, First in Peace, And in his Countrymen Hearts." Beneath a portrait of Chief Justice John Marshall is a silver wine cooler given to the doctor by Marshall in 1831 when Physick brought him through a difficult illness.

The doctor was often presented with gifts by grateful patients. In the dining room is a handsome silver pitcher given to him by Commodore John Barron. On its face is the couplet:

> *The offer of feeling to the Surgeon who feels*
> *As much pleasure in healing as he whom he heals.*

We remember Barron with mixed emotions today because it was he who caused Stephen Decatur's untimely death in the Maryland duel.

The dining room is dominated by a Valley Forge marble mantel with inset mirrors on one side and a sideboard which is one of the finest examples of Federal style, circa 1820, on the other. The sideboard has striking Atlantes columns (with the figure of Atlas), another evidence that our ancestors went to history and mythology for their decorative motifs.

Another of Dr. Physick's gifts from his patients is the painting of the Roman ruins hanging in the drawing room, which was presented by Joseph Bonaparte. This room is dominated by a Grecian couch of blond mahogany made in Philadelphia for the Custis family (Martha Dandridge had married a Custis before Washington became her second husband). It and a Pompeiian stool, also made in Philadelphia in 1805, indicate the heights Philadelphia furniture-makers achieved in the Federal period. This was an age of elegance.

The recently opened second floor contains a bedroom, and here, besides the spectacular bed, is a linen press which was owned by the mother of Henry Hill, the original occupant of the house.

The Society of Cincinnatus, one of the oldest and most distinguished in the United States, has its headquarters in the upstairs parlor and all of the furniture in this room belongs to the Society. Candlesticks presented to Washington by Lafayette flank an inkstand which still bears Benjamin Franklin's thumbprints! This seems difficult to believe, but Franklin used both hands in opening it—after many years his thumbs left impressions—and if we open it with both hands, we see his thumbprints where ours have been. Franklin, who had a great sense of history, scratched his name on the back.

The Hill-Physick-Keith House is an outstanding example of the preservation work going on in Philadelphia. The Annenberg Fund purchased the property and with a grant for its restoration then presented it to the Philadelphia Society for the Preservation of Landmarks, which also maintains the Powel House, seen on this walk, and Grumblethorpe, which will be visited on Walk 12.

In Society Hill we have looked into many gardens and walked through several. However, there is none quite so evocative of the past as the last one. This romantic *garden* of a romantic age follows a serpentine path—Hogarth's "Line of Beauty"—and we follow it, too, and pass an Etruscan sarcophagus, Pompeiian statues (one in a natural grotto), antique cannon and a rustic bench. The plants are all those grown in early 19th century gardens, and the lasting effect is one of civilization at its highest order. It is a fitting finale to a walk through Society Hill.

Hill-Physick-Keith House

Deep in the Heart
of Southwark

Southwark (or *Wicaco*, to give it its Indian name) is one of the oldest parts of Philadelphia. It was named for that part of London on the southside of the Thames. Under a grant from the Dutch governor in 1664 the Swedes were already here when the English came. The Swedish influence is still evident in many of the street names—Swanson, Christian, Queen—and traces of the original character remain long after other parts of the city have gone through constant and frequent change.

The English bought lots along the river front, below South Street, for warehousing and stores. Edward Shippen, a vital force in Colonial Philadelphia, bought 50 acres in 1694, a purchase confirmed by patent in 1701. Other families whose names became important—Whartons, Mifflins, Penroses, the Reverend William White—began to buy and use property for wharves, warehouses and other commerce. When Christopher Swanson, whose father Andreas was an original Swedish settler, died in 1735 he owned the area from Gloria Dei to Pemberton Street, an extensive tract. By the middle of the 18th century it was so developed that, in 1743, one writer said, "Southwark is getting greatly disfigured by erecting irregular and mean houses; thereby so marring its beauty that when he shall return, he will lose his usual pretty walk to Wiccaco [*sic*]."

In the 17th century Southwark's housing was of a primitive kind, with few doors and windows. The window openings were usually loopholes with sliding shutters. The original Swedish settlers built their homes of wood, smearing clay between the logs. Peter Kalm, the Swedish botanist (1716–79), who made a three-year-long survey of American natural history, visited Philadelphia beginning in 1748. He reported in his book, *Travels into North America*, that the Swedes who were settled in Pennsylvania built wooden houses because they "knew nothing of brick making or burning lime."

The houses were smaller than those in Society Hill for the tenants were artisans. This was an area in which mariners, sea captains, pilots, sailors, shipwrights and riggers lived and it was said that one pirate—probably a retired one—resided here as well.

Hundreds of 18th century houses stand in Southwark today. Since they were built by workingmen, staying within their own class rather than rising as Benjamin Franklin did (his genius had something to do with it!), the houses were seldom torn down to make room for larger ones; instead a small house was enlarged. Often the kitchen was built first, then the rest added later.

Philadelphia was the major seaport of the British colonies in the 18th century and later the first United States Navy Yard in Philadelphia was built in the district at the foot of Federal Sreet. It was in Southwark that the city's first playhouses were located, both Hallam's and the Southwark Theatre, and it was an active, bustling, thriving area—in 1790 there were 27 inns or lodging houses in the district. Southwark may be a less-grand part of the city than Society Hill, but it is no less historic.

We begin at *Head House Square*, which we visited on Walk 3, **1** but our starting point now is the southernmost end of the market. From where Lombard and South 2nd Streets cross, we make our way

Head House Square

toward South Street. Should a good lunch or dinner be desired, there are restaurants of every kind and in every price range on South Street, in Head House Square, and also at New Market. With some of these it is very wise to make reservations and to avoid all the busiest times. At the north end of the Square, at

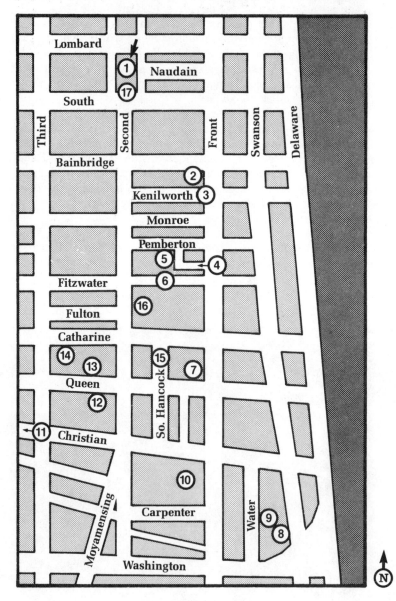

the Head House itself, is Head House Tavern, where light lunches (sandwiches, salads and beer) can be gotten. There is one French restaurant, Le Champignon at 122 Lombard, but this is more expensive, takes a little longer and is suggested for the evening. Another French restaurant on the Square itself is the Lautrec, where lunch and dinner are served.

Don't be discouraged by the look of the neighborhood. This is the way Society Hill looked in the 1950s and 1960s, before its restoration. We shall walk south with our ultimate destination Old Swedes' Church, one of the oldest and most historic buildings in America.

Turn left and walk toward the river. At Front and South Streets a wonderful panorama is visible, the *Delaware* with the Benjamin Franklin Bridge on the left, the *Penn's Landing Marina* nearer at hand, and slightly to the right is Pier 30, which has been converted into a tennis club. The skyline and shoreline of Camden, New Jersey, the home of Walt Whitman, are in the distance. The poet often took the ferry across and celebrated both the Philadelphia and Camden shorelines in his work.

To the left, almost at the corner of Lombard Street, at what was later *502 South Front Street*, was the cave of Francis Daniel Pastorious, the founder of Germantown. He and the heads of thirteen families met in the cave in 1683 and selected the lots which were to be theirs in Germantown.

Walk straight along Front Street toward Christian Street, seven blocks to the south. At times we shall diverge slightly and wander up interesting small streets along the way, where ship's chandlers and seamen lived. Although particular families might die out or move on, the character of the area was fairly constant, for the men who dwelt here made their living from the sea and the port.

At Front and Bainbridge Streets are two restored houses—*100 and 102 Bainbridge*—on the southwest corner. They are typical of **2** the hundreds in this area that have survived from the 18th and early 19th centuries. There is probably a greater collection of unrestored houses of the period here than anywhere else in America—more than in Boston, Charleston, Savannah and other old cities. Number *107 Bainbridge* is typical of the unrestored houses, but the lines, the old brick, the pitch of the roof, the dormer tell its story.

One street south of Bainbridge is *Kenilworth*. At number 106 the **3** overhang and the dormer catch the eye. It and 109 and 117 on the other side are restored. In the next decade all of the unoccupied ones will be restored and many of those already occupied will be as well. Most of these have been restored by individuals, acting on their own, rather than by builders and architects in some instances, as happened in Society Hill. In the 1970s many younger people in their twenties bought properties and did the work themselves.

The area abounds in restored houses and we shall see more examples as we proceed. The walker is advised to keep his eyes open

Mifflin Houses

at all times, for among the worst examples of present-day building materials—asbestos siding, shingles, plastic awnings—a perfect gem of an old building will suddenly appear, its lines intact.

4   Two blocks farther south, at Pemberton Street, is a collection of buildings that is a marvel. *Workman Place* has stood the vicissitudes of a century and a half. This group—the ones on Front Street were built by John Workman in 1812—is maintained by the Octavia Hill Association, which has provided low-cost housing for families since the 19th century.

Along Pemberton Street, follow the brick wall with ivy climbing over it that encloses the common ground within. Two buildings which Colonial Williamsburg would treasure stand here, dwellings which face each other, with an iron gate between to help keep undesirables

5   out after dark. On one of the *Mifflin Houses,* in the brick of the upper wall, are the initials *G.M.* and on the other *1748*—the year George Mifflin built them. He was the grandfather of Thomas Mifflin, the general who built Fort Mifflin and was governor of Pennsylvania from 1790 to 1799.

On the southeast corner of Front and Fitzwater Streets, at 757 South Front, is a building erected in 1801, housing Rick's Cabaret, a delightful French pub and restaurant. Turn right and wander along

6   the one block of *Fitzwater Street.* Here are the small-street modest houses of the 18th century. The brick is old here, it hasn't been cleaned, repointed or tampered with. This enclave out of the past is not a restoration. Two steps off Front Street into Fitzwater and we are back in the 18th century, a section that is known as *Queen Village.* It was so named in the 1960s and extends from the southside of Lombard Street to the southside of Washington Avenue and from Front Street to 5th, much farther westword than we shall explore.

Back on Front Street again, we find a pair of beautifully restored houses—three stories each, with a dormer window in the attic and the charming overhang that is typical of the time and, at 776 South Front, there are excellent examples of window caps of the period. Between Catharine and Queen Streets are other fine examples of houses erected at about the same time.

The *Church of the Redeemer* for Seamen and Their Families, a **7** wonderfully Victorian structure by Frank Furness, the 19th century architect, stood at the corner of Front and Queen Streets. The cornerstone was laid in 1878, and the church was consecrated the following January. It was unlike the churches we are used to seeing in the historic parts of the city in its variety of peaks and gables and because it had no tower or steeple. The church and the adjacent Charles Brewer School were destroyed by a fire of mysterious origin in September, 1974.

Walk one block farther to Front and Christian Streets, then go left across and under the still-unconnected section of highway I-95 (its completion is being vigorously protested by civic groups) to Water Street. Here is the tiny Gloria Dei, or *Old Swedes' Church*, the **8** oldest church in Pennsylvania. It was founded in 1642, and the present church was built in 1700. Originally serving a Swedish Lutheran congregation, it is now an Episcopal church and a national shrine.

Entering the compound from Water Street, stand for a moment looking down the brick path to the church. The industrial area beyond is forgotten. Two centuries or more in time have slipped away. In the spring when the trees are in blossom and the forsythia as well, with crocuses and hyacinths beginning to push up among the graves, the place is pervaded with a feeling of quiet and serenity and rebirth. At the end of summer, there is a dark green lushness over all. In the 17th century when the first church was erected and at the beginning of the 18th when the present one was built, the Delaware River flowed at the east end of Christian Street where Swanson crosses it. In the more than two hundred and seventy years since, there has been a great deal of land filled in, and what is now Delaware Avenue, between the church and the river, is new ground.

The house directly alongside the church is the rectory, built early in the 19th century, and behind it is a small building used for exhibits and teas. To the rear of this is the tiny custodian's house which looks much more ancient than the parsonage. Gloria Dei was considered a country church in the 18th century because of its distance from the center-of-town activity.

Of particular interest is the *churchyard*. There is a monument to **9** John Hanson, first president of the United States under the Articles of Confederation in 1781 and 1782, or, as he is usually referred to, "first president of the United States in Congress Assembled." Around the base of the monument are bas reliefs to other Swedes who helped make American history: Johan Printz, governor of New Sweden; Johan Risingh, last governor of New Sweden; John Dahlgren, admiral of the United States Navy; John Ericsson, inventor; John Nystrom, engineer; and John Morton, Signer of the Declaration of Independence. Another point of interest is the grave of Alexander Wilson, father of American ornithology. Born in Paisley, Scotland, in 1766, he emigrated to the United States in 1794 and died in 1813. A new stone placed over his grave was made possible by contributions from school children in Wilson's native Scotland.

Here also is the spot where the blockhouse church stood in 1677, and just beyond the hallowed ground where eight Revolutionary soldiers are buried. Their stones originally stood in Ronaldson's Cemetery and were removed when the burying ground was being closed. The tallest monument marks the grave of one romantically referred to as "the Scottish Stranger."

As we enter the church a small stone outside the entry reads:

> This is none other
> But
> The House of God
> And this is
> The Gate of Heaven

The church is charmingly simple inside. It was here that Betsy Ross, widow of John Ross, married Captain Joseph Ashbourn, on June 15, 1777.

One room of the church is set aside as a small museum. Among the photographs are those signed by King Gustav VI Adolf and Queen Louise of Sweden, when they visited the church as Crown Prince and Princess with Prince Bertil in 1938 for the Swedish tercentenary in America. A delicate small silver crown given by Carl Milles, the Swedish sculptor, is also on view. Any girl being married in Old Swedes' can wear the crown on her wedding day.

After leaving Old Swedes', return to Front Street, turn left and walk one block to Carpenter Street. Enter this old street which has a number of beautifully restored houses and note others awaiting

10 restoration. Commanding this street is the 142-foot brick shot tower, the first such tower erected in the United Sates. It was built in 1807 by John B. Bishop and Thomas Sparks and used until 1907. At the time the tower was built shot was poured into molds and while cooling was dropped from the height of the tower into cold water. By the time it had reached the bottom it had cooled and was ready for use. The tower dominates the recreation center which has been developed around it.

Walk along Carpenter to Second Street, turn right and, at 2nd and Christian, proceed to the first crossing, Moyamensing Avenue, which soon becomes 2nd Street again. In the distance are the Society

Gloria Dei Church

Carving in
Gloria Dei

Hill Towers, which can serve as a guide even when wandering in streets to the left and right. Although it is not on our way, one could

11 walk along Christian and come to the *Italian Market* on 9th Street, open air, bustling, filled with the aroma and smells of its European origins. Market days are usually Friday and Saturday although the market is in operation every day of the week. There are marvelous cheese and bread shops and others specializing in Italian pastries, and all sorts of special vinegars, oils and spices not available elsewhere. Numerous Italian restaurants dot the area.

Turn left at Queen Street, crossing 2nd, and just below the

12 corner is the unexpectedly handsome façade of *St. Philip Neri Church.* The red sandstone front, with its severely plain pediment, is not in keeping with the other Catholic churches we have seen. It has no tower and the only relief to the standstone are IHS and the date in gold—A.D. 1840—and the gold cross which seemingly floats above the pediment.

The small park opposite the church is a surprise. (This far south we miss the many squares and parks found in Society Hill or

13 the Independence Hall area.) *Mario Lanza Park* was dedicated, in 1967, to the tenor (1921–59), who will always have a place in the hearts of South Philadelphians. The old trees lend it a quiet dignity, and its being just opposite the church helps give perspective to the church front as well.

Walk along Queen Street to 3rd and before reaching the corner pass a number of restorations which have helped make Queen Village a residential area which will soon take its place beside Society Hill. Continue on 3rd to Catharine, turn right and between 228 and 230

14 Catharine Street is a courtyard which was recently restored. It is the sort of spot which was found in Society Hill twenty to twenty-five years ago in a similar condition.

St. Philip Neri Church

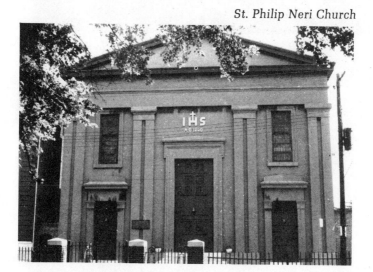

Chandelier,
Neziner Synagogue

Returning to 2nd Street, on our left we can see Society Hill Towers. Before continuing in that direction, cross 2nd Street and walk to the first small street beyond. Here on *South Hancock Street* are **15** several of the remaining small wooden 18th century houses.

Back on 2nd Street, walk along toward Society Hill Towers. At 781 South 2nd is a *courtyard* reminiscent of some of the smaller ones of New Orleans. Behind the iron gates is a collection of homes typical of Queen Village, and this restoration and preservation process will be apparent again and again as we walk back and forth along these streets.

A few steps farther on is the *Neziner Synagogue* at 771 South **16** 2nd. Founded in 1889, the congregation until recently occupied this historic building. The structure, dating from about 1810, was erected by the Third Baptist Church, the first all-stone building completed in the Southwark district. The First Polish National Society of Philadelphia occupied it from 1898 until it was sold to the Congregation Ahavas Achim Nazin Misach Hoarce. Painted grey and protected by a handsome iron fence with the Star of David worked into the pattern on the gates, the yard provides a delightful pocket garden-park among the houses of the street. Inside, the original atmosphere has been retained—there is a gallery around the sanctuary itself and a handsome brass chandelier hangs from the ceiling.

A few blocks farther and we are back on South Street, facing the market at *Head House Square*. A turn to the left *along South* **17** *Street* will bring the unguided walker who is inquisitive and anxious to explore even more to a collection of antique, craft, flower, and natural food stores. There are a number of art galleries and the area has become the Greenwich Village of Philadelphia, especially since Pine Street has become more respectable and conservative and its stores more establishment-minded and expensive. South Street is a section that most people enjoy; different and colorful with a relaxed charm all its own.

A Long Stroll Through Washington Square West

Frances Trollope, that inveterate critic of Americans and their ways, wrote in her *Domestic Manners of the Americans* in 1830: "This pretty Washington Square is surrounded by houses on three sides, but has a prison on the fourth; it is, nevertheless, the nearest approach to a London square that is to be found in Philadelphia." The Walnut Street Prison she noted stood across from the northeast corner, with its yard extending through to Locust Street. Its most famous prisoner was Robert Morris, in debtors' prison in 1798 after he had helped finance the Revolution. Washington did not forget Morris' services and loyalty and often visited him while he was jailed. And it was from this prison yard that Jean-Pierre Blanchard made his epochal balloon ascension in 1793 with Washington and hundreds of Philadelphians watching him. His flight was successful and he thus became our first aeronaut!

As one of William Penn's five squares this one was simply called the southeast square, for Quakers did not believe in naming places

1 after people. The trees in *Washington Square* are older, widerspreading and taller than those in Rittenhouse or Independence squares, and the square itself has a more open, spacious quality— but then it started as a pasture. Later the square served as a burial ground—potter's field—and many American and British soldiers of the Revolution lie here, along with victims of the yellow fever epidemic of 1793. In 1833 it was renamed. From the time of the Revolution through the early 19th century, it was a hub of activity with a distinctly residential character. Then for many years, its residents moved away, but, since the recent renaissance of Society Hill, the residential character of the square is returning.

Standing in the center at the *fountain*, turn slowly around to see the landmarks on the square. Turning east toward 6th Street, you will see the Penn Mutual Life Insurance building at the corner of 6th and Walnut Streets, site of the old prison. Next to it at 219 South 6th Street, on the corner of St. James Street, is the Athenaeum of Philadelphia. The Colonial house between it and the offices of J. B. Lippincott Company, book publishers, was the home of the late Richardson Dilworth, former mayor of Philadelphia. It is neither a restoration nor a reconstruction, but an imitation, and it replaced, alas, two handsome 19th century town houses, which had fine balconies extending across their width.

To the north, the square is dominated by the former Curtis Publishing Company building and on the west side of the square on the corner of 7th and Walnut Streets, is the Philadelphia Saving Fund Society, which opened here in 1869. A 19-century grey stone pile, it has been designated an historic building, as it is a fine example of the period.

Just behind it on 7th Street is the monolithic former headquarters of N. W. Ayer, the advertising agency, and on the corner of 7th and Locust Streets is the home of W. B. Saunders Company, the world's largest medical publisher.

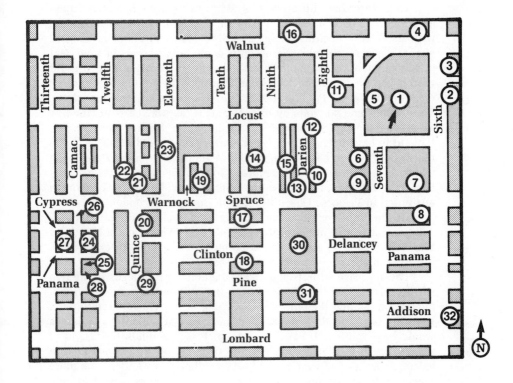

Hopkinson House, the large modern apartment complex on the south side, has as its neighbor in a pseudo-Italian palazzo, Lea & Febiger, publishers. When Philadelphia was a great publishing center, Washington Square was "publishers' row" and, surprisingly, there is a good deal of publishing activity here today.

2   The first stop on the square is the *Athenaeum of Philadelphia*, 219 South 6th Street. (Monday through Friday, 9:00-4:00; closed Saturday, Sunday and holidays. Group tours by reservation: WAlnut 5-2688.) A proprietary library founded in 1814, it has been housed in this beautiful Italianate building, designed by John Notman (1810–65), since 1847. Its purpose is "to maintain a reference library for members and the public, a depository of rare books and periodicals of interest to scholars, to join actively in the cultural life of Philadelphia by participation in historical and educational activities and in the recognition of outstanding literary achievement in Philadelphia."

During the 19th century there were Athenaeums in many large cities. Now only a few survive besides Philadelphia's, notably the Boston Athenaeum, the Wadsworth Atheneum (now a museum) in Hartford, Connecticut, and the Society Library of New York. Election to membership involves purchasing a share of stock which can descend through the stockholder's family in successive generations.

There are few libraries like it anywhere. Immediately upon entering, the visitor is struck by its air of serenity. The entrance hall with its Empire furniture helps give it this special aura—an elegant pier table, a lovely old mirror with a charming scene in gold leaf (a sentry guarding an ancient fort), the chairs with the ever-present golden bee on the green background, a copy in marble of Canova's reclining nude of Pauline Bonaparte, Napoleon's infamous sister. Three handsome portraits by John Neagle (1796–1865) are outstanding as are a splendid Empire desk attributed to Michel Bouvier and thought to have been in Joseph Bonaparte's home, and a pair of chairs that was known to have been. A gold escutcheon from the state coach which bore Napoleon to his coronation on December 2, 1804, has found its way here, too, and a charming watercolor of a noblewoman attributed to Princess Charlotte, Joseph Bonaparte's daughter.

At the first floor rear, overlooking an intimate garden, is the circulation room. Not only are there books everywhere, but a Neagle of Mrs. Julia Wood as Amina in *La Sonnambula* and, as an extra fillip, a tray with sherry decanter and glasses!

The staircase with its square skylight on the roof leads to the two spacious rooms on the second floor—the old reading room overlooking the garden and the old reference room facing Washington Square. Here the past and the present meet in a way of which Henry James would have approved. Pause a moment to contemplate the island of repose which is Washington Square, or stand on the theatrical iron balcony shrouded in wistaria and let your thoughts wander back more than a century to the time when the garden was first laid out.

Archeologists have located the foundations of part of the Walnut Street Prison beneath it.

Although the library is not open to the public at large, but for the use of shareholders, the Athenaeum is available for all qualified non-member students of Anglo-American and Anglo-French cultural history of the 19th century. It does have a noteworthy collection of architectural drawings and architects' papers.

Now walk to the corner of 6th and Walnut to the Penn Mutual **3** Life Insurance building. There is an observation deck on the eighteenth floor which provides an overall view of the square and old Philadelphia, and an enclosed one on the top of the new tower. At present they are not open to the public. Note the preserved Egyptian Revival façade of the building which was razed when the new tower was built. It was designed by John Haviland.

What is particularly pleasant about the view from this point is that all of the landmarks we saw on the first four walks can be seen from the vantage of an aerial view. It seems as if we can reach out and touch some of the buildings, and Independence Mall seems like a miniature from here. We can see the Walt Whitman Bridge to the south, beyond Old Swedes' Church, and although there is a great concentration of houses and buildings everywhere, the abundance of trees is more noticeable from here, the tiny gardens, green walks and the touch of green here, there and everywhere.

Directly across the north side of Washington Square at 6th and Walnut Streets is the Curtis Publishing Company building, formerly **4** the home of The Saturday Evening Post, The Ladies' Home Journal and Country Gentleman magazines. Inside the lobby (Monday-Friday, 9:00-5:00; closed Saturday, Sunday and holidays) is "The Dream Garden," a spectacular glass mosaic of 260 different colortones made for Curtis by the Louis C. Tiffany Studios. It was based on an original painting by Maxfield Parrish. Each of the thousands of separate pieces was hand fired to achieve the proper color and texture. The only similar glass mosaic is a mural by Tiffany in Mexico City's National Theatre. The Curtis one is an art work that many Philadelphians haven't seen, but, with the renewed interest in Tiffany's work, it is drawing people from all over the world.

Now, instead of walking around the square, we shall walk through the 6th and Walnut entrance and continue on the axial walk, circle the fountain, pick up the axial walk on the other side of the fountain, passing the memorial tomb to the Unknown Soldiers of the **5** Revolution, until we reach the diagonally opposite corner of the square. This southwest corner retains its character and a feeling of the 19th century. Here a block of four-story red brick mansions suggests the period of Henry James or Edith Wharton, but the buildings are actually much earlier.

Christopher Morley once lived in the third house from the corner of 7th Street, facing the square, and for a time in later years it was

"Unknown Soldiers of the Revolution"

6 known as *"The Christopher Morley Inn."* This was before he achieved fame with *Parnassus on Wheels* and *Kitty Foyle.* Morley confessed to a passion for city squares and he said no Walden sky was ever more blue than "the roof of Washington Square."

Stroll east past Hopkinson House and the Lea & Febiger building to 6th Street and the southeast corner of Washington Square.

Although the house is no longer here, Marshal de Grouchy, one of Napoleon's 26 marshals, lived at 245 South 6th Street; the site is occupied by the condominium Washington Square East. He had to flee France after his non-appearance at Waterloo—one of history's enigmas—caused feeling against him in France to run high.

As we walk on 6th Street to Spruce we pass the *graveyard* of

7 *Holy Trinity Catholic Church.* Opened for services in 1789 by a German congregation, the church established the first Catholic orphan asylum in America in 1797. In 1831 Stephen Girard, the banker and philanthropist, was buried in the cemetery, but his body was later removed to Girard College. There is a small area in the cemetery where Acadians are buried. About fourteen hundred of them came to Philadelphia from Nova Scotia and New Brunswick in 1755 when the British took over French Canada. Called "the French Neutrals," they were housed in a cantonment at 6th and Pine Streets while waiting for transportation to Louisiana. Many are buried here, and this is "the little Catholic Churchyard in the heart of the city" in which the lovers of Longfellow's poem "Evangeline" are said to be buried.

Directly opposite on the southwest corner of Spruce Street is the *birthplace of Joseph Jefferson* (1829–1905), the American actor who **8** made *Rip Van Winkle* famous. Francis Wilson, the actor, and a group of friends had a bronze tablet put on the house during Jefferson's lifetime, and, when that disappeared another was placed there, only to be stolen. Jefferson, always loyal to the city of his birth, played a week's engagement every theatrical season either at Mrs. John Drew's Arch Street Theatre, razed in the 1930s, or at the Walnut Street Theatre, which still stands. Jefferson was the fourth member of that theatrical family to bear the name, and his daughter Margaret, friend and confidante of Asia Booth, was entrusted with the Booth family papers about Lincoln's assassination. Jefferson's granddaughter was Eleanor Farjeon, the playwright and well-known author of children's books.

One of the great pleasures of walking in Philadelphia is looking at houses, not only 18th century houses but all sorts of houses, for the city is a delight for architects and buffs alike. Continue leisurely along Spruce Street to number 715, the *home of Nicholas Biddle* (1786– **9** 1844), banker, scholar and author. He was editor of *The Port Folio*, a director of the Bank of the United States, and, in 1823, was elected president of the bank. He lived here during the crisis which ended with the fall of the Second Bank of the United States. The double dwelling was erected in 1821 by Whitton Evans, a wealthy merchant, and for many years in the present century it was the home of the American Catholic Historical Society. Christopher Morley, who could see the back of the Biddle House from his rooms on Washington Square, referred to it and the others in the row as "that delightful cluster of back gardens, old brick angles, dormer windows and tall chimneys."

Along the 700 block of Spruce Street, opposite the Biddle mansion, are some handsome Greek Revival fronts that were saved because of the strong and concerted protest of area preservationists. They are owned by Pennsylvania Hospital and serve at present as offices.

At 8th and Spruce Streets, turn right to 256 and the classic front of *St. George's Greek Orthodox Church*. It was built in 1822 as St. **10** Andrew's Episcopal, with John Haviland (1792–1852) as the architect. The present congregation plans to restore the interior to that of former days. Haviland, incidentally, is buried in a crypt beneath the church. The iron fence is one of the most noteworthy in a city of handsome ironwork.

Walk north to Locust Street, but glance back at Manning Street. Again, the backward glance is rewarding, as always while sauntering in this city. These small houses back on the ones Christopher Morley loved.

At 8th and Locust Streets, continue on the east side of the street to the *Morris House* at 225 South 8th. It was built by John Reynolds **11** in 1786 just after the Treaty of Paris (1783) brought an end to the Revolution. There was great activity in Philadelphia in the postwar years and a building boom of sorts was in progress. In 1817 Reynolds sold the house to Luke Wistar Morris, the son of Captain Samuel Morris of the First City Troop (whose portrait hangs in the Deshler–Morris House, seen in Germantown on Walk 12). It passed through generations of Morrises until, at the time of World War II, it was owned by a Morris triumvirate, a brother and two sisters. For some years the house was used by N. W. Ayer, the advertising agency, as a guest house for visiting dignitaries. It is now a private residence again and not open to the public. Built in Flemish bond of alternating red stretcher and black header brick (as so many of the houses hereabout were), it has a handsome doorway of notable proportions, set between fluted and quilled pilasters. There is a fine pediment over it and the lock and brasses on the door are worthy of note. One thing to remember about the Morris House is that it never fell into disrepair, since the generations of Morrises who owned and loved it very carefully kept it much as we see it today. Before continuing, look at the garden of boxwood, ancient trees and old roses.

Although it is no longer standing, the house where Amos Bronson Alcott's school stood was at 222 South 8th Street. The Alcotts will be heard from on Walk 12 through Germantown.

Returning to 8th and Locust Streets, turn right toward 9th Street. **12** At Locust and Darien Streets is the *Musical Fund Hall*, 806 Locust street, designed by William Strickland in a rather severe style. The present façade is a much later one by Addison Hutton grafted onto Napoleon Le Brun's rebuilding of the front in 1847. Thackeray, who referred to the city as "grave, calm, kind old Philadelphia," gave six lectures here on the "English Humorists" in 1853 and a second series on "Charity and Humor" in 1856. Dickens lectured here in 1842. Among the others who performed in this hall were Ole Bull, the Norwegian violinist (who once sought to establish a colony in Potter County, Pennsylvania); Jenny Lind, the Swedish nightingale, whom Barnum brought to America; and Adelina Patti, the legendary coloratura of the 19th century. In June, 1856, the first Republican National Convention held its sessions in Musical Fund Hall. It has been converted into condominiums and all that is authentic now are some sections of the walls. Note the lyre on the pediment. It is not difficult to imagine Philadelphians of the gaslight era, alighting from their carriages and entering this old music hall.

By continuing down Darien Street to Spruce toward Pennsylvania Hospital, you come to one of the city's most hallowed spots— **13** the redbrick-walled *Mikveh Israel Cemetery*, dating from 1740. It is burying ground of the Sephardic Jews (Portuguese-Spanish), and here in an unmarked grave lies Haym Salomon (c. 1740–1785), the Pole who placed his fortune at the disposal of the Colonies and, like Robert Morris, helped finance the Revolution.

Rebecca Gratz by Thomas Sully

Most famous of all who lie here is Rebecca Gratz (1781–1869), the daughter of Michael Gratz, who emigrated from Upper Silesia in 1759, and Miriam Simon of Lancaster, Pennsylvania. Her father and uncle were prominent merchants and the family was very much involved in the commercial, social and political life of the city.

Rebecca's great friend Matilda Hoffman, the fiancée of Washington Irving, died before they could marry. Irving was bereft and never married. He and Rebecca remained friends all their lives. Rebecca didn't marry either but she, who was Jewish, had been in love with Samuel Ewing who wasn't. Although she couldn't bring herself to marry outside her faith, she and the Ewing family remained fast friends and Samuel's children called her "aunt."

Later, on a visit to Scotland, Irving described Rebecca, who had been painted by Sully and Malbone, to Sir Walter Scott, who was then writing *Ivanhoe*. When *Ivanhoe* was published, Scott sent a copy to Irving, asking him how he liked his Rebecca. As devout and good as her fictional counterpart, Rebecca Gratz devoted her life to charitable causes, establishing homes for orphans and unwed mothers of all faiths. Here, in the heart of the city, in one of the nation's smallest burying grounds, lies one of the great romantic heroines of Philadelphia's past. Standing outside the gate, note the gnarled tree inside. Even in winter this ancient tree is a marvelous accent to the stones, especially when etched in snow, but in spring, when first in flower, it is worth a visit to see the tree alone.

Opposite the burying ground is the Pennsylvania Hospital, the oldest in America, but we shall see that later in our walk.

14 At 9th Street, however, turn right and proceed to 260 South 9th, the *Bonaparte House*. There will always be something extremely appealing and romantic about this dwelling because Joseph (1768–1844), elder brother of Napoleon and deposed king of Naples (1806–08) and of Spain (1808–13), lived here.

When Joseph reached Philadelphia in September, 1815, after Waterloo, he was known as the Comte de Survilliers. On his way

Bonaparte House

from New York to Washington to call on President James Madison, he stopped over in Philadelphia. The cautious Madison feared diplomatic repercussions and discouraged his arrival in the capital, so Joseph, with the help of the French immigrant Stephen Girard, made what arrangements he could in Philadelphia. He rented this house, which had been built in 1812 or 1813, from Chandler Price until he moved to his magnificent estate at Point Breeze, on the Delaware near Bordentown, New Jersey.

We are told that Girard had panels, designed by David—at the instigation of Napoleon—on the "Cupid and Psyche" theme, installed in the dining room, and they remained there well into this century. The house became a gathering place for Bonapartist refugees and for any French nationals who had emigrated in the 18th or early 19th centuries for the two years Joseph remained in Philadelphia. Today it serves as a union headquarters.

Look back into the garden—the entry is from the side—to the outbuildings. An immense barn once stood here, and there is a romantic story of love lost and of a ghost that often walks from the barn to the rear door of the house. The ghost once lived and had the improbable name of Chloris Ingleby. A girl of the neighborhood, she was in love with Amedée La Fourcade, steward and major domo to Joseph. Fourcade was in love with a Corsican girl related to the Bonapartes whom he hoped to marry after the Restoration, but Chloris was ardent and hated being spurned.

Chloris had stowed away on *Jean Barth* and when she reappeared in a starving condition after fifteen days (the ship hadn't sailed and Fourcade had it watched in order to apprehend her), the irate Fourcade dragged her by her hair to the barn and placed her in a box stall on bread and water. However, her guards gave her decent food and someone must have supplied her with tools . . . for she escaped. As she ran to the house and entered by the rear door, Chloris lost one of her slippers. A guard heard her, and fired. When a search was made she could not be found.

Legend differs as to Chloris' fate. Some say she joined the man who supplied the tools to saw her way to freedom. Others believe when she heard the shot she hid behind a panel and was smothered, or that she was shot by the guard. Whatever the fate of this girl who danced in the waterfront taverns 150 years ago, older residents of the neighborhood believe her ghost can still be seen darting across the garden on certain still nights.

At *264 South 9th Street*, Frank R. Stockton (1834–1902) once **15** spent a year. He was born in Philadelphia, but moved on, returning at last to a grave in Woodlands Cemetery. His "The Lady or the Tiger?" is a classic and his comic *The Casting Away of Mrs. Lecks and Mrs. Aleshine* was a favorite of Eleanor Roosevelt. His *Stories of New Jersey* are still in print today, too, and provide fairly accurate history laced with the humor he is better known for.

16 Before going south to Clinton Street, you can continue north on 9th to Walnut and visit the *Walnut Street Theatre*, the walls of which make it the oldest theatre in the English-speaking world. It was first opened in 1808 as the New Circus, in 1811 a stage was added and it was renamed the Olympic and the first play, Richard Brinsley Sheridan's *The Rivals*, opened on January 1, 1812. In 1820 it was given its present name. Edwin Forrest made his debut here; Edmund Kean, Rachel, Otis Skinner, Edwin Booth, Dion Boucicault, John Drew, Ada Rehan, the Four Cohans and Ethel Barrymore in *Captain Jinks of the Horse Marines* all played here. The interior was remodeled in 1920 and just recently it has been made into a contemporary playhouse with the façade restored to look like the John Haviland original. However, the spirit of the great who trod the boards here can be felt and the sounds of their voices almost heard.

17 From the Bonaparte House, however, proceed to Clinton Street, south of Spruce on the way to Pine. Stop at the corner of 9th and Spruce, though, look up to *922 Spruce* on the south side; this is the house where Sarah Josepha Hale (1788–1879), one of the first successful women magazine editors (*Godey's Lady's Book*) lived from 1859 to 1861. It has almost been forgotten that Mrs. Hale was the first proponent of a national Thanksgiving Day. Although she wrote to Congressmen for years and bombarded each successive president with letters, her dream wasn't realized until, after the Battle of Gettysburg in 1863, President Lincoln issued a proclamation for the regular observance of Thanksgiving. Mrs. Hale's fame today, despite her zeal and dozens of books, rests on the poem, "Mary's Lamb," the childhood classic which begins "Mary had a little lamb. . . ."

Continue to *Clinton Street*. The 900 and 1000 blocks of this sleepy, quiet, tree-shaded street would be delightful in any city. This could be old New York, Boston or London—but it is old Philadelphia. The houses are unchanged outwardly, the trees have the authority of years, and at the 9th Street entry to the street is another horse

Walnut Street Theatre

fountain, beneath the walls of Pennsylvania Hospital. It bears the inscription: "A Merciful Man is Merciful to His Beast."

Until just recently there was a gnomon, or sundial pointer, and the dial itself painted on the house at 905. It was a great curiosity for it was the only sundial on the wall of a house in this part of the city. Unfortunately, the present owners had it covered over when the house was repainted, but the pointer itself can still be seen.

Many today fail to remember that *920 Clinton* was the home for **18** years of Agnes Repplier (1855–1950), the foremost woman essayist of her time in America. Miss Repplier was truly a Lady of Letters with a salon of sorts, where the great men and women of the Republic of Letters came to tea. Miss Repplier, as befitted a Philadelphia lady of quality, wrote one of the most delightful books imaginable about tea.

On reaching 10th and Clinton Streets, turn right to return to Spruce Street. Between 1003 and 1005, notice the distinctive iron gates. Some of the finest ironwork—balconies, gates, fences—was produced in Pennsylvania, and many who visit New Orleans do not realize that the ironwork decorating those houses came from here, too. Once our eye is trained to see the ironwork about the city, we find it at unexpected places.

Next to 1007 Spruce is a tiny passage between it and the house at 1009. A lettered sign arched over the entry proclaims that this is *Jefferson Village* (also South Alder Street). There are only eight **19** houses within the village, which is truly hidden away behind Spruce Street on one side and the buildings of Thomas Jefferson University on the other. This is typical of the streets to be seen in this section of the city.

Back on Spruce Street itself, there is a row of impressive 19th century brownstones, larger than the houses seen before on this walk; continuing along Spruce, we come to *South Warnock Street*—only one block in length here—and of a similar character to Jefferson Village.

Between 11th and 12th on Spruce, strolling past handsome old town houses that have fallen on hard times but are due to be restored, we reach Quince Street. To the left, south of Spruce, can be seen the tiny theatre which houses the *Mask and Wig Club,* the University of **20** Pennsylvania's musical comedy group. It is European in character and beguiling to the theatre lover.

But it is *Quince Street,* between Spruce and Locust, or to the **21** right, that is of most interest. This rabbit warren of tiny streets is the sort of area Americans go abroad to see—and it is right here in the heart of Philadelphia. These houses are only historic in that they are old and have passed through time. They did not house Washington, Jefferson or Franklin, but run-of-the-mill Philadelphians working and living in the city. We walk along Quince, dart into *Manning* and **22** *Sartain,* or wander the tiny block of *Irving Street,* note the iron balcony on one of Philadelphia's most enchanting houses, and find

23 *Jessup Street*—a cul-de-sac with ivy running over the walls, doors, windows and fences. At Manning and Quince there is an old slate marker—which might have been placed there to keep horses from the narrow sidewalk. It is difficult to believe we are only a few blocks from Broad, Chestnut and Walnut Streets—the heart of the business district. By working our way back to 12th and Spruce Streets and going south to Cypress, then turning right and then left, we enter the **24** one-block cobblestones of *Fawn Street*. We are back in an area similar to the one we have just left.

At the foot of Fawn Street, enter Panama—which runs for two blocks here like so many Philadelphia streets, is then lost and picks up again several blocks away. To the left on Panama, before reach- **25** ing Camac, is *Lantern Court*—the tiniest and, perhaps, the least-known courtyard in the city. Five houses look onto the courtyard, which has a single lantern near the gate. One of the houses has always had a riotously gay Pennsylvania Dutch motif as its decoration.

26 *Camac Street* in the area between Spruce and Pine has all the charm of Clinton Street, except that the houses are smaller and on a more intimate scale. The row on the west side of the street has a beautiful communal garden behind it.

We are still on Panama and have crossed Camac and found **27** *Iseminger Street* (like Fawn Street, one block long here). When gas lamps lighted the area—up until the 1950s—this street was one of the most photographed in America and pictures of it were used in magazine stories and advertisements. The houses are three story— "Father, Son and Holy Ghost"—and each has its own firemark and "busybody." A busybody is an appurtenance peculiar to Philadelphia. It consists of three mirrors on an iron rod, so placed that the viewer on the second floor of a town house can see the visitor on the doorstep reflected in the mirror. The gardens are tiny—no more than a patio at times—but the charm of Europe or a vanished America has been caught, held and nurtured here.

At the end of Panama Street, facing us as we emerge onto 13th Street, is the classic front of *St. Luke and the Epiphany Church*, which is discussed on Walk 6. The façade and the churchhouse adjoining it provide a theatrical accent after the order and sameness of some of the small houses nearly.

Turn left once more, walk to Pine Street and turn left again. Now we are facing east and will walk along Antique Row until we reach the Pennsylvania Hospital.

At the corner of Camac, which we are passing again, we pay **28** particular attention to the building numbered *1221 Pine*, or *343 Camac Street*. It is one which has an entrance on the other side, which opens on Lantern Court. The store window, the old brick, the graceful fanlight at the attic, the fine woodwork all attest that it has seen better days—one of those buildings with fine lines that stands out even in decay.

Pennsylvania Hospital, southeast view

At the corner of 12th Street the *antique shops* begin and con- **29**
tinue intermittently down through 9th Street; interspersed among
them are art galleries, book shops, flower shops and a particularly
good ice cream parlor. There is great variety of antiques here—some
shops specialize in European furniture, others in American, still
others in everything and anything. Some are a potpourri, others concentrate on china and glass or pictures. If there is no hurry, wander at
will. On the corner of Pine and Quince, there is an old school, next to
a small park; with its square tower and old brick it gives a positive
accent to the rows of houses.

If walking here in the spring, keep an eye out for the tree which
hangs over the garden fence at 925 Pine Street. In bloom it is one of
the glories of the neighborhood.

The block between 8th and 9th on Pine contains *Pennsylvania* **30**
Hospital, which gives it a special character all its own. (Tours by
reservation: 829-3971.) When the United States celebrated the 200th
anniversary of Independence in 1976, the Pennsylvania Hospital,
founded in 1751 by Benjamin Franklin and Dr. Thomas Bond, marked
its 225th birthday. Philadelphia is like that: many of its great institutions are older than the United States itself.

Benjamin Franklin, who seems ever more remarkable as we
encounter his works on these walks, was the first president of the
hospital but he relinquished the post when he was appointed Provincial Agent to England in 1757.

The oldest buildings are the ones seen through the fence, the East
Wing, nearest 8th Street, having been built in 1755. The Center House
in 1804, and the West Wing eight years earlier in 1796, but it is impossible to believe they were not all built at the same time, so cleverly

have they been melded together. The first building of its kind in America, it is still considered one of the classic examples of American architecture. Notice the bay of four marble pilasters contrasting with the red brickwork on the Center House.

The first patient was admitted in 1756 and up until 1972 the wards of the East Wing were still in use. On its first floor were rooms for the mentally ill—Pennsylvania Hospital was a pioneer in the treating of the insane—the second floor was the men's ward and the top floor the women's.

On the tour of the older part of the hospital you can see the *Historical Library,* the oldest collection of medical books in the United States, and also a similar collection of herbals and horticultural volumes. Housed in the center building of 1805 and paneled in old, richly patinaed wood, the library has a graceful gallery running around all four sides. Here are found two charming primitives painted by Benjamin West before he went to England at the age of twenty-one and became a recognized academic, a chair of William Penn's from Pennsbury, the cradle said to have been used for Mary Girard's baby, and a Rittenhouse grandfather's clock. There are small wooden trunk-like cases, containing plaster casts of a fetus or a pregnant mother which were used in the instruction of the medical students.

Leave the library, passing Sully portraits of Dr. Benjamin Rush and Samuel Coates, and climb the stairs to the circular room, the oldest clinical amphitheater in the United States. A glass skylight provided natural light for the operations, instead of the dome originally specified for the building. The first operation planned specifically for appendicitis was performed here as was the first gall bladder operation.

The treasures of the hospital are many and various, but perhaps none is of greater importance than the painting "Christ Healing the Sick" done by Benjamin West in 1817. This was West's second version of the same subject, for, although he was asked by the hospital for a painting as a donation and agreed to this subject, once the work was finished, its popularity was so great in London that West was forced to leave it there and paint another—and somewhat different—version for the hospital.

Be sure to see also the old bell, which called the staff to meals, and the *Treaty Elm.* For generations schoolchildren have been familiar with the painting of William Penn concluding the treaty with the Indians. The old tree in the gardens is a direct descendant of the Great Elm of Kensington. When the original elm was destroyed by a storm in 1810, its rings were judged to be about 238 years old and the tree to have been seeded around 1527. A part of the root was presented to the hospital and another elm sprang from it. When Clinton Street was opened in 1841, the new elm had to be cut down, but a number of cuttings were taken and one of these was planted just inside the 8th Street gate, near the entrance to the old Center

House. This "grandson" of the original tree carries on a great tradition and is a living link with William Penn.

The Pennsylvania Hospital owned the entire facing block below it on the south side of Pine Street to Lombard Street, until 1850 when the Board of Managers decided they no longer needed it. Hence, the houses on the block involved are of a somewhat later vintage than many of the houses to be seen a few blocks to the east.

The superb iron fence that encloses the flagstone at *810 Pine* **31** creates a small courtyard before the house, and the ironwork on the first floor balcony, along the top of the garden wall, and the gate itself at 814 are equally fine. In fact, the brownstone at 814 is complemented by the row 820, 822 and 824 that is occupied by the Sisters of Mercy. The latter three have fortunately been scaled in the past several years, and although time and weather have eroded the decorative features, the elegance is still there.

The *gardens of the hospital* seen from these houses are among the most beautiful in any city, particularly the azaleas which are masses of brilliant color in the spring and the wistaria which is well over one hundred years old. Mary Girard, the wife of Stephen, is buried in these gardens. In 1777 Stephen married Mary Lum, daughter of a Kensington shipbuilder. She suffered from what was then called acute melancholia and was committed to the hospital on December 31, 1790, described as "a lunatic." In 1791 she gave birth to a daughter there, but the child only lived five months. Mary lived on until 1815, buried in an unmarked grave in the gardens at her husband's request. Perhaps this tragedy is the source of Girard's benefactions which were legion.

*Dr. Benjamin Rush
by William Rush*

Benjamin Franklin's signature

The *statue of William Penn,* which was presented to the hospital by his grandson John Penn in 1804, was found by the younger Penn in a London junkshop. A legend persists to this day that at midnight on New Year's Eve, as the clock strikes, ushering in the new year, the statue descends from its pedestal and walks about the hospital grounds.

The ironwork on the *700 block* of Pine Street is in somewhat different form and is a little lighter in treatment than that of the 800 block. On the north side are eight houses between 705 and 719 that have railings on each side of the marble steps leading to the houses. Each is a different lace-like tracery. Opposite, at 702, there is an unsual fanlight over the front door. It is, in fact, a glass fanlight within a larger brick fan-shaped recess. Between it and the door is a fine piece of carving, distinctive from the other doorways on the street.

32 At 6th and Pine Streets, you can turn right and just beyond the corner of 6th and Addison stands *Mother Bethel African Methodist Episcopal Church,* founded in 1787 at this location by Bishop Richard Allen, who was mentioned in connection with Old St. George's Church on Walk 2. The church occupies the oldest piece of ground in America continuously owned by black people. It was here that black Masonry was started.

Bishop Allen, a former slave who had become a preacher, is buried in a tomb in the basement. He and other Negroes had held services at Old St. George's at five o'clock in the morning, but the day came when they were told they could use only the balcony. Allen led his flock out of St. George's and soon afterward purchased the lot at 6th and Addison. The present church, built in the 1890s, is the fourth to stand here. Allen's first church was an abandoned blacksmith's shed hauled by horses to the site. He did have support from Dr. Benjamin Rush, the Signer, who admired Allen's handling of those ill with yellow fever in the epidemic of 1793. Remarkable in many ways, Allen ran a school where he taught slaves to read and write and he even started a burial service—the first black funeral director—for the victims of 1793.

Just across Lombard Street is an institution of another kind, but a Philadelphia one for all that. Levis' is where the first ice cream soda is said to have been concocted. The sodas *are* different from those to be had elsewhere, and a hot dog at Levis' is a must.

Back at 6th and Pine Streets, continue along 6th, passing the McCall School on the left, and on the right will appear some charmingly restored houses. The one on the corner of Delancey Street had been in ruins before it was restored. At Cypress Street, to the right, is another row on a quiet backwater.

At 6th and Spruce Streets we are back at the Joseph Jefferson House again, with Holy Trinity Church opposite. A few steps bring us to Washington Square once more.

From City Hall South to Pine Street

Philadelphia's "downtown" area—known as "center city" to Philadelphians—is dominated by City Hall. It occupies the Centre Square of William Penn's original plan for five public squares.

At the close of the 18th century, this square was selected as the site of the engine house of Philadelphia's first municipal water works, for the city didn't extend so far west in the early years. By 1801 water was carried by gravity through a conduit to the Centre Square pumping station from the Schuylkill River near 22nd and Chestnut Streets. It became a favorite recreation area for the city and was fenced in and landscaped, with a graceful fountain by William Rush. The engine house was abandoned in 1815 and demolished in 1828.

Centre Square

Following that, Broad and Market Streets cut through the square, forming four similar plots which were officially named Penn Squares in 1829.

1   In 1870 Philadelphia voted to erect a *City Hall* on the spot, and the structure was completed principally between 1871 and 1881, but was not officially finished until 1901.

There was a time in recent years when Philadelphia's Victorian "wedding cake" of Renaissance styles was in danger, for there were

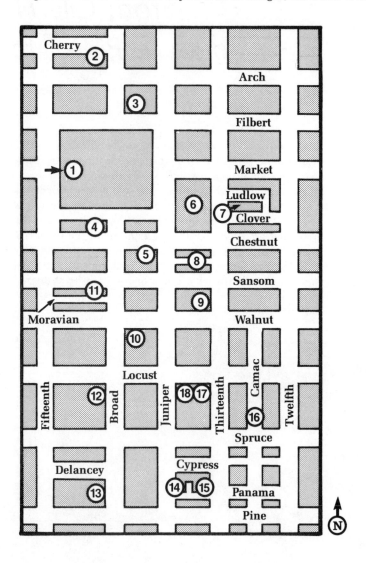

people who wanted to see it razed and Broad and Market Streets going through the square at right angles again. However, the preservationists prevailed, and it is now certain that City Hall will stay. In recent years it has been cleaned, and even more recently new lighting enhances the façade at night.

City Hall provides an unique pivot for the city. It is in essence the city's hub, and although many people won't be able to tell visitors where other places of interest are, everyone knows City Hall. At the Christmas season there is a large tree in the inner courtyard and choral and instrumental groups play at intervals during the day and early evening.

During the annual Mummer's Parade on New Year's Day, the "shooters," accompanied by string bands (generally playing songs such as "I'm Looking Over a Four Leaf Clover"), strut up Broad Street to City Hall, where the judges' stands are located. In the spring the tulips and hyacinths are particularly lovely and give the quadrangular courtyard with entrances at four sides a feeling of intimacy, which invites the walker to stop a moment. Moreover, City Hall has been with Philadelphia the better part of a century now and has, like an old friend, grown familiar.

The architect John McArthur, Jr., was assisted in the detailing by Thomas U. Walter, architect of the dome and the House and Senate wings of the national Capitol. Alexander Milne Calder, grandfather of the 20th century Alexander who is famous for his mobiles, was responsible for the bronze *statue of William Penn* on the tower, which wasn't put in place until the 1890s. At one point the statue was assembled in the courtyard and Philadelphians came by the thousands to see it.

Incidentally, City Hall is the tallest structure in Philadelphia and there is an unwritten rule, observed by the Art Commission, that no structure will be any taller. The tower is 547 feet, 3½ inches tall, including the statue of William Penn, and the view is spectacular. (For tour information, phone 567-4476.)

Leaving City Hall, walk north and be sure to stop and read William Penn's "Prayer for Philadelphia," which is to the right on the wall as you go through the *North Arch* to Broad Street. It has poignancy for today's Philadelphians, and great meaning. It was written in 1684:

> *And thou, Philadelphia, the virgin settlement*
> *of this province named before thou wert born,*
> *what love, what care, what service and what*
> *travail has there been to bring thee forth*
> *and preserve thee from such as would abuse*
> *and defile thee. O that thou mayest be kept*
> *from the evil that would overwhelm thee,*
> *that, faithful to the God of thy mercies,*

in the Life of righteousness, thou mayest
be preserved to the end. My soul prays to
God for thee that thou mayest stand in the
day of trial, that thy children may be
blest of the Lord, and thy people saved
by His power.

2   *The Pennsylvania Academy of the Fine Arts,* Broad and Cherry
Streets, is just two blocks north of City Hall. (Tuesday through
Saturday, 10:00-5:00; Sunday, 1:00-5:00. Closed Monday and holidays.) Founded in 1805 and thus the oldest institution of its kind in
the United States, it has been at its present location since 1876. This
was the year Philadelphia was the focal point of America because
of the Centennial Exposition, held in Fairmount Park, to mark one
hundred years of Independence.

We seldom see a museum building like the Academy today.
In a time when buildings are created almost without decoration, its
detailed façade is a delight. The interior is spacious beyond expec-
tation, and the staircase, elaborately—even extravagantly—decorated, is unalloyed pleasure. Designed by Frank Furness and George
Hewitt, the building reflects the later Victorian taste in architecture
and is a monument to a vanished age.

Only a small part of the vast and choice permanent collection of
the Academy is on display at one time. Some of the American
artists represented in the collection are: John Vanderlyn, Benjamin
West, George Inness, Gilbert Stuart, Charles Willson Peale, John
Neagle, Charles Sheeler, Cecilia Beaux, Thomas Eakins, George
Luks, Rembrandt Peale, William Rush, Peter Hurd, Andrew Wyeth,
Rockwell Kent and the present-day Alexander Calder. Although
American art has always been its main objective, there is a fine collection by European artists as well. It was the Academy which first
mounted the large Andrew Wyeth retrospective show some years
ago and produced the catalog which became a national best-seller.

Exhibits change constantly, and the Academy is one of those
marvelous spots in the heart of the city where office workers can
pop in for a short visit at lunchtime. It is one of the pleasures of
Philadelphia often overlooked by out-of-town visitors and it
shouldn't be. Dr. John P. Coolidge, of Harvard University, has summed
it up this way:

*It is that spirit which explains a Greek statue between Gothic columns
under a Mansard roof, a Baroque staircase leading to Moorish
arcades, an hydraulic elevator; tile, sandstone, brick, iron, glass; a
floor of custard yellow with scarlet accents, raspberry walls above
a Delft-blue dado, chocolate spandrels diapered in gold leaf; all of
these elements which, as the astonished visitor perceives, make up
the Pennsylvania Academy.*

*The Pennsylvania Academy
of the Fine Arts*

Staircase and detail

From May 1974 to February 1976 the present building was closed in order to restore it to its original condition. Under the direction of Hyman Myers the building came alive once more. Colors were restored, gilt refurbished, new lighting installed.

Retrace your steps back toward City Hall. On the southeast corner of Broad and Arch Streets is the Arch Street Methodist Church, built in 1868. Just beyond it at 1 North Broad Street is the *Masonic* **3** *Temple.* (Tours Monday through Friday, 10:00, 11:00, 1:00, 2:00 and 3:00; and on Saturday, 10:00 and 11:00. Closed on Saturday in July and August.) The temple was built between 1863 and 1873, and within are Renaissance, Ionic, Oriental, Corinthian, Gothic, Egyptian and Norman halls as well as a library with more than 70,000 volumes.

The first Masonic Lodge in America was organized on June 24, 1732 (also the year of George Washington's birth) at Tun Tavern in Philadelphia so it is only fitting that a museum relating to the

City Hall from Kennedy Plaza

Masonic order should be here. The museum is a fascinating mélange —William Rush figures in wood of Faith, Hope, Charity, Virtue and Silence, which were carved between 1811 and 1819 for the old Masonic Hall on Chestnut Street; ancient gilt vessels; a candlestick used in window illumination during Lafayette's reception in 1824; a cross of matched rubies which belonged to William McKinley; specimens of the last money used by the Grand Masters of the Knights of Malta, 1741 to 1773; and letters of Benjamin Franklin, Washington, Andrew Jackson and Lafayette. A curious piece of memorabilia is the application for membership of Charles A. Lindbergh, who listed his age as "24-2/12" on March 30, 1926, along with cases of commemorative china and glass, bearing Masonic symbols and oftentimes the likenesses of well-known figures in history who were Masons.

Pass through City Hall courtyard again and walk south on Broad Street to Broad and Chestnut Streets. The Roman building with the dome on the northwest corner is the *Girard Bank's* head- **4** quarters. It was modeled after the Pantheon in Rome except that it is square and has windows. It and the tall building next to it, also owned by Girard, were designed by McKim, Mead and White. (Stanford White was the architect shot by Harry K. Thaw on the roof of the old Madison Square Garden in the love triangle over Evelyn Nesbit, "The Girl in the Red Velvet Swing" of theatrical fame.)

Each of these four corners is occupied by a bank. There are banks everywhere in Philadelphia, one of the nation's centers of banking. The Provident National and the Philadelphia National Banks usually have interesting art exhibits on their first floors, and the Philadelphia Savings Fund Society always has an exhibit— china, stamps, silver, paintings or even dogs for adoption by the Pennsylvania S.P.C.A.—in the window on the Chestnut Street side.

Cross Broad Street and walk along Chestnut Street toward 13th Street. On the south side of the street, on the front of Woolworth's store, there is a *bronze tablet* marking the site of the *studio of Thomas* **5** *Eakins* (1844–1916), one of America's greatest painters who went unrecognized for much of his lifetime. His studio was here from 1884 until 1900, and his home at 1729 Mt. Vernon Street is now owned by the Philadelphia Museum of Art and used as a study center. There is an extensive collection of his work at the Philadelphia Museum of Art, much of it given by his widow.

On Chestnut Street, occupying the block between Juniper and 13th Streets, is *John Wanamaker's,* Philadelphia's landmark depart- **6** ment store. It is well worth a stroll around inside, for in this day of suburban shopping malls Wanamaker's is unique. Once inside, direct your steps to the center of the building and the Grand Court, which is always spectacularly and seasonably decorated. At Easter two paintings, "Christ Before Pilate" and "Christ on Calvary" by the Hungarian artist Michael de Munkácsy, are displayed. The history of the paintings is dramatic in itself. The first was painted in 1880–81 and the latter in 1884. John Wanamaker, founder of the store, purchased them in Paris in 1887 and 1888. They went on tour throughout the country before they were finally hung in the Wanamaker home where they remained until it burned in 1907. During the fire they were cut from their frames and saved. Today they are valued at one million dollars each.

The brilliant and unusual fountain shows, fountains playing to the music of the huge organ, start the day after Thanksgiving and continue at least until Christmas Eve and usually until New Year's Eve. Watching and hearing these *son et lumière* shows is a Philadelphia habit, and a schedule of the fountain displays is always widely advertised.

The Wanamaker Organ, the largest in the world, was installed in

1911—it had been made originally for the St. Louis Exposition in 1904. It took thirteen flatcars to transport it to the store and it was then doubled in size so that today it consists of 30,000 pipes. The daily organ concerts, a Philadelphia staple, are usually at ten o'clock in the morning, at noon and at five-thirty in the afternoon. Another noontime feature here in the Grand Court is the interviewing of celebrities—authors, film and stage stars, sports figures—usually about a quarter-past twelve.

A Philadelphia by-word is "Meet me at the Eagle." Everyone meets everyone else at the large bronze eagle here in the Grand Court. Nearby is a brass plate in the floor commemorating a visit by President William Howard Taft on December 30, 1911, when he dedicated the building.

7 Leave by way of Chestnut Street. Just north of the corner of 13th and Chestnut Streets is *St. John the Evangelist Roman Catholic Church,* built in 1832. It was the second Catholic cathedral in the city, but was not used as one until 1838. The original building contained a painting by Caracci, given to the church by Joseph Bonaparte during his residence in Philadelphia. That painting and the frescoes by Nicola Monachesi (1795–1851) were ruined when the church burned early in this century.

The tiny *burying ground* next to this, which consists of vaults only, is the resting place of a tragic and historic family—that of Agustín Iturbide (1783–1824), who in 1822–23 was Emperor of Mexico, long before the Austrian Maximilian and the Belgian Carlotta were placed on the Mexican throne by Napoleon III.

Agustín Iturbide was executed, but his wife Maria Huarte and their children eventually came to Philadelphia to live. A grandson, Agustín, was adopted in 1865 by the childless Maximilian and Carlotta as their heir. The Iturbides were unfortunate when it came to dynastic succession, and Prince Agustín before his death was known as Professor Iturbide (of Spanish and French) at Georgetown University. During the Mexican War of 1845–46, the former Empress Iturbide appealed to President Polk to intervene with the Mexican authorities and see that her pension was continued. At one time she and her children lived at 13th and Spruce Streets, later at 226 South Broad Street. The Empress died March 21, 1869, at the age of seventy-nine. A son Agustín, a daughter Sabina, and two other children brought here from Mexico for reburial in 1849 lie in vault number nine with their mother.

8 Walking down 13th Street to *Drury Street,* we find a spot for lunch, which is one of Philadelphia's favorite (and one of the few remaining) pubs. McGillin's Old Ale House at 1314 Drury Street is just behind the Blum Store at 13th and Chestnut Streets. The tavern had been in the McGillin family for almost a century when the present owners bought it. The interior was burned several years ago and since then it has been remodeled, but the atmosphere has not

been lost. The tavern licenses for past years are displayed and the gaslights are still in the ceiling. A buffet, much like those in English public houses, is set up on a bar at lunchtime (11:30-2:15 except Sunday). There is a dining room on the second floor with a "Tiffany Bar," which has the same lunch hours as the pub, but also opens between 5:00 and 9:00 for dinner.

If a more elaborate lunch is desired, walk a half-block to Sansom Street, cross to the left, and at 1214 Sansom Street is the Hoffmann House, with an old world German atmosphere of dark paneling, steins, and excellent food and drink. It is one of the most noncommercial restaurants to be found in this part of the city.

Continuing down 13th Street, on the northwest corner of Walnut Street, we come to one of the handsomest clubs in Philadelphia and the most exclusive—the *Philadelphia Club*. It is the oldest such club **9** in America (1834), and the building was once the home of Thomas Butler, whose nephew married Fanny Kemble, the great 19th century English actress. The club is not open to the public, but it is a building worthy of study architecturally. Note that there is no marker on it except a discreet *PC* on the doormat.

Now walk on the south side of Walnut Street, cross Juniper Street, and just before Broad Street, we find a small (and unmarked) *Indian campsite*. It is the tiny entryway between the Christian Science **10** Reading Room and the corner building on Broad. John Penn, the grandson of William Penn, gave the ground to the Indians in 1755. According to Struthers Burt, an historian of Philadelphia and its ways, five Seneca chiefs came down from New York in 1922 for a ceremony here. John Penn-Gaskell Hall, a direct descendant of William Penn, presided. Few Philadelphians even realize the campsite exists, let alone that it still belongs to the Indians!

To our right, at the corner of Broad and Walnut, on an angle across Broad Street, we can see the *Union League* of Philadelphia, **11** between Moravian and Sansom Streets. A private club (Republican), the building was erected in 1865 and is an ornate structure of red brick and sandstone in the French Renaissance style that was so popular at the time.

The interior (which is not open to the public) is truly magnificent on a grand scale: the library has more than 20,000 volumes, there are four dining rooms downstairs that seat some 500 members simultaneously (there are more than three thousand members), and paintings, sculpture, fine furniture, and superb paneling and marble reflect the wealth that originally built it and still enables it to operate as one of the most beautifully run private clubs in America. The League was formed originally to support the Union and contributed $100,000 to that cause during the Civil War. There is probably no more elegant staircase in Philadelphia than the double one leading to the front entrance, sweeping gracefully up from busy Broad Street.

We now cross Broad Street and pass by the Bellevue-Stratford

Hotel, one of Philadelphia's oldest and most cherished hostelries. It is here that the Charity Ball is held every December, the Academy Ball every January and, of course, the Assembly, which is the most exclusive ball given in Philadelphia. Its rules are rigid and only families which have been members for years may attend. It is the scene of many of Philadelphia's debutante dances, too. Walk to Broad

12 and Locust Streets and behold the *Academy of Music*, "the grand old lady of Locust Street." Philadelphia, which claims many a first and oldest among buildings and institutions, points with pride to the Academy of Music, opened January 26, 1857, as the oldest concert hall and opera house in America.

Designed by Napoleon Le Brun and Gustav Runge, it has acoustics which are reputed to be second only to those of La Scala in Milan. It might be well to consider these acoustics. Every artist who has performed here has remarked about them and the Philadelphia Orchestra holds its recording sessions here. The architects placed a dry well under the main floor, known as the Parquet, to balance the dome on the roof which, the experts tell us, contributes to the spectacular sound. In December 1871, the Academy was the scene of a spectacular ball in honor of the Grand Duke Alexis of Russia, son of Czar Alexander II. The parquet was floored over for dancing, and ladies of the highest social caste were chosen to dine in the green room with the Grand Duke.

Edward VII of Great Britain visited here (as Baron Renfrew) in 1860 when he was Prince of Wales and today the right balcony box, as we face the stage, is referred to as the Prince of Wales box. In

Academy of Music

Academy of Music

1872 Ulysses S. Grant was nominated the second time at the Academy, and President and Mrs. Nixon attended the gala—the 113th anniversary concert—in 1970.

Almost every musician of note has played, conducted or sung here, including Tchaikovsky who conducted in 1891. The major orators—William Lloyd Garrison, Edward Everett, Henry Ward Beecher —and Presidents Cleveland, McKinley and Wilson are a few of the notables of the past who have faced the Academy audience.

The Grand Ballroom, which is used for recitals or private parties and dances, is modeled on the Hall of Mirrors at Versailles. The very elegant crystal chandelier in the Academy can be lowered electronically down onto the seats for cleaning.

The Academy of Music, with its gilt, festoons, griffons, shells and other carvings, is older than Covent Garden Opera House or the Paris or Vienna operas and has its own particular aura, its own special glamour. Ask any Philadelphian and he will tell you so.

Tours of the Academy of Music are given to groups and can be arranged by calling 893-1935. Academy House, the apartment complex behind the Academy itself, contains a rehearsal hall which is often used for small recitals, storage rooms for scenery and a lounge for members of the Philadelphia Orchestra.

Walking south on Broad Street to Pine, we come to the *Philadel-* **13** *phia College of Art.* Originally the Asylum for the Deaf and Dumb, it was erected in 1824 and 1825, with John Haviland (who also designed the Walnut Street Theatre and the Atwater Kent Museum) as architect. The simplicity of the building in front contrasts with the Victorian additions by Frank Furness in the rear. Exhibits of student work are held periodically—usually between October and early June —and the public is welcome.

Crossing Broad Street and walking east along Pine, we come to Juniper Street again. Turn left and walk to the first turning, which is a fragment of the ever-appearing, ever-disappearing Panama Street.

14 Turn right on Panama and we are now at *Butler Avenue*. Few Philadelphians even know of Butler Avenue, and what a misnomer it is! It should be called "Butler Corner" or "Butler Way" for this tiny block of houses is a dead-end street, directly behind St. Luke and the Epiphany Church. It isn't a distinguished street, and the houses on it haven't the architectural interest that some on Juniper Street may have, but it is unique—a Philadelphia "elbow alley" we have purposely detoured to see. After making our way back and turning into Panama Street, on which no doors open, we should pause and examine the handsome Palladian window on the back of 1325 Pine Street. Palladian windows were popular in Philadelphia and many will be seen on our rambles about the city.

Back on Pine Street, look at the front of 1325 and the handsome garden wall as we make our way to 13th, turn left at the corner and, just above it, come to one of the most impressive façades in Phila-

15 delphia—that of *St. Luke and the Epiphany*. This lovely old Greek Revival church dating from 1839–40, with its cast-iron columns and narrow rectangular windows, represents the last phase of the Revival. The trees and the paved garden between the church and the offices give the street an almost-European character. The small street across 13th from the church is Panama, which leads to Iseminger, Camac, Lantern Court and Fawn, which we saw on Walk 5.

Now walk north on 13th Street up to Locust, turn right and

16 walk the short block to Camac. Turn right and enter *Camac Street*. On this small street of clubs note the Plastic Club at 247 South Camac, the Charlotte Cushman Club at 239 and the Sketch Club at 235. On entering Camac we can see the sign of Deux Cheminees, a rather elegant and quite romantic French restaurant. It and the building across from it, Venture Inn, are examples of charming architectural treasures that need saving. Notice the della Robbia-style medallion on the wall of Venture Inn.

The *Plastic Club,* art club for women, is the oldest club of its kind and was founded in 1897. Although not regularly open to the public, it is when an exhibit is hung. The upper floor is one large studio, with skylights, and is often used for receptions as well as art exhibits. The Miniature Camera Club of Philadelphia holds its meetings here.

The *Charlotte Cushman Club* is a private club, named for the 19th century American actress. It has an extensive library, a collection of memorabilia and some fine paintings of actors of the past. The pleasant and helpful executive secretary will show visitors and researchers through the library and collections. (Monday through Friday, 2:00-5:00, except June through August when it is closed.) The Charlotte Cushman Award is presented each year to an actor, actress or technician for service to the American theatre. Among those who have won the coveted honor are Helen Hayes, Judith Anderson, Helen Mencken, Mary Martin, Jo Mielziner, Julie Harris and Cyril Ritchard.

The *Sketch Club* is the oldest of its kind in the United States, having been founded in 1860 by George Bensell and five other students of the Pennsylvania Academy of the Fine Arts. Most Philadelphia artists have belonged to it and an annual show of members' work is a feature of the club's activity. It has occupied its present location since 1903 and among its members have been Joseph Pennell, Thomas Eakins, N. C. Wyeth, Thomas Anshutz and Howard Chandler Christy. The hours vary, but when a show is open to the public they are posted on the door and widely advertised in the newspapers.

Just behind the buildings on the northeast corner of Camac and Locust Streets is the *Franklin Inn Club*, Philadelphia's literary club, founded in 1902. It, too, is not open to the public. Among the celebrated writers of the past who have been members were S. Weir Mitchell, Struthers Burt, Christopher Morley, Joseph Hergesheimer and Howard Pyle, as well as the actors George Arliss and Otis Skinner, and playwright Edward Childs Carpenter.

St. Luke and the Epiphany

William Penn, artist unknown

Penn's coat of arms

On the southeast corner of Camac and Locust Streets is a Philadelphia institution of another kind—*Polly's Spinning Wheel Tea Room.* For years Philadelphians who want their tea leaves read have gone to Polly's for lunch. The area is one in which renovation, restoration and preservation are making great headway.

We now continue west on the south side of Locust Street to the corner of 13th Street and at 1300 Locust we find the *Historical Society of Pennsylvania.* (Monday, 1:00-9:00, Tuesday through Friday, 9:00-5:00. Closed Saturday, Sunday, holidays and during the month of August. $1.00 for non-members.)

17

The *HSP,* as it is familiarly called in scholarly circles, houses one of the most important collections of documents, microfilms, books and prints in the nation and is a center for scholars doing research or laymen seeking genealogical records. Although we won't have the time to examine this aspect of the Society, we can look into the museum on the first floor. It has an amazing collection of furnishings which belonged to, among others, Washington, Lincoln, Franklin, James Logan and William Penn.

There are many portraits of Washington and also some of the furniture—a desk, a mantel, chairs—from the Executive Mansion on Market Street, between 5th and 6th (the house is gone and the spot is a part of Independence Mall), which had been put at his disposal by Robert Morris. There is even a bust of Jacques Necker, the French banker and father of Madame de Staël, a gift from Admiral d'Estaing, commander of the French fleet sent to aid the Americans; Washington kept the bust in his library at Mount Vernon in his lifetime.

A waistcoat, silver and china belonging to Robert Morris are here as well as his strong box (after all, he was at one time one of the wealthiest men in Philadelphia, although all that changed before he died). The bent hickory chair Lincoln was sitting in when he received word of his nomination in 1860 and life casts of his face and hands are among the more intriguing objects. We see William Penn's chairs, desk, family chest, family cradle; Franklin's music stand; and a portrait of Margaret Shippen (1760–1804) and one of her children—this was the tragic Peggy who married Benedict Arnold. Perhaps most marvelous of all is a portrait by John Singleton Copley of Thomas Mifflin (1744-1800) and his wife Sarah Morris, painted on horizontally striped blue and white bed ticking in 1773. We can't buy bed ticking like that today. Mifflin was a Quaker until read out of meeting in 1775 when he joined those who were fighting England. He was a fashionable man for all that as his handsome clothes attest. Other paintings are by Hesselius Elder and Younger, the Peales, Sully, Stuart, West— the entire pantheon of American painting.

James Logan's furniture is here—it isn't all up at Stenton in Germantown. And there is a sewing stand which is thought to have been made by Michel Bouvier, the great-great-grandfather of Jacqueline Kennedy Onassis. This was given to the Historical Society in 1936, which proves that Philadelphia appreciated Bouvier's furniture long before President Kennedy entered the White House. This is borne out, also, by the fact that there is a Bouvier Street in the city.

The miscellany is never ending—a French Empire clock given to Joseph Bonaparte by Napoleon; a burning glass owned by George Fox, founder of the Society of Friends; Gilbert Stuart's snuff box which was owned later, appropriately enough, by Thomas Sully; William Penn's razor and Stephen Girard's door knocker. For the curious who love old things, just looking at these mementoes of the past can be a joy. And among the thousands of manuscripts, diaries, letters and documents are James Wilson's first and second drafts of the Constitution.

Leaving the Historical Society and walking toward Broad Street, the next building we come to is the *Library Company of Philadelphia* **18** at 1314 Locust Street. The Library Company has been in so many locations in its 200-odd year history that it seems to have had more homes than the peripatetic Washington and Dolley Madison.

Founded in 1731 by Benjamin Franklin and members of his Junto (a club whose members read and discussed matters of a philosophic and political nature and were also to found the American Philosophical Society), it was the first public library in America. Only shareholders could take books out in those days and most books had to be imported, but the public could come to the library and read them there. Francis Hopkinson, who signed the Declaration and was our first native-born composer, was an early librarian. One of its first locations was in Pewter Platter Alley, today's Cuthbert Street which was visited on Walk 2, certainly one of the most colorful of early Philadelphia street names.

The Library Company has untold treasures within its walls, but the greatest of these is undoubtedly the Loganian Library, that of James Logan of Stenton and his brother, Dr. William Logan of Bristol, Pennsylvania. These books came to it in 1792 and comprise 2,185 titles or 2,652 volumes, probably the finest library in the Colonies because Logan had been the greatest scholar of his time on this side of the Atlantic.

We won't enter the Library Company because its major purpose is for historical research and, although it does not discourage visitors, the staff is small and the library is really open only to those whose main object is research. Its strengths are in American history, science, medicine and architecture, and there is a superb collection of early

Head of Liberty

prints. Among the paintings in the collection is the earliest known one of Philadelphia painted in 1720. Widely reproduced, its title is "The South East Prospect of the City of Philadelphia by Peter Cooper Painter." It is a far different skyline than we see today!

Among its holdings are portraits by Sully, Franklin's electrical machine (which created static electricity by using Leyden jars), a giant head of Liberty by Giuseppe Ceracchi (1751–1802) which formerly sat beside the Speaker's chair in the House of Representatives in Congress Hall, William Penn's desk purchased at the sale of the furnishings of Pennsbury, John Dickinson's music stand, and the remnants of an air pump—books might have been more appropriate—sent by John Penn in 1738. The case for the air pump is far more interesting to us than the pump itself, or Penn's reasons for sending it. Built in 1739–40 by John Harrison, it is the earliest known example of American Palladian furniture.

All this lies beyond the modern, vault-like façade. However, if we stop and look through the slit in the front wall—almost like those tiny windows lepers used to peer through to watch church services in England—we discover a little-known fact about Philadelphia. Right here on Locust Street are buried two bodies. Dr. James Rush and his wife, Phoebe Anne Ridgway, are interred beneath the *marble slab* in the courtyard. Dr. Rush, a Philadelphia eccentric, left one million dollars to the Library Company when he died in 1869, but he specified that his body and that of his wife would be buried at the library. For many years they rested in the Ridgway Branch on South Broad Street with the books, but in 1965 they were disinterred, the remains examined by a number of witnesses, and reburied here. It is an intimate touch and gives Locust Street an added charm.

Before we leave Locust Street, we should examine the former headquarters (between 1925 and 1980) of the *Poor Richard Club*, once the most distinguished advertising club in the world, which is directly opposite at 1319 Locust Street. Designed by the great Wilson Eyre, Jr. (1858–1944), the building was from 1885 until 1925 the residence of Dr. Joseph Leidy, Jr., a socially prominent Philadelphia physician.

At 1316 Locust Street is an interesting Victorian house now owned by the Library Company. Until the death of its last owner, Mrs. Walter Wheeler, during the 1960s, it was furnished exactly as it had been in the 19th century.

We now walk the short half-block to Broad Street and are again facing the Academy of Music. To our right, several blocks away, is City Hall. We are back in the heart of the city's busiest area again.

Center City and
Around Rittenhouse Square

Rittenhouse Square, one of William Penn's original five, was known as the southwest square until 1825 when it was named for the astronomer-clockmaker, David Rittenhouse (1732–96). This amazing man of universal talents—there were many such in 18th century Philadelphia —was a descendant of William Rittenhouse, who built the first paper mill in America in Germantown. He was at various times a member of the General Assembly and the State Constitutional Convention, a vice-president of the Committee of Safety and president of the Council of Safety. His survey of the Maryland-Pennsylvania boundary in 1763–64, to settle a dispute between the Penns and Lord Baltimore, was so accurate it was accepted and followed by Charles Mason and Jeremiah Dixon when they surveyed the "line" for which they are still remembered. Professor of Astronomy at the University of Pennsylvania and inventor of the collimating telescope, he was also president of the American Philosophical Society and the first director of the United States Mint.

1   *Rittenhouse Square* was once enclosed by a board fence and, later, with an iron railing described as "tall, grotesque and fanciful." In 1834 city commissioners were ordered to lay out a street 50 feet wide on the west side and another on the south side. The first house facing it was erected in 1840, when the residential movement was west, and during its next century the square kept its residential quality. In 1913, the architect Paul Cret, who was one of the men responsible for Benjamin Franklin Parkway and many of the buildings there, designed the present entrances, the central plaza with the stone railings, the pool and the fountain.

The Square has always denoted quality in Philadelphia much as Louisburg Square has in Boston. To have lived near or on the Square was a mark of prestige, more so until the 1930s, when the Depression marked a change in fortunes, and World War II, which leveled all strata of society. The private homes are gone except for one lone survivor, that of Henry McIlhenny, but it still counts for something to live on the Square. There are two other houses still standing, but they have been converted into apartments. With cooperative apartments and condominiums displacing private dwellings in the last two decades, some of the Old Guard still live on here—in these homes in the sky rather than family mansions.

The Square evokes two overworked terms of the 1970s, "ambience" and "charisma." If a *place* can have the latter quality, then Rittenhouse Square has a good deal of both. Artists, writers, musicians and actors have all lived near here. It wasn't uncommon, too long ago, to observe Rudolf Serkin, the pianist, walking with his baby daughter and holding her up to stroke the trunk of a tree; or see Frank Lloyd Wright dashing ahead of his party to examine something that interested him; to spy Katharine Cornell, the distinguished actress—who like so many celebrities stayed at the Barclay—walking her dogs between performances.

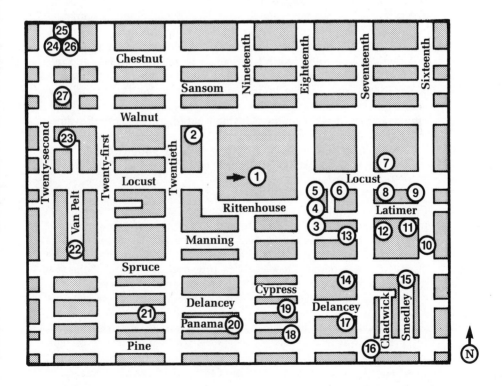

Clothesline Exhibit,
Rittenhouse Square

Part of the square's charm is many activities of a civic or cultural nature. One of the most colorful is the Flower Mart, usually held the third Thursday in May. Starting in 1914, it has become a Philadelphia tradition. Then the square is alive with gaily decorated booths selling flowers, plants and vegetables, with the proceeds going to a number of hospitals; and thousands of Philadelphians converge here to suck peppermint sticks stuck in lemons (another tradition), or eat leisurely in a temporary outdoor café. Following, early in June, is the annual Clothesline Exhibit of paintings started in 1931, and, all summer long, concerts, opera and ballet are given on a temporary stage. In the autumn dog lovers converge here for the annual dog show, and at Christmastime there is a tree-lighting ceremony with carols, and on Easter Sunday a fashion parade. Some activities here will be curtailed as the refurbishing of the square goes forward.

The square is always alive with activity, if nothing more than a lone guitarist, an artist sketching or a child releasing a balloon and watching it soar above the trees.

Around the square itself, there are few old buildings left, but the **2** *Church of the Holy Trinity* on the northwest corner is another of John Notman's, this one dating from 1857–59. One of the city's most fashionable congregations, it had for rector the Reverend Phillips Brooks (1835–93), best remembered today for the words to "O Little Town of Bethlehem." When, early in July, 1863, he heard of the victory at Gettysburg and the turning of the tide, the Reverend Mr. Brooks stopped the Communion service to announce the news to his congregation.

At the southwest corner is 1914 Rittenhouse Square, the red-brick 19th century town house of Henry McIlhenny, whose art collection is one of the finest in America. His house, the one to the left of it, and the Monticello-like pavilion to its right are all furnished in

The Philadelphia Art Alliance

French furniture from the reign of Charles X and contain works by Chardin, Ingres, Cézanne, Manet, Renoir, Matisse and others. It is, of course, not open to the public.

Facing the square on the northeast corner is the former home of Alexander Van Rensselaer, a financier and supporter of Leopold Stokowski and the Philadelphia Orchestra. One of the few splendid old mansions to survive, it housed the Pennsylvania Athletic Club until recently. Now the club's members use their building on boathouse row in Fairmount Park as headquarters. The *Alison Building* next door contains the offices of the Presbyterian Ministers' Fund, the oldest life insurance company in the world (1717), and adjacent to it, at 1811 Walnut Street and also facing the Square, is the *Rittenhouse Club*, another of the city's old and exclusive clubs. Henry James used to sit at a window and view this square, too, with his worldly eye.

Rittenhouse Square itself is enduring. Children still climb on the Albert Laessle goat, the lion or the frog, and young lovers sit along the edge of the pool, with the statue of the girl and the duck watching them. No one tells time by the handsome sundial, but everyone admires it, especially the older bench sitters basking in the sun.

The walk begins on the southeast side of the square at the *Philadelphia Art Alliance*, 251 South 18th Street. Founded by Christine Wetherill Stevenson in 1915, it is now housed in the former Samuel Price Wetherill mansion—he was a descendant of the Wetherills who were active in the "Fighting Quakers" Meeting (Walk 2). One

3

of the most active organizations of its kind, the Art Alliance sponsors art exhibits, drama, literary, dance, musical events, architectural displays and lectures of all kinds. To wander through the galleries or attend one of the musicals or lectures, which are open to the public and usually free, is a delight. (Monday through Friday, 10:30-5:00; Saturday-Sunday, 1:00-5:00.) The dining room is for members only. The Art Alliance Medal of Achievement has gone to many men and women prominent in the arts, among them Eugene Ormandy, Marian Anderson, the Curtis String Quartet and Catherine Drinker Bowen.

On leaving the Art Alliance, turn right and the building just across the street—also called Rittenhouse Square (it runs for a num-
4 ber of blocks beyond the square itself)—is the *Barclay Hotel*, one of the most fashionable and elegantly run hostelries in America. It was owned by John McShain, the millionaire Philadelphia builder who also owns the Lakes of Killarney in Ireland. The scene of some of society's most glittering private parties, it has also housed almost every distinguished celebrity who has traveled to Philadelphia. The dining room, while expensive, is perhaps the most beautiful in Philadelphia and the service is impeccable. No sign of commercialism taints the beautiful lobby. With its handsome paneling, draperies and comfortable chairs, it could be the living room of a private mansion.

5 At the corner of 18th and Locust Street find *The Curtis Institute of Music*. Founded in 1924 by Mrs. Mary Louise Curtis Bok Zimbalist, it is an unique conservatory of music for it is entirely a scholarship school. Some of the musicians who have graduated from Curtis are Gian-Carlo Menotti, Samuel Barber, Leonard Bernstein, Anna Moffo and Gary Graffman. The building was the home of George Childs Drexel, the banker, and in addition to the lecture rooms, practice studios and administration offices, it has a charming small music hall for concerts over which is a fully-equipped operatic rehearsal hall. The school is not open to the public. There are many fine works of art inside, the gift of Mrs. Zimbalist (daughter of the founder of Curtis Publishing Company; her first husband was Edward W. Bok, the humanitarian and author of *The Americanization of Edward Bok;* her second Efrem Zimbalist, the violinist). The Institute can point with pride to the Leopold Stokowsky Collection of music scores, letters, papers, recordings and memorabilia of the legendary maestro who conducted the Philadelphia Orchestra from 1912 until 1936.

Across Bouvier Street is a smaller building, also belonging to
6 Curtis, known as *Knapp Hall*. Originally it was the home of Theodore F. Cramp, the shipbuilding magnate, and later the salon of Elizabeth Arden, the cosmetician. A copy of a French town house, as is the one adjoining it, it strikes a note of elegance along the quiet street. Opposite Knapp Hall, at one time during the 19th century, there was an unique group of houses called Harrison Row, but it has long since been supplanted by the Warwick Hotel.

Just below the corner of 17th Street on Locust is *St. Mark's* **7** *Episcopal Church,* founded in 1848. The church building was begun that year, dedicated in 1850, and finished in 1851 when the tower was completed. The architect was John Notman, also responsible for the Church of the Holy Trinity on Rittenhouse Square, and the Athenaeum which we visited on Walk 5. The church, an example of the Gothic Revival, has long been one of Philadelphia's most fashionable. A strikingly lovely chapel within has a silver altar. The parish buildings and the garden create an effect not unlike that of an English church, and the complex complements the *brownstones* facing it.

These houses date from the Civil War period and later. *1622* **8** *Locust,* which once housed the Women's City Club, has been handsomely restored by a firm of lawyers. The Rosenbach brothers conducted their rare book business from number *1618,* which has a small projecting bay onto Locust Street, where a rare book or an illuminated manuscript was displayed. There is an unusual stained glass fanlight over the bay.

The *Locust Club,* at 1614, blends in with its neighbors; the direc- **9** tors had shown the plans to other owners on the street before its construction, a gesture not untypical of certain Philadelphia institutions and organizations.

George W. Childs (1829–94), the publisher of the *Public Ledger* and one of the most influential men in America, made his home at *1606 Locust* from 1865 to 1872. La Panetière, a fine but expensive French restaurant, occupies the former *Sinkler mansion* at 1602. The elegant chandeliers, the beautiful molding, the unrushed atmosphere—even when observed from outside—blend with the quiet dignity of Locust Street.

Next we shall go in and out and around the corners of a series of small streets in pursuit of the charm of this part of the city, which is different from Society Hill and Southwark. The garden at the northwest corner of 16th and Latimer Street, just behind 1600 Locust, can't be seen from the street, but the tree which towers over the wall can, and at night the graceful wall lantern gives it a continental aspect.

Just below Latimer Street, on 16th, is a *series of small shops—* **10** silversmiths, clothiers, an art gallery—and 256 South 16th is the headquarters of the Eisenhower Exchange Fellowships, while 250 is the home of the Republican Women of Pennsylvania in the Hannah Penn House, named for William Penn's second wife. Both these houses, which were once private homes, have beautiful gardens behind. We'll see some of these gardens as we wander west on Latimer Street. Opposite, at 247 and 249 South 16th Street, are wrought iron gates which have been preserved in good condition.

Latimer Street itself—a backwater, true—is a street of private gardens. Typical is the one at 1610 with its brick walk, ivy, old trees and a sense of peace, and we can peer through the gate to see it. Two iron rings in the wall on either side of the gate are held by provoca-

tive figures. Although one wouldn't expect to find a distinguished art
11 gallery here, 1614 Latimer is the home of the *Print Club*, a Philadelphia institution since 1915. (Tuesday through Saturday, 10:00–
5:30. Closed during July and August.) This famous organization
has more than a thousand members from all over the world, composed of artists, collectors and others whose interest in prints has
brought them together. There are shows continually throughout the
year, and it is extremely pleasant to stop by and browse in the first
and second floor galleries. From the second floor we can see not
only the charming small statue against the wall in the Print Club
garden, but the gardens of other houses on Latimer and Spruce Street
as well.

The *Cosmopolitan Club*, a women's club with a long history of
interest in the arts, politics and the humanities, has its clubrooms
at 1616. Art exhibits and lectures—for members and their guests
only—are held periodically. By walking through the slight alley to the
side and around to the back of the Cosmopolitan Club, we can see
the al fresco dining area of The Garden, a new restaurant on Spruce
Street.

12 The last *garden* on Latimer Street, and in many ways the most
spectacular, is that of the National Society of the Colonial Dames
of America (founded in 1891). Walkers in Philadelphia often find
themselves peering into gardens, formal ones, old-fashioned ones,
neglected ones, and marveling that so many green places are to be
found in the heart of the city. Few are more inviting than this garden.

Turn left on 17th Street and walk toward Spruce Street. Just
opposite, behind the parking lot, is a series of "Father, Son and Holy
13 Ghost" houses on *Manning Street*. Each is painted a different color,

Etching from Print Club

with a still different hued trim, and the effect is rainbow-like. The row is typical of those found here and there in this section of the city.

Down the street on the southwest corner of 17th and Spruce Street is the *Tenth Presbyterian Church*, one of the handsomest to **14** be found in this part of the city. Built between 1850 and 1875, it is beautifully maintained; note the ironwork in the fence, in the gates before the front entrance and in the fixtures for the lanterns. At *1710 Spruce*, next to the church, is the mansion in which Harry K. Thaw— remember his love triangle with Evelyn Nesbit and Stanford White?— once lived. Still a private house, it has been lovingly restored, and inside are beautiful woodwork, pediments, pillars between the dining room and living room, and fine fireplaces—all the accoutrements of a gracious age.

A leisurely stroll about the area will take ten or fifteen minutes. Turn left and walk along Spruce Street until we come to The Garden at 1617, a new and different restaurant occupying the former premises of the Philadelphia Musical Academy. On pleasant days eating in the garden is *de rigueur*, and the atmosphere is still old fashioned, for the garden hasn't been redone by a landscape designer.

Opposite The Garden is the one-block segment of *Smedley Street* **15** that out-of-towners always like. Smedley Street runs throughout the city, but not continuously. Sometimes it disappears and is picked up again many blocks away. This particular block has long been the home of artists, writers and members of the Philadelphia Orchestra. There is a charming restaurant, the Three Threes at 333 South Smedley, that is a favorite of many Philadelphians. Lunches are served from 11:00 to 3:00 and dinners from 4:30 until 11:00 Monday through Thursday, and as late as midnight on Friday and Saturday—a rarity in Philadelphia.

Walk through Smedley Street to Pine, then take a right and make a sharp right at *Chadwick Street*, the next small street—one most **16** people miss. Chadwick has several intriguing houses. 303, a white house with a black horse's-head hitching post in front, is one of the most elegant of town houses. Next to it, at 305, is the home of Frank Weiss, a Philadelphia architect, who has been in the process of finishing it for many years. It looks like a beehive—or even a dovecote, a little reminiscent of Gaudí, the Barcelonan genius. Walk to the corner of Cypress—we have to turn, there is no other way to go—and we are now facing the east side of the Tenth Presbyterian Church again.

Diagonally opposite from the Cypress Street corner is the entrance to *Delancey Place*. Before we enter there are several small shops that beckon from below the corner—antique, candle, flower— and behind us at 231 South 17th is an extravagant Spanish house— incongruous here, perhaps, but it has been here long enough to have become part of the scene. Every alternate block of Delancey is narrow, the following one wide. The wide blocks held the homes of the wealthy, the smaller ones were really mews with occasional stables and dwellings for the lesser folk and servants. Of course, now, all these houses are desirable.

The *1700 block* of Delancey Place has several pleasant town

17 houses to show and the home of *Plays and Players*, the city's oldest little theatre group. Note the terra-cotta frieze above the marquee and the ancient carriage house next door at 1718. On the other side, in what was the stable of the Thaw House, there is a marvelous little bay window on the second floor with a horse's head beneath. Farther along on the same side of the street are stables which have become architect's offices.

Having passed Bouvier Street we have come to the corner of 18th and Delancey Place. Before turning into this really elegant street, cross over, turn left and go to the next corner, passing Panama Street which is an alley here. There make a sharp right and go to *The War*

18 *Library* and Museum of the Military Order of the Loyal Legion of the United States at 1805 Pine Street. Few Philadelphians know of this museum and more should. (Monday through Friday, 10:00–4:00. $1.00. Appointments should be made for groups of more than six. Groups are limited to fifteen persons.)

Organized in 1896, the museum is devoted to memorabilia of the Civil War with a library of 10,000 volumes on the War and related subjects. It is open to scholars, students and others doing research on the period. The Military Order of the Loyal Legion was founded on April 15, 1865, the day Lincoln died, by three former commissioned officers who had served the Union. Major General Winfield Scott Hancock was the first Commander-in-Chief in 1885. Three years later The War Library and Museum was chartered under the laws of Pennsylvania. It has been in its present location since 1922.

The contents of the museum are staggering. There are a Meade Room, a Lincoln Room, a Naval Room among others. The Lincoln Room, in addition to numerous photographs and portraits, does have a life mask done in 1861 and another made two months before his assassination, as well as casts of both his hands. The life masks are strangely compelling—much more so than the photographs—and there is a lock of the President's hair. One of the broadsides has photographs of Surrat [sic], Booth and Harold [sic] at the top and offers a $100,000 reward, since "The Murderer of our late beloved President, Abraham Lincoln, is still at large." It is one of the very few copies of this broadside extant.

There are drums, hundreds of guns, swords, epaulettes, a cast of Grant's left hand and his death mask in the Grant Room, and a genre painting by William Spang of a Sea Island slave with a braided beard.

General Meade's complete uniform and his magnificent jeweled presentation sword and another jeweled one which belonged to General Francis P. Blair of Missouri are here, too. Things haven't changed much in more than a century, for there is the Paisley dress-

Panama Street

ing gown in which President of the Confederacy Jefferson Davis fled the Union Army. When the news flashed through the North that Davis was captured, "impersonating a female," it furnished a field day for satirists and cartoonists. The museum has a Currier and Ives, entitled "The Last Ditch of the Chivalry, or a President in Petticoats."

Retracing our steps around the corner, we come once more to *18th and Delancey Place.* This is the street enjoyed so much by R. F. **19** Delderfield, author of *God is an Englishman.* When he and his wife were being shown it in 1971, the novelist turned to his guide and said, "I never thought I'd see anything like this in America. It is like Dickensian London." With that Mrs. Delderfield spoke up and said, "Only better." No greater tribute to an American street has been paid by British visitors.

The Victorian house on the northwest corner attracts every walker. It is a series of cupolas, bays, towers, balconies and even has a small secluded garden within the outer garden. At night small lights glow in one of the trees, and from time to time bits of Victoriana are displayed in the small bay on 18th Street.

There are a myriad of things to see in this block of Delancey Place: the caryatids as mullions on the window of 1810, perhaps the only ones in the city; the acanthus leaves and grape design on the ironwork fence at 1823; the leaded and stained glass windows at 1821; or the small garden with the iron fence at 1835. From the vantage point of the garden we can have a fine view of 1900 Delancey Place, now the office of the law firm of Anapol, Schwartz, Weiss & Schwartz. Designed by Frank Furness, it is generally considered one of the finest examples of his town houses. The ornate decoration, the little balcony, the frame of carved stone around the oval window above the entrance door give it a distinctive appearance in this age of austerity in architectural decoration. Be sure to observe the cherubim and seraphim on the pediments. This is appropriate because the Savoy Opera Company, Philadelphia's distinguished Gilbert and Sullivan troupe, often rehearses inside and the voices of the singers can be heard throughout the night.

20   Cross over 19th Street diagonally and enter *Panama Street,* one of the most charming of all Philadelphia streets, and long the home of artists and writers and musicians. The tall poplars enhance its charm. Be sure to notice the lion's head on the wall of 1928—it becomes a medallion between the second and third floor windows.

We reach 20th Street, take a sharp right on a diagonal and enter another elegant block of *Delancey Place.* This block has back gardens, something the 1800 block doesn't have to any extent; and S. Weir Mitchell (1829–1914) wrote about the roofs and gardens he could see from Delancey while looking back toward Pine. Dr. Mitchell, a famous neurologist and a pioneer in the treatment of nervous disorders, was also like so many doctors—Oliver Wendell Holmes, A. J. Cronin, W. Somerset Maugham—a man of letters. His books are all but unread today, but his most famous—*Hugh Wynne, Free Quaker,* an historical novel of the American Revolution—has not been entirely forgotten.

The *chef d'oeuvre* of Delancey Place, in fact one of the glories of
21 Philadelphia, is the *Rosenbach Museum & Library* at 2010. (Tuesday through Sunday, 11:00–4:00. Closed on national holidays and during the month of August. $2.50; students and senior citizens, $1.50.) Attractively housed in a town house of the 1860s, the museum contains the treasures acquired by the Rosenbach brothers, dealers in antique furniture, silver, painting, drawings, rare books and manuscripts. The furniture is mainly 18th century English—Chippendale, Adam, Hepplewhite and Sheraton—and it is breathtaking. It is especially so in its natural setting, and we appreciate it the more being able to stroll through the house and examine things at close hand. One of its most valuable objects in the front parlor is an olive wood box with silver gilt mounts made for Charles II. We hardly expect to see such a superb historical piece in a Philadelphia town house.

The silver by Paul Storr, Hester Bateman and others is masterly and there are more than a thousand portrait miniatures (not all on view), including one of James I of England, the only known portrait of Cervantes as a young man and a self-portrait of Major André done shortly before his execution.

It is impossible to see *all* the rare books—30,000 volumes—and the nearly 120,000 pieces of manuscript material, but there are always special exhibits and displays. The particular strengths of the collection are Americana, British and American literature, and book illustration. Some of the highlights of this collection are letters of Cortez, Pizarro and De Soto; copies of the first three extant books printed in the Western hemisphere: the Bay Psalm Book: the first book

The Rosenbach Foundation

printed (1640) in what is now the United States; the only known copy of the first book printed in Pennsylvania (1685); and the only known copy of the first issue (for 1733) of Benjamin Franklin's *Poor Richard's Almanack*.

For literary scholars there are the first copy known of the first edition of *Don Quixote*; a first edition of *Pilgrim's Progress*; a manuscript of *The Canterbury Tales*; leaves from the manuscript of *The Life of Samuel Johnson*; Dickens, Lewis Carroll, Oscar Wilde, Joseph Conrad, Robert Louis Stevenson are all represented; and the original manuscript of James Joyce's *Ulysses*.

Upstairs are the living room and bedroom of the American poet Marianne Moore, just as they were in her New York apartment when she died—the furnishings of the last home she lived and worked in.

For lovers of children's books the Rosenbach Foundation has John Tenniel's drawings for *Alice in Wonderland* and *Through the Looking Glass*, those of Ernest Shepard, and over two thousand drawings of Maurice Sendak. In short, the Rosenbach has everything and it is as difficult to leave as to stop marveling..

Mrs. Clarence C. Brinton, who lives on Delancey Place, told in her charming memoir, *Their Lives and Mine*, how she and the late Clarence Brinton didn't buy Upsala in Germantown, which we will see on Walk 11, but their Victorian house here instead.

Across the street from the Rosenbach, at *2003 Delancey*, is the birthplace of C. Stuart Patterson, Jr. (1875–1933). A well-born, brilliant and highly eccentric lawyer, "Chippy" was a defender of criminals (and usually succeeded in getting them off scot free or with light sentences). The story of Chippy, another of Philadelphia's legendary characters, is told by Arthur H. Lewis in *The Worlds of Chippy Patterson*.

Perhaps no other home in the country can boast of what lies behind the exterior of *2014*, with the gas lamps guarding its entrance. A former owner had the lobby of the old Lyric Theatre, which stood on North Broad Street between Arch and Cherry, installed in the house. At 2019 Delancey Place, Pearl S. Buck once lived. The Nobel Prize-winning author of *The Good Earth* and other novels divided her time, during her later years, between this town home and her farm in Bucks County, Pennsylvania. Rudolf Serkin, the piano virtuoso, also lived on this block at one time.

Turn right at 21st Street and stop, preferably across the street, to examine closely the house at *315 South 21st Street*, on the northeast corner of 21st and Delancey. There is a small garden in the back, opening onto Cypress Street, and the second floor bay when lighted with its magnificent chandelier is a favorite of the entire neighborhood.

Walk the short block to Spruce, passing the old carriage house on the northwest corner of Cypress that has been made over into a private dwelling. At 21st and Spruce turn left and walk the short **22** block to *Van Pelt Street*—one of Center City's streets that is the envy of visitors from all parts of America. These two short blocks contain every conceivable kind of architectural style, all very elegant, and this diversity certainly lends enchantment. Among the private houses, at 254 is the home of the *Orpheus Club*, that distinguished amateur male choral group founded in 1872. Since then it has delighted Philadelphians with its concerts in the Academy of Music— a ritual for some admirers—and the "revels" in the clubhouse.

Continuing on Van Pelt Street, cross Locust Street, and just before the dead-end, turn left through the archway and enter the *English Village*. A collection of town houses, facing the courtyard **23** from both sides, each dwelling has only a small garden but the privacy and the sense of serenity in the heart of the city make up for the lack of individual space.

Leaving the English Village by way of 22nd Street, turn right, walk the three blocks to Chestnut Street and the *Church of the New* **24** *Jerusalem* (Swedenborgian). Its crenelated towers and turrets and soot-stained granite give it a highly romantic Gothic appearance. Emanuel Swedenborg (1688–1772) would have been pleased with the angels facing his church. The red sandstone exterior of 32 South 22nd Street opposite has cut into it the legend *Anno Domini MDCCCL-XXXVIII*, a child-like mermaid and the heads of angels.

The *College of Physicians*, at 19 South 22nd Street since 1908, has been described as "a scientific body dedicated to the reception and discussion of papers on medical, surgical and allied subjects." Founded in 1787, it is the oldest institution of its kind in the United States.

That part of the College open to the general public is the **25** world-famous Mütter Museum. (Tuesday through Friday, 10:00– 4:00. Closed Sunday, Monday and holidays.) The museum, still one of the best of its kind, was established in 1849. It was named for Dr. Thomas Mütter and is a fantastic collection of medical lore—there is no other description for it. Some of it is not for the faint-hearted, but those specimens are reserved for medical students or persons doing medical research. Among the rarities exhibited are part of President Grover Cleveland's jawbone removed during an operation on the yacht *Oneida* in the East River, New York, in July, 1893. Because the United States was in a dire financial crisis at the time, it was feared a panic would ensue if the country knew of the operation. So, utmost secrecy was maintained. The President lived for fifteen years afterward.

There are bones shattered by bullets, others showing wounds, breaks, etc., and skulls bearing the personal data and medical history of their owners. Particularly fascinating is a cast of the original Siamese twins, Chang and Eng Bunker, who were sixty-three at the time of their death in 1874. The chair they used is here, a pathetic small wooden one, and their liver has been preserved in a jar.

Much is here to remind us of the medical problems of today— an acupuncture display, instruments for producing abortion which were sold in the market places of Paris in 1903, and exhibits of the lesions of syphillis and tuberculosis. There is an early Electrocardiograph, and we realize on looking at it that we've come a long way in a short time.

In the College itself are a number of portraits by masters of the art—Thomas Eakins, John Neagle, Charles Willson Peale, John Singer Sargent, Gilbert Stuart and Thomas Sully. In Philadelphia, not all fine paintings hang in the art museums.

Co-founder Dr. Benjamin Rush had recommended from the beginning that the College plant an *herb garden*. The one we stroll through was planted early in this century and is cared for by the Philadelphia Chapter of the Herb Society of America. It is now a memorial to the Honorable Owen J. Roberts (1875–1955), Philadelphia lawyer and prosecutor in the "Teapot Dome" scandals, later Associate Justice of the United States Supreme Court. A statue of a young girl holding a bowl by Edward Fenno Hoffman, one of Philadelphia's outstanding contemporary sculptors, gives the garden a focal point.

Leaving the College of Physicians, turn left, walk again to Chestnut Street, go east past the Church of the New Jerusalem, and on the

26 corner of Van Pelt is Frank Furness' *First Unitarian Church* of Philadelphia (founded 1796). The Parish House was finished in 1884; the cornerstone for the church was laid in 1885 and it was dedicated in 1886.

At Van Pelt Street cross Chestnut and continue up Van Pelt Street past the Sidney Hillman Medical Center to Sansom Street. At the corner of Sansom and Van Pelt is a block of houses, undistinguished architecturally, but with charm. Between Van Pelt Street and 22nd

27 can be seen a sign, *Beechwood Street*. It is far from being a street— it is nothing more than a woodsy walk alongside the entrances to some of the houses. The walk, the shrubbery, the flowers all create the smallest, but most intimate of city gardens—almost a private greenwalk. It is yet another oasis in the heart of the city.

Continuing along Sansom to 21st Street and crossing over into the block between 21st and 20th, we enter what was popularly known

28 as "*Hippie Village*" for many years. Its character has changed, as has that of many such sections, and all that remains are a silversmith, a furniture craftsman, several outré clothing stores and one or two oriental bazaars. However, long before the hippies found this and made it their village, La Chaumière—Restaurant Francais—at 2040 Sansom was serving excellent food, and that food in an *intime* atmosphere that Philadelphians find irresistible. Lunches are not served, but dinners are (except Sunday and Monday) from 5:30 on. It is best to phone LO 7-8455 for reservations.

A few steps more bring us to 20th Street and if we turn right and proceed to Walnut, we see the Church of the Holy Trinity and Rittenhouse Square just beyond.

West Philadelphia: In Particular, University City

West Philadelphia—an area that stretches from the Schuylkill River roughly thirty blocks west—also extends southwest to the borders of Southwest Philadelphia and to the northeast to the outer reaches of Fairmount Park. It is a sprawling region that lacks the definition or homogeneity other parts of the city have, but University City, the part of West Philadelphia we are concerned with, does have that quality.

This ground was part of 1500 acres purchased from the Indians by William Warner in 1677, before the arrival of William Penn. Originally called Blockley, it was named for Warner's native parish in Worcestershire. In 1783 there were 632 souls residing here and by 1790 the total had reached only 733.

Because there was no bridge over the Schuylkill the region developed slowly, although Penn had authorized a ferry earlier. The district was farmland, until 1805 when the first permanent bridge was erected over the river, and by 1810 the population had doubled. From then on growth and expansion were rapid.

Named for William Hamilton of The Woodlands, Hamilton Village, which is now part of University City and the area in which we shall concentrate our walking, was once a summer colony. As the 19th century progressed, the name West Philadelphia came into general usage for the entire area and, little by little, the names of the villages and towns, like Mantua, Greenville and Hamilton Village, were forgotten by all but the residents. The area was incorporated into the city in 1854.

Probably the greatest impetus to expansion, after the construction of the bridge, was the moving of the University of Pennsylvania from 9th and Chestnut Streets to West Philadelphia. Students first attended classes on the new campus in the fall term of 1872. Twenty

117

years later, Drexel Institute of Art, Science and Industry—later Drexel Institute of Technology and now Drexel University—was founded by Anthony J. Drexel (1826–93), who was encouraged and supported by his friend George W. Childs. The Institute was also located on the west bank and opened for classes in 1892. The two educational institutions became the nucleus of University City as it is seen today.

We shall walk from 42nd and Spruce Streets to the Schuylkill River, stopping along the way to diverge left and right. The easiest way to reach the starting point is to take a number 42 bus at any point on Walnut Street in Center City.

1 On a rise and dominating the northwest corner of 42nd and Spruce is the *Philadelphia Divinity School*, an Episcopal seminary. The main church, St. Andrew's Collegiate Chapel, although begun in 1923, could easily be transplanted to an English cathedral town and, inside its walls, this illusion of antiquity is even stronger. The carved screen, the magnificence of the wood and stone, the banners on each side of the aisle easily transport us to the Old World. Unfortunately, the seminary and chapel are now closed.

The Victorian row of houses opposite on Spruce Street—dating from the mid-1880s—is typical of the dark red-brick buildings of the late 19th century in this vicinity, with their peaked pediments over the windows and ornate trim.

Walk through the school property along the 42nd Street side and

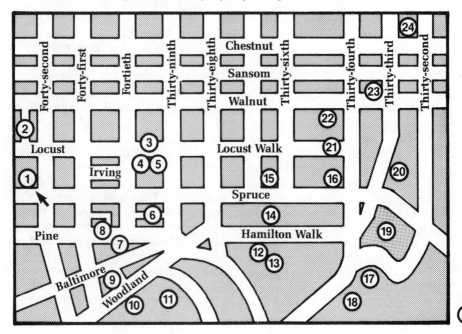

observe the Italianate villas facing the seminary grounds. They are similar to the spacious homes in generous tree-shaded yards which were popular before and immediately after the Civil War.

At the corner of Locust Street, turn left and walk one block to St. Mark's Square—historically certified—the last unchanged row- **2** house street of its kind in Hamilton Village. The façades remain practically unchanged since they were built in 1877–78, and they have been described as a mixture of modified Romanesque brickwork and Gothic wood porches. Older residents say the houses were built of material taken from the Mechanics Building at the 1876 Centennial and were designed by Frank Furness. As an infant the anthropologist Margaret Mead lived here.

The poet laureate of St. Mark's Square, Ruth Branning Molloy, has celebrated its virtues in verse:

> Happy the dwellers of St. Mark's,
> Their lawns are all like little parks . . .
> The houses snuggle side by side,
> Like one continuous groom and bride . . .
> And yet the residents, thank God,
> Are not like peas within the pod . . .
> Some get up early, some sleep late,
> One has a mean or noble trait . . .
> Some go to work, some sponsor causes,
> Some spend their days in restful pauses . . .
> St. Mark's Square, you must have heard,
> Runs a little east of 43rd . . .
> And though it's neither long nor wide,
> It, for a fact, is certified!

Now return to Locust Street, turn left and cross 42nd. Continue on Locust Street and between 41st and 40th—on the left side—the line of houses shows the individuality that is achieved when a row such as this is in the process of being renovated by interested owners. At the end of the row, the rotunda-like, red-tiled Mediterranean roof is the First Church of Christ, Scientist.

At 40th Street Locust Street becomes *Locust Walk*, a part of the **3** major expansion of the University of Pennsylvania. The concept of town planning here has not only created a new city, but has allowed the campus-within-the-city an unhurried pace it formerly lacked.

St. Mary's, the church we approach, as a parish dates back to a **4** grant of land (1807) by William Hamilton, whose home we'll see in Woodlands Cemetery. The present church was built in 1872 and is characterized by its square tower without a steeple. The high altar was designed and built in Rome and later exhibited at the Centennial of 1876. The church actively serves the University community and is often used for the presentation of experimental theatre.

The charm of this crossroads of the University is that enough old buildings have been preserved to contrast with the soaring skyscrapers that dominate the complex. Next to St. Mary's is a charming **5** 19th century villa, now the offices of the University's Department of Public Safety. Its charm is its Victorian Gothic quality, with lacelike fretwork and the remnants of old-time chimney pots. The benches on the stoop before the entry contribute a welcoming quality, and the openwork crosses lend an ecclesiastical flavor.

Where 39th Street crosses Locust Walk, the former *Drexel mansion* is now a fraternity house. The iron balconies at the floor-length windows and the ornate coping are in contrast to the severity of the modern structures around it.

Two blocks to the left at 3910 Chestnut Street is an ideal spot for lunch—Pagano's Casa Vecchia—and at the corner of 38th and Walnut is Smokey Joe's tavern, one of the most colorful of the student hangouts. It is worthwhile stopping in for a drink just to savor the local color.

Continue on Locust Walk, past the side of the Drexel mansion, to the arched bridge which soars over 38th Street. Behind the Drexel residence are two appealing "cottages"—smaller than their more ornate neighbor yet reflecting the age of extravagance in a simpler way. They were designed in the 1850s, and now one is a fraternity house and the other the chaplain's residence.

Instead of crossing the *bridge,* return to 39th Street, turn left to Spruce and cross to the other side and continue walking to 39th Street and Delancey Place.

The former convent of the Good Shepherd stood here until it was demolished, when the University's new Veterinary Hospital was built. Now there is a quiet enclave with almost secret exits and entrances. **6** Walk along this one block of *Delancey Place between 39th and 40th.* Few Philadelphians from other sections of the city even know of it, yet it holds one of the most charming, colorful rows of houses to be seen in the city. Each is painted and trimmed differently and each has its own pair of window boxes. The effect is beguiling, in sharp contrast to many of the other houses on these streets. Society Hill's restoration is widely publicized, but the University City houses are unfortunately often overlooked.

Now walk back along Delancey Place to 39th Street, turn right and walk to Pine Street and continue along Pine to 41st Street. The *3900 block of Pine Street,* while not as much of a piece as its companion block on Delancey, is in the process of being revitalized, and interested young University-connected couples have taken over these late Victorian houses and are refurbishing them.

7   At *4002 Pine* is one of the most magnificent, spacious dwellings to be found in the area. The three-story house sits on a rise and must be approached by a flight of steps from the sidewalk to the front garden. Truly beautiful wrought iron supports the roof of the porch;

the first floor has graceful floor-to-ceiling windows; smaller ones with ornate Victorian window caps mark the second, and even smaller casements are on the third. The larger houses in West Philadelphia were—and are still—referred to by architectural historians as Italianate villas. This one, although not Italianate, is certainly a splendid example of the villas of the period and the place.

Opposite at 4037 Pine is the *Provost's House*, once used by the **8** University for that purpose, but now a private home. A house in the antebellum style, with fine pillars and the extreme simplicity of the Greek Revival, the only decorative addition is the lattice of the balustrade above the veranda roof.

The street is a quiet backwater, green in feeling because of the heavy growth of trees and shrubbery everywhere, and punctuated by individual styles of architecture, the Italianate predominating.

At 41st and Pine, turn left and walk one block to Baltimore Avenue, cross over to the other side, turn left and walk one more block to Woodland Terrace.

Here, backing on the entrance-exit tunnel of the subway surface cars, and the decay on Baltimore Avenue, is one of the glories of Philadelphia city living. *Woodland Terrace* is an entity, designed with **9** an eye for space, balance, formality and grace by Samuel Sloan about 1861. The street contains twenty-one residences—ten semi-detached houses on either side, with one half of the eleventh remaining on the west side at the corner of Woodland Avenue. In the spring wistaria covers most of the porches, crepe myrtle, tulips and hyacinths bloom in all of the gardens. In the autumn the fall flowers predominate amid the ivy which has taken over as groundcover.

At the south end of Woodland Terrace, *Woodlands Cemetery* **10** stretches up and down the other side of Woodland Avenue. The cemetery itself contains *The Woodlands*, the house William Hamilton **11** built in 1788, incorporating a simpler house his grandfather had built earlier. Andrew Hamilton the first, who purchased, in 1735, 300 acres in Blockley Township on which he built a summer home, was the lawyer who successfully defended John Peter Zenger that year in New York. The trial became a landmark case in preserving the freedom of the press. He is also credited with designing the State House—Independence Hall—and was chief member of the committee which determined its site and used the funds appropriated for its construction. He died in 1741 before the State House was finished.

It was his grandson, "William of The Woodlands," son of Andrew the second, who developed the house and grounds from 1788, when he returned from living in England, until his death in 1813. Andrew the third, his brother, married Abigail Franks, whose home, Woodford, will be seen on Walk 10 in Fairmount Park.

The house itself, now used as a residence by the cemetery superintendent, commands a fine prospect of the river and is noted for its graceful entrance hall, ballroom and, in particular, the southwest bedroom with a secret door beside the fireplace which conceals a ladder leading to the cellar. The house is not open to the public.

William modeled his spectacular gardens after the great English ones, introduced the ginkgo tree and the Lombardy poplar to America. The coachhouse and stable, which is near the house, were also built at the time The Woodlands was enlarged.

Interred in the cemetery are members of some of Philadelphia's most illustrious families—Stotesbury, Drexel, Newbold, Price and Da Costa. The largest monument is to Dr. Thomas William Evans (1823–97) and his wife Agnes Doyle (1822–97). The founder of the Thomas W. Evans Museum and Dental Institute, now part of the University's dental school, Dr. Evans was a confidant of royalty and dentist to many crowned heads, including the Empress Eugénie whom he helped escape from Paris in 1870. His collections of jewels, snuff boxes, trinkets and gem-studded bibelots were gifts of these members of the *Almanach de Gotha*. In 1983 they were sold, as were two Manets that were his, and the proceeds went to the Dental School.

A rather endearing monument was erected by the St. Andrew's Society of Philadelphia (founded 1747). Its inscription reads: "This lot is reserved as a last resting place for friendless Scotchmen dying far from home and kindred." There are seven stones before the larger monument, the last dated 1940. Two men of letters—S. Weir Mitchell and Frank Stockton—are buried here, also. Stockton's career took him away from Philadelphia, but like all good Philadelphians he came home to be buried.

Woodlands Cemetery is a natural bird sanctuary, and the continuous chatter of hundreds of birds can be heard when walking through it. This stretch of the Schuylkill was once one of the most beautiful in Pennsylvania. Farther down the river (at 54th Street and Elmwood Avenue) are the *house and garden of John Bartram* (1699–1777), the great American botanist. Bartram's gardens and Woodlands Cemetery are the only enclaves of nature on this part of the river that still remain intact amid the urban blight and industrialization of West Philadelphia.

Return now to Woodland Terrace and, on reaching Baltimore Avenue, cross and turn right. Walk to 39th Street. Opposite are the gates to Hamilton Walk, one of the pedestrian paths inside the University of Pennsylvania campus. Walk past the zoology building. The second building on the right is the *Alfred Newton Richards Medical* **12** *Research Laboratories* (1959), designed by Louis Kahn, one of the leading architects of the world and a resident of Philadelphia. Ironically enough, it is one of the few Kahn structures in the city for this prophet had to go elsewhere for recognition.

Turn right, walk through the brick courtyard and up the steps. **13** The *botanical garden* beyond is always a complete surprise to those who come upon it for the first time. A small pond complete with water

The Woodlands

Richards Medical Research Laboratories

Dormitory Quadrangle

lilies and gold fish is circled by a web of wooded paths, forest glades and expanses of open lawn—all in miniature, of course. This is a favorite retreat for students wishing to study out-of-doors on mild days. It is a lost green world at the heart of the University campus. Louis Kahn, his genius showing, took every advantage of this natural setting in designing the contemporary building which overlooks it.

14 Leave the garden and return to Hamilton Walk. Just a few steps away on the left is a passage to the *Main Quadrangle,* designed by the firm of Cope and Stewardson and built in 1895. Around the quadrangle are dormitories, reminiscent of Oxford and Cambridge in England. On entering, note the *statue of George Whitefield (1714–70),* the firebrand minister who during his seven tours of America was largely responsible for the Great Awakening in the Colonies. It was done by R. Tait McKenzie, sculptor, physician and educator at the University of Pennsylvania from 1904 to 1938. A collection of his sculpture, mostly of athletes and glorifying sport, are in the *Lloyd P. Jones Gallery,* which is housed in the Gimbel Gymnasium at 37th and Walnut Streets.

Before reaching the gate to Spruce Street, turn right and enter the arch leading to another quadrangle to the east. Here, shrouded by the arch and mounted on a drinking fountain is a sculpture by Alexander Stirling Calder, "The Scholar and the Athlete," a gift of the class of 1892. The middle Calder of three generations of sculptors, it was he who designed both the fountain and the Shakespeare Memorial at Logan Circle, which will be seen on Walk 9. Descend the steps, proceed to the arch ahead, leave by this gate, turn left and walk the few steps to Spruce Street.

Opposite on the northwest corner of 36th is the Wistar Institute, **15** the oldest independent biomedical research institute in the United States, incorporated in 1892. Dr. Isaac Wistar, a Civil War general, named it for his great-uncle, Dr. Caspar Wistar (1761–1818), whose home, the Shippen-Wistar House, was seen on Walk 3.

The Museum of Anatomy and Biology is open to the public. (Monday through Friday, 9:00-4:00. Children must be accompanied by an adult.) This appealing museum has been redesigned and the effect of the exhibits is striking. It houses the Wistar and Horner anatomical collection started by Dr. Caspar Wistar in 1808 and continued by Dr. William Edmonds Horner (1793–1853), his assistant who was elected to the chair of anatomy after Dr. Philip Syng Physick's resignation in 1831.

The development of the embryo and the fetus; fetal skeletons; development failure in fetal growth; growth failures or deviations in humans due to endocrine dysfunction; the evolution of posture; figures showing the normal male, dwarfs, giantism and obesity; skeletons showing experiments in dog crossbreeding and growth in rats are among the many exhibits to be seen. It is all very educational in a simple, uncomplicated way, and the explanations are understandable to all.

Between 36th and 34th Streets on Spruce (there is no 35th Street on campus), the University Hospital is on the right, and Houston Hall, a commons for students, and Irvine Auditorium (1928) are on the left. **16** The ornate and highly individual auditorium on the northwest corner of 34th is generally believed to have been the rejected project of an architectural student who later became successful. This is an appealing story and adds to the building's legend. In actuality, however, the auditorium was designed by Horace Trumbauer, a respected and distinguished architect who had designed several Philadelphia hospitals and hotels. Inside is the Curtis Organ, the world's largest university-owned pipe organ. The 10,973-pipe organ was built at a cost of $150,000 to entertain fairgoers in 1926 at the Sesquicentennial. The Sesquicentennial was a financial fiasco, but Cyrus H. K. Curtis, an organ buff who was named for Hermann Kotzschmar (also an organist), gave the organ to the university. The Curtis family loved to give organs to institutions. Cyrus' own organ is in Christ Church (Walk 2), he also gave one to The Curtis Institute of Music (Walk 7) and his daughter gave one in his memory to the Academy of Music (Walk 6).

From 34th and Spruce Streets turn right. The quietly imposing
17 white building ahead is the *Civic Center Museum* (Monday through
Saturday, 10:00–5:00; Sunday, 1:00–5:00). The museum's exhibits, which
are challenging, lively, contemporary and of wide range and scope,
change periodically. There are often programs of chamber music,
opera and folk dancing. Next to the museum is the *Civic Center Audi-*
18 *torium,* marked at its entrance by the handsome fountain by Harry
Bertoia (1915–1978) on the plaza. Large exhibitions and conventions
are held here, and every March the Pennsylvania Horticultural Society holds its annual flower show. Philadelphia is the only major
city on the East coast that still has a flower show.

Return to 34th and Spruce, turn right and walk to the corner of
33rd. Just below the corner, opposite Franklin Field (the scene of the
University's football, soccer, lacrosse and track events) is the
19 *University Museum,* devoted to archeology and the study of ancient

University Museum

and primitive man. (Tuesday through Saturday, 10:00–4:30; Sunday 1:00–5:00. $2.00 donation suggested.)

Founded in 1887, the first section of the museum building was opened in 1899. The museum now contains one of the largest collections in the United States of ancient and primitive cultures and is certainly one of the world's leading archeological museums. We can find galleries devoted to Oceana, South America, Middle America, Egypt, China, the Classical World, Persia and Mesopotamia. There is an American "gold room" housing objects made of gold from ancient American civilizations; another room devoted to pottery of the Amazon; religious motifs in pottery and weaving; paddles, canes staves, shields and war clubs of primitive cultures; stelae from Honduras and Guatemala; and an amazing new display on the art of Africa—handicrafts, musical instruments, dancers' masks and costumes; gods and fetishes; homes and tools of the people of the Dark Continent. In its history more than two hundred and fifty expeditions have gone out all over the world to investigate such civilizations and regions as Ur of the Chaldees, Egypt, Etruria, Crete, Palestine, Persia, Babylonia, Alaska, Guatemala and Southeast Asia.

Very special indeed is the *Nevil Gallery for the Blind and Sighted*. The wonder of it is evident to the sighted at once and must be to the blind as they uncover the magic of archeology through touch. Along a handrail are conveniently placed tags in braille, and before these are objects of pottery, soapstone, wood, shell, brass, alabaster, and a variety of musical instruments: a gong, a zither and a primitive xylophone. The blind visitor can handle these things on revolving pedestals, which can be turned at will. The stratification display, showing archeological levels, enables him to touch successive shelves and sense the layers unearthed. The gallery is a further indication of the progressive policy the University Museum pursues. It is not only up to the minute, but a step or two ahead.

There is an excellent place to eat lunch in the museum, the Potlatch Restaurant, which is open Tuesday through Saturday from 10:30 to 4:00. The food is good, the prices are reasonable, and the name is singularly apposite.

Leave the museum by the central court, which sets the tone of the entire complex. Around the pool are ancient sculptures in a beautifully landscaped setting. The museum has shown remarkable growth in recent years and has opened a new wing, an extension designed by Mitchell and Giurgola, which contains the Pyramid Shop for children—all sorts of toys and imaginative games and books—the Froelich Rainey Auditorium, named for the museum's director, laboratories, curatorial offices, classrooms and the Kress Gallery devoted to a display on the American Indian.

Turn left and return to the corner of 33rd and Spruce Streets. Cross Spruce, walking north, keeping Franklin Field on the right until reaching the statue of *"Benjamin Franklin in 1723"* by R. Tait **20**

McKenzie, which lends a human touch to the blocks of buildings. After all, it was Ben who founded the University as well as almost everything else of note in Philadelphia. Here he is a youth just arriving in Philadelphia and all that is still ahead of him.

Cross 33rd Street, ascend the steps and continue past the statue of John Harrison (1773–1833), the first manufacturing chemist, until reaching 34th Street once more. Cross and take the path between
21 Irvine Auditorium on the left and the old *University Library* on the right. The library, considered one of architect Frank Furness' best buildings, is now the home of the Department of Fine Arts and the library of the Graduate School of Fine Arts. (Monday-Thursday, 9:00-11:00; Friday, 9:00-10:00; Saturday, 10:00-5:00; Sunday, 1:00-11:00.) It is richly decorated, a monument to an extravagant age when architects weren't afraid to express themselves by decorating buildings. The stairway in the tower should be examined for it, too, has an openness and sweep that contemporary ones seldom have.

Leaving the library, turn right and walk through the campus. The next building on the left, toward 34th Street, contains the *Institute of Contemporary Art*, which has changing exhibits all during the academic year. (Tuesday, Thursday and Friday, 10:00–5:00; Wednesday, 10:00–
22 7:00; Saturday–Sunday, 12:00–5:00.) Continue along the path and on the left is the *Van Pelt Library*. (Monday through Thursday, 8:45–12:00; Friday, 8:45–10:00; Saturday, 10:00–6:00; Sunday, 12:00–12:00.)

The *Rare Book Collection* is of special interest because it, like so many Philadelphia ones, contains riches—a hoard to make even proud prossessors of the past envious. Take the elevator to the sixth floor. The magnificent panels and doors carved in relief are as old as they look. They were taken from a 15th century house in Chester, England, and are a gift of Robert Dechert, an emeritus trustee. They, the oriental rugs, the superb collection of portrait miniatures, the paintings, including a fine Gilbert Stuart of Provost William Smith, provide an appropriate setting for the changing displays of rare books and manuscripts in the recessed cases.

The Collection itself, which is open to students and scholars but not the general public, is monumental. Some of its highlights are the papers of such American writers as Theodore Dreiser, James T. Farrell, Van Wyck Brooks, Waldo Frank, Burton Rascoe and George Seldes. Two Franklin desks—one known to be his and one from the Franklin family—a 16th century clock in an 18th century case, the Herbert Gilchrist portrait of Walt Whitman, a Thomas Phillips portrait of Lord Byron, the Henry Inman portrait of William Wordsworth (the one in England is a copy), and a Thomas Cole depicting a scene from *The Last of the Mohicans* grace the room.

Back on the ground floor again, before leaving the building, turn right and walk through the lounge, turning right again. *The Orrery,* constructed by David Rittenhouse in 1771, showing the planetary system, is on display here. The mechanical universe is con-

"Benjamin Franklin in 1723"

tained in a Chippendale case constructed by Folwell and Gibbs (John Folwell was also responsible for the Wine Glass pulpit in Christ Church and the Rising Sun Chair in Independence Hall). During the Revolution, the orrery was respected by the occupying British forces and returned safely to the Philadelphians.

Continue along to the corner of 34th and Walnut Streets. Here cross over 34th, walk to 33rd and Walnut. On the left, on the north-west corner, is Eero Saarinen's *Hill Hall,* a dormitory with an unusual **23** courtyard within. Almost theatrical, the court is a planned contrast with the severity of the exterior and gives the student quarters a sur-prising intimacy.

Turn left, cross Walnut and continue on to 33rd and Chestnut Streets. This is the heart of the new campus of Drexel University. We can stroll at will along the paths of this almost completely new

Franklin Desk

Main Hall, Drexel University

modern complex. One of the few original buildings left, *Main Hall*, stands at 32nd and Chestnut Streets. The building, constructed of light buff brick with terra-cotta ornamentations, is classic Renaissance in style, contrasting to the newer buildings around it, all made of a salmon-colored brick. Inside there is a spacious central court, 65 feet square and open to the roof, surrounded by galleries, enclosed by arcades. It is on such a grand scale and so elaborate that it should be visited. The Drexel Museum Collection is in this building, too, and it can be seen by calling the curator for an appointment at 895-2423. (Monday and Wednesday, 11:00–3:30; Friday, 1:30–3:30.) In the collection are Napoleon's chess table and a mirror from his house on St. Helena and *"The Water Boy"* by Auguste Bartholdi (1834–1904), the French sculptor responsible for the Statue of Liberty in New York harbor. "The Water Boy's" right toe has been burnished to a shining bronze by generations of students who traditionally rubbed his toe for luck before taking examinations.

Also of interest is the *Rittenhouse Clock,* which tells the time of day in seconds, minutes and hours, strikes on each quarter-hour and plays any one of ten tunes. Devised by David Rittenhouse (Walk 7) in 1773, the clock also indicates the day and the date, the phases of the moon, the orbit of the moon around earth and earth's around the sun, the signs of the zodiac, equations of time and the then-known planets, excluding Uranus and Pluto. Rittenhouse was indeed a genius! It might also be mentioned in passing that Cyrus H. K. Curtis, after giving an organ to the University of Pennsylvania, was persuaded to give one to Drexel, which was not to be outdone.

Leaving Main Hall, it is a simple matter to return to Center City by walking across the bridge over the Schuylkill or taking any bus on Chestnut Street.

The Benjamin Franklin Parkway

Benjamin Franklin Parkway is Philadelphia's Champs Elysées—or its Pennsylvania Avenue. True, there is no Arc de Triomphe or White House, but there are such fine buildings as the Philadelphia Museum of Art, the Rodin Museum and the Cathedral of SS. Peter and Paul. Fountains, small parks, statues and monuments all lend a formality that gives the Parkway its own special aura. This, of course, was not an accident. Photographs of the area before World War I show the Cathedral and a stretch of road from Logan Square to Fairmount Park, but a mass of buildings with no space at all between them extended from Logan Square to what is now John F. Kennedy Plaza.

By 1919—the Parkway was begun in 1917—a stretch of Parkway could be seen from the beginning at 16th Street to the site of the Museum of Art, but none of the public buildings we know today had yet been erected. The designers of the Parkway were Paul Cret and Jacques Gréber, who were also responsible for the design of the Rodin Museum. By 1935 the Franklin Institute, the Free Library of Philadelphia, the Philadelphia Museum of Art at the head of the avenue, and the Rodin Museum could be seen, but the trees at that time were still young, and today's landscaping was not evident. Paul Cret was the architect of the Federal Reserve Bank at 10th and Chestnut Street, the Benjamin Franklin Bridge, and it was he who designed the central plaza, the pool and the entrances to Rittenhouse Square. The development of the Parkway took vision, and Cret, Gréber and Eli Kirk Price, a public-spirited citizen whose forebears had done much for the city, were among the proponents of the plan.

In the years since World War II blocks of apartment flats have risen along the Parkway, a motel overlooks the Rodin Museum and the Philadelphian apartment house intrudes on the Museum of Art. It is true that 2601 Parkway was erected before the war, but it is actually off the Parkway and was shielded by a growth of trees that prevented it from spoiling the view of the Museum. John F. Kennedy Plaza with its fountain, complementing the Calder fountain at Logan Circle and the three before the Museum of Art, has helped unify the whole in spite of its encroachments.

The "Parkway"—as it is always called, many forgetting it was named for Franklin—is a busy traffic artery leading as it does from Center City to the East and West River Drives. It is also a place of

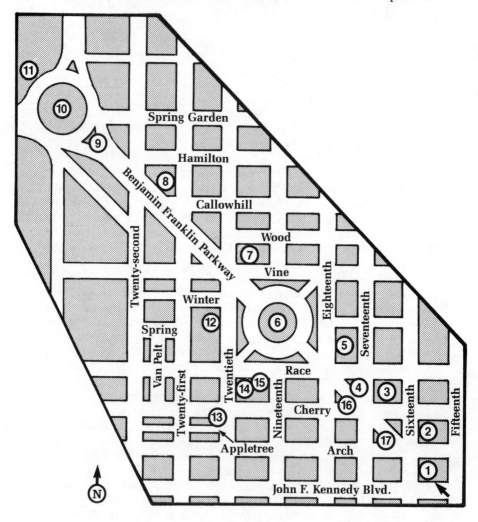

Benjamin Franklin Parkway

parades—the St. Patrick's Day, Columbus Day, Pulaski Day and Veteran's Day. Most groups march down the Parkway except the Mummers who confine their strutting to South Broad Street.

In the autumn there is "Super Sunday" held in October, with all the public institutions participating and Philadelphians, usually a quarter-million or more of them, joining in. Concerts, puppet shows, films, storytelling and a flea market appear along the Parkway from Logan Circle to the Museum of Art. The Festival of the Fountains, which is held in the spring, with special lighting effects has attracted similar thousands as has the largest street painting in the world, done in vari-colored stripes before the Museum of Art.

The Parkway has recently been taken over as much by cyclists as by motorists and is serving a new and unexpected purpose for younger Philadelphians. It will soon be sixty years old and most citizens of advanced age find it difficult to recall when it wasn't there.

1 Begin at *Kennedy Plaza* on the west side of City Hall. On the corner of 16th is the circular glass Tourist Center, where information on events and places of interest can be obtained.

During the milder days of the year there is usually entertainment of some sort here—rock concerts, evangelical and gospel singers, political speeches, folk dancing, string bands, exhibition basketball games, boxing, wrestling and gymnastic exhibitions. Lunchtime crowds flock to see and hear these groups and senior citizens make up much of the audience for the summer-evening concerts. The fountain is a thing of beauty, but it has a lighter aspect, too. High

"Three Way Piece" by Henry Moore

school girls regularly celebrate the end of the school year by taking off their shoes and stockings (some don't!) and cavorting in the fountain.

Fine pieces of sculpture are placed strategically, notably "Three Way Piece (Points)" by Henry Moore (1898–   ), near the corner of 15th and Arch Streets. Perhaps Kennedy Plaza is most beautiful at night with the globes that serve as lamps in the square and the buildings around it—Penn Center, City Hall, the Masonic Temple, the Arch Street Methodist Church—lighted, and in the distance the floodlighted Museum of Art. At this time, when Philadelphia becomes a City of Light, the relationship between Center City and the Parkway is even more evident as is that of Philadelphia to its Parisian model.

For those who find it difficult to walk long distances, take the Fairmount Park Trolley at John F. Kennedy Boulevard, with stops at the Free Library of Philadelphia, the Franklin Institute, the Academy of Natural Sciences, the Rodin Museum, the Museum of Art and the Zoo. A $1.75 ticket entitles the rider to use the trolley all day, getting off and on at whichever point he desires. The bus originates at Independence Hall, then stops at City Hall, and the Pennsylvania Academy of the Fine Arts before reaching the Tourist Center. It makes the return trip, starting at the Zoo, in reverse order. It is the best bargain available in transportation in Philadelphia. After its success here for a number of years, New York took notice and inaugurated a similar service.

From the north side of the Parkway at 16th, begin walking at

"Festival"

Sculpture in Penn Center

2 the *Bell Telephone Company Building.* The statue of "Man" by Joseph Greenberg (1963) stands above the reflecting pool, and the prophetic words of Theodore N. Vail (1912) are incised in the wall above him: "The growth and evolution of man—of civilization—have gone—step by step—along the trail made by communication."

Cross 16th Street to the small park, one of the most judiciously landscaped spots in the city. To the right between 16th and 17th

3 Street is the *Pennwalt Building.* That part nearest 16th Street houses offices; the 17th Street side is occupied by the Friends Select School (founded 1689). At one time the entire block, between 16th and 17th, the Parkway and Race Street, was occupied by the school and its grounds. The old log cabin, now at Stenton, which once stood on the grounds of the earlier school, can be seen on Walk 12. When the cabin was here, it served as a home for the caretakers of the Friends Burying Ground, then as a home for faculty members. For one year (1968), the 5th and 6th grades used it as a school, while the present building was being built, and children of the 1960s can tell their children that they went to school in a log cabin in the center of Philadelphia! Just inside the door of the school, in a severe and functional hallway, stands a grandfather's clock made by John Child of Philadelphia. A brass plate on the clock tells us the school first came into possession of it in 1839. For many years it had belonged to the Friends School at 4th and Chestnut Street and was used in regulating the clock in the tower of Independence Hall.

Farther along at Cherry Street, before the new United Fund

4 Building, is the steel construction to *Copernicus,* the Polish astronomer. A plate at the base denotes that soil from his birthplace at Torun, Poland, is placed here. German and Polish groups had a lively battle, in and out of the press, before the monument was even in place as to whether Copernicus was a German or a Pole. The Poles evidently triumphed for his name on the marble base is spelled *Kopernik.*

Opposite the monument, across Race Street, was the residence of the cardinal of the Roman Catholic Archdiocese of Philadelphia.

5 Behind the residence, the reddish brownstone *Cathedral of SS. Peter and Paul,* built between 1846 and 1864, dominates the area. Napoleon Le Brun, who designed the Academy of Music, and John Notman, whose buildings include the Athenaeum and the Church of the Holy Trinity, were the architects. Its Palladian façade and copper dome are in the Italian Renaissance manner, and the interior is spacious with magnificent proportions reminiscent of Roman churches. It was largely decorated by Constantino Brumidi (1805–90), who painted the dome of the Capitol in Washington. A baldachin over the main altar and the three altars on each of the side aisles point up this Italian Renaissance flavor. Unfortunately a chapel was added in 1954 which completely destroyed the symmetry of the entire structure and marred the north wall of the cathedral.

SS. Peter and Paul,
1872

Just in front, in the small park opposite, is a *statue of Thomas FitzSimons* (1741–1811), born in Ireland and a Signer of the Constitution, a member of the Constitutional Convention and of the 1st, 2nd and 3rd Congresses. He is buried in St. Mary's burying ground, visited on Walk 3.

Now follow the path along the outer edge of the drive around Logan Circle, passing the monument to Galusha Pennypacker, Brevet Major General, United States Army, and the *Shakespeare Memorial*, "Hamlet and the Fool" by Alexander Stirling Calder. Erected in 1928, it commemorates Philadelphia's Shakespearean scholars and such actors as Joseph Jefferson, John Drew, Louisa Lane Drew and Edwin Forrest among others.

Logan Circle is one of Penn's original five squares, and it, too, **6** was once used as a burying ground. In 1821 the ground was being used as a pasture—difficult to imagine today—and on February 7, 1823, William Gross was hanged here—the last public execution held on the spot. Whether William was also buried in the square we don't know. In 1825 it was renamed for James Logan and seventeen years later it was a punishable offence to take a cow, horse, cart, wagon or carriage into the square. Eventually the graves, mounds and hillocks were removed or leveled. And now it is one of the most beautiful spots in the city. The square has become a circle, the *Swann Memorial Fountain* by Alexander Stirling Calder, a graceful aerial water ballet, the flower beds among the most brilliant in Philadelphia. It is a medallion in the Parkway's necklace of gems.

7   *The Free Library of Philadelphia,* to the right of the Shakespeare monument (its balancing building is the County Court Building behind the Pennypacker monument), is one of the great libraries of the country. The main library of the Philadelphia system, anyone may use its resources on the spot. (Monday-Wednesday, 9:00-9:00; Thursday-Friday, 9:00-6:00; Saturday, 9:00-5:00; Sunday, 2:00-6:00.) There are always exhibits of interest in the entrance hall, concerts, lectures and films throughout the year. A roof garden for reading is also a splendid spot to view this part of the city. There is a cafeteria on the roof as well, and during the summer you can eat al fresco and enjoy the panorama of Philadelphia.

One of the riches of the Free Library is the Rare Book Department, which has holdings spanning 5000 years, from cuneiform tablets, European manuscripts dating from the 9th through the 18th century, examples of calligraphy, Oriental manuscripts and miniatures, incunabula, Pennsylvania German frakturs from the notable collections of Henry S. Borneman and Levi E. Yoder, an extensive collection of children's books and illustrations (Arthur Rackham, Kate Greenaway, Howard Pyle and Beatrix Potter) and the William McIntire Elkins library. This handsome Georgian room was removed from Mr. Elkins' home in Whitemarsh, on the outskirts of Philadelphia, and installed in the library in 1949. Richly paneled, the room contains Mr. Elkins' own fine library, a notable collection of Dickens' letters and editions, Dickens' desk and candleholder and even his pet raven which was stuffed in 1841! There is a Poe connection, too, for Poe had reviewed *Barnaby Rudge* and didn't feel Dickens had done justice to the raven in his portrait of it. "The Raven," more in keeping with Poe's idea of the bird, was the result. The library also has the gravestone of Dickens' pet canary ("Dick the Best of Friends"), something of which no other rare book department can boast.

Leaving the library, turn right, cross 20th Street and pass the Youth Study Center, with the *two sculptural groups* of 1955, "The Doctor" and "The Healer" by Waldemar Raemisch, to the right.

Just beyond 21st and Callowhill Streets, which both enter the **8** Parkway here, is the *Rodin Museum.* (Daily 10:00–5:00. Closed Mondays and holidays. Admission by donation.) This small museum is like a jewel box in design and contents. "The Thinker" broods before the entrance, an architectural fragment which is a reproduction of parts of the old Chateau d'Issy. (Auguste Rodin (1840–1917) had re-erected the original near his studio at Meudon.) It provides an im-

Swann Fountain,
Logan Circle

William Elkins Library

pressive entry to the formal garden with its lily pool which, in turn, draws the visitor naturally to the portico, containing the original casting of "The Gates of Hell." The garden is another natural, unplanned bird sanctuary.

Given by Jules Mastbaum, the theatrical magnate, to the citizens of Philadelphia (he died in 1926 before it was begun), the museum contains some of Rodin's greatest figures—"The Burghers of Calais," "Adam," "Eve," "St. John the Baptist Preaching," busts and figures of Balzac, and busts of Mahler, Shaw, Victor Hugo, Georges Clemenceau, Pope Benedict XV and Puvis de Chavannes. Sketches, drawings, books and papers of Rodin's are on deposit as well as plaster casts and a fine series of mood photographs of Rodin at Meudon by Edward Steichen. The plaster of "Eternal Springtime" is the original Rodin sculpture which the artist presented to Robert Louis Stevenson in 1885.

Now walk the remaining stretch of the Parkway to the plaza before the Philadelphia Museum of Art, which Lord Dunsany called the most beautiful building in America. At the foot of the plaza stands
9 the tiny *Victorian Gothic guard house,* which stood to the east of the

Rodin Museum

Gothic Guard House

museum for many years. It was built about 1850 and its present location has given it greater emphasis and made it a positive accent to the spot where the roads swirl around the plaza.

The plaza, named for Thomas Eakins (1844–1916), the great Philadelphia painter who is best known for "The Gross Clinic" and "The Agnew Clinic," leads to the three fountains which begin the natural sequence of water, seeming in fact to cascade here from every direction.

The *center fountain,* dedicated to Washington, was erected by **10** the Society of the Cincinnati of Pennsylvania. The four figures and the animals overlooking the pools at the base represent four great waterways of America—the Mississippi, the Potomac, the Delaware and the Hudson. The fountain to the left is a memorial to Eli Kirk Price (1860–1933), who was a major force in developing the Parkway and the Museum of Art. That on the right is to the memory of Captain John Ericsson (1803–89), scientist and inventor of *Monitor* which engaged the Confederate vessel *Merrimac* in an historic naval battle at Hampton Roads, Virginia, in 1862.

The *Philadelphia Museum of Art* is almost too large to compre- **11** hend and the best way to savor it is to ascend the steps slowly, taking in the prospect in stages. (Tuesday through Sunday, 10:00–5:00. Closed Monday. Sunday until 1:00 free. Adults, $2.50; students, senior citizens and those under eighteen, $1.25. Frequent guided tours available.) The tunnel-like entrance on the left, past the majestic statue of Joan of Arc by Emmanuel Frémiet, leads to the elevators.

The arrangement of sculpture around the pool and about the forecourt allows again for savoring the museum façade. Begun in 1919, the first section was opened in 1928. The Minnesota dolomite building covers ten acres of space and is breathtaking when seen floodlighted at night.

The pediment or tympanum on the north wing was done by C. Paul Jennewein and illustrates the theme of sacred and profane love. There are thirteen classical figures, the central one of Zeus signifying the creative force, with Demeter, the laurel tree, Theseus, Aphrodite and Eros to the sides. Unfortunately, funds were never available to complete it with similar groups on the central and south buildings.

Inside, the Great Stair Hall is awesome in its magnitude and provides a fitting setting for the thirteen magnificent tapestries from the Palazzo Barberini in Rome (a gift of the Samuel H. Kress Foundation), "Diana" at the top of the stairs whose poised figure once graced —as a weathervane—the first Madison Square Garden in New York (Gotham would like to have it back) and "Ghost," a mobile by the present-day Alexander Calder, son of the sculptor of the Logan Circle fountain and grandson of the man who created William Penn on the top of City Hall. Because of the name of the mobile, the three sculptors have often been irreverently called "the father, son and unholy ghost."

It is impossible to begin to catalog its contents fully, but the museum's great treasures are the John G. Johnson collection of early Italian art, notably religious; the English, Dutch, French and American rooms which have been installed intact in the museum; the Arensberg collection of pre-Columbian and modern art; the Gallatin collection of modern art; the Titus C. Geesey collection of Pennsylvania Dutch folk art; and the fragments of medieval chapels, cloisters, and the Romanesque fountain and courtyard from the abbey of Saint Michel de Cuxa (12th century), Pyrénées-Orientales.

Every museum has its most popular works and the Philadelphia Museum of Art is no exception. Through the years it has found the favorites of the public to be: "Nude Descending a Staircase" by Marcel Duchamp, Van Gogh's "Sunflowers," the large "Bathers" by Cézanne, Picasso's "Three Musicians," and Brancusi's sculptures, variations on his "Bird in Space" theme and "The Kiss."

Children seem to respond in particular to the Japanese ceremonial tea house and garden and the Chinese scholar's study. The museum has a superb costume collection, print department and distinguished collections of china, porcelain, jade, glass and silver. It is wise not to try and see it all at once. Between 1974 and 1976 some galleries will be closed from time to time, because the entire museum is being air conditioned. It is best to note special shows—and the galleries open—on the bulletin boards at the entrances before planning your itinerary.

Two recent amenities are an excellent cafeteria—the food is not the standard museum cafeteria fare—and the museum restaurant, which is more expensive but certainly worth it. Decorated in the Bauhaus tradition, it has chrome and cane chairs which are a Marcel

Philadelphia Museum of Art

Great Stair Hall

Breuer design. The carpet was inspired by the weavings of Anni Albers, and the white curtains at the windows on a sunny, cloudy or rainy day give the room a particular glamour.

Leaving the museum, descend the steps, cross over to the fountains and take the righthand walk down the Parkway. Walking along this side gives us the opportunity to observe the buildings we saw on the way up in a different perspective.

Pass the Rodin Museum and the Youth Study Center and at the Civil War Memorial Gates, which lead into Logan Circle, the *Franklin Institute* is on the right. Turn right at 20th Street and enter **12** by the main entrance. (Monday-Saturday, 10:00-5:00, Sunday, 12:00-5:00. Adults, $3.50; children 4–11, $2.50, and 12–18, $3.00; senior citizens, $2.00.)

Founded in 1824, in honor of Benjamin Franklin, by Samuel Vaughan Merrick and William H. Keating, the institute's first permanent home was the present Atwater Kent Museum, 15 South 7th Street, visited on Walk 1. In 1974 it marked its 150th anniversary. The cornerstone for the present building was laid in 1932, the Fels

Planetarium opened the following year and the Science Museum a year later.

The Franklin Institute is a museum-goer's paradise. It is a living, vital museum of energy, motion and sound. These qualities are transferred to the children who, presented with such a wealth of things to do, become frantic at times. They begin at one thing, see another and in great excitement rush off madly to have a go at that. The excitement is intense.

Sound, from radio to electronic music, is one of these excitements. The exhibition features a theremin, an electronic flute, a telephone with musical dial tones, an electronic music studio, a keyboard illustrating rhythm, melody and harmony, and it is even possible to type a tune ("Mary Had a Little Lamb," "Joy to the World" and "Swanee River"). It is also exciting, stimulating and marvelous. Anyone may whack and strum a bass fiddle in time to the electronic sounds heard everywhere.

The trains and planes have the same appeal. In all these exhibits the visitor participates. A Link Trainer in the Hall of Aviation can be used by anyone between the ages of thirteen and twenty who is at least five feet tall, and it is possible to clamber into a United States Air Force plane, sit behind the controls and get the feel of it.

In the same vein we can climb aboard a 1926 Baldwin locomotive or an earlier American engine (1842) to the sound of train whistles and bells, although the "Rocket"—constructed in London in 1838—is just for viewing and not for climbing into.

The pilot house and bridge of a ship in the marine museum are open in the same way, and the models of John Fitch's steamboat (1796) and Robert Fulton's *Clermont* (1807) are activated when a button is pushed. Fitch and Philadelphia have never gotten full credit for Fitch's having invented the steamship before Fulton.

Here, where nothing is static and everything is manipulatable, there is even recorded ragtime music in the stamp exhibit! The regular rhythm of the Foucault Pendulum, which hangs four stories, illustrates the earth's rotation, and a drop of water falling into a basin illustrates yet another principle. The simple movement of the drop of water, perhaps, crystallizes the philosophy of the Franklin Institute, whose credo could easily be expressed in the words of Thomas Huxley inscribed around the lip of that basin:

> *Sit down before a fact as a child,*
> *be prepared to give up every preconceived notion,*
> *follow humbly wherever nature leads,*
> *or you will learn nothing.*

It is difficult to leave the Franklin Institute, with its statue of a seated Benjamin Franklin surrounded by his belongings in the main rotunda. Some of the money from Franklin's estate, in trust, helped build Franklin Institute. The remainder will be distributed on the 200th anniversary of his death in 1990. A Philadelphia anomaly is that the trusts set up in Benjamin Franklin's and Stephen Girard's wills are still being administered. The Fels Planetarium, with its own entrance facing the Parkway, gives regular shows. (Monday through Friday, 12:30 and 2:00; Saturday, every hour on the hour between 12:00 and 4:00; Sunday, 2:00, 3:00 and 4:00. Adults, $1.00. Saturday morning children's show at 10:30, $.75.

Leaving Franklin Institute turn right, cross Race Street, pass the Franklin Institute Research Laboratories and at the corner of Cherry Street (actually between Cherry and Appletree) is *St. Clement's* **13** *Episcopal Church*. The Episcopalians have some of Philadelphia's most interesting and historic churches and by and large the ones with the greatest architectural beauty, such as this John Notman one of 1859.

Walk to Appletree Street, and just around the corner is the entrance to the garden and the church itself. The high altar has a fine triptych and the stained glass, even on a dull day or when the church is unlighted, is especially notable. St. Clement's was once in a fashionable neighborhood, then the city changed and Arch Street became a warren of cheap hotels and rooming houses. Now, on the edge of the Parkway in an area which is becoming revitalized and near the apartment houses on Kennedy Boulevard, it is having a revival. There are charming small houses on Cherry and Appletree Streets, which border the church.

At 20th Street cross, turn left and walk to Race, passing on the right the buildings of *Moore College of Art*. Turn right at 20th and **14** Race, passing the front of Moore College. At the corner of 19th and

Benjamin Franklin
by James Earle Fraser

Academy of Natural Sciences

15 Race Streets stands the *Academy of Natural Sciences*, the oldest institution of its kind in America, founded in 1812. (Monday through Friday, 10:00–4:00; Saturday and Sunday, 10:00–5:00. Adults, $2.75; children 3–12, $2.25; senior citizens, $2.50.)

The Academy, one of Philadelphia's most active and progressive museums, houses cases of stuffed birds and animals displayed in backgrounds simulating their natural habitats, fossils—including a collection of Thomas Jefferson's—models of extinct animals, insects and shells. An exhibit such as "What's inside a python?" shows the skeletal structure without the skin. A show-stopping sign says: "Look." When the viewer looks into the glass the size of an eye, he is gazing into the eye of an owl!

Another sign brings the visitor up short: "A tiger can leap 30 feet to pin his prey." This startling thought is pointed up by prints of a tiger's paws on the floor and thirty feet away another set of prints. Drugs are covered—hashish and the pipe, and there is an exhibit devoted to the evolution of an elephant.

The gems, minerals, fluorescent minerals and a model of the massive gold nugget found in 1858 at Bakery Hill, Australia, are alone worth a visit. Cut but unset gems are displayed to great effect.

The Academy, like the Franklin Institute, endeavors to make natural science a simple, understandable thing on an everyday level, explaining it in a way that relates to the world around us. The American Indian practice of burying a fish in each hill when sowing corn—a practice the Pennsylvania Dutch borrowed—provides us with a simple example of the fertilization process.

Leaving the Academy of Natural Sciences, cross 19th Street, walk along to 18th and then cross that street. The *Palace Hotel*, formerly the Plaza apartments, displays another sculpture worthy of note. At the rear of the building, on the point of land where Cherry Street

16 crosses the Parkway, we find the handsome *sculpture-fountain* by Oskar Stonorov and Jorio Vivarelli, with water cascading over a male figure holding a young girl aloft, as two others prepare to help lift her from the pool below. This is an example of the benefits of the

Philadelphia one-percent-of-building-costs rule. This city regulation commits architects and builders to set aside that percentage for decoration—sculpture, a mural, a bas relief—on buildings constructed within the city limits. It is responsible for some of the more exciting contemporary art seen on or in our new buildings.

Opposite it is Mace's Crossing, a tavern which refused to leave when the apartment building behind it—The Windsor—was constructed. It provides one of those accidental but delightful accents which enliven a city. It is also a rather old-fashioned watering spot, rather than a cocktail lounge like those in the fashionable buildings nearby.

Walk along to the corner of 16th and Arch Street, with the Pennwalt Building and Friends Select School on the left. Here is the monument by C. Natan Rapoport (1964) in memory of the six **17** million Jewish martyrs who perished at the hands of the Nazis between 1933 and 1945. It is a powerful statement of struggle and agony. Among the striving figures can be discerned the Torah, an old scholar wearing his prayer shawl and an arm holding a sword for freedom.

We are now opposite John F. Kennedy Plaza, our starting point. The Parkway is behind us now. The bold angling off was the first deviation from William Penn's original city plan as shown on Thomas Holme's famous map of 1683. Penn visualized his city as a tidy and orderly one, with the streets four-square (except where the rivers dictated otherwise). The break with tradition presaged things to come. As the new country became older, life in the city changed, the tempo accelerated. Non-residential areas became livable, and neglected ones became desirable again.

In the Logan Square area a new look has come to Philadelphia. Facing the Parkway, between 18th and 19th Streets and just opposite the Academy of Natural Sciences, is the Four Seasons Hotel, which opened in 1983. The hotel, built of handsome beige granite, is a hostelry of great sophistication. Its adjacent courtyard is a garden which echoes the flowers-and-water motif of Logan Square. Fountains and waterfalls, trees, flowering shrubs and plants make it a modern oasis in the heart of the city.

An heroic statue of Thaddeus Kosciuscko by Marian Konieczny glorifies the Polish military genius whose house we visited on Walk 3. The white and red base of the monument symbolizes the colors of the Polish flag. It was given to the United States by the Polish people as a sign of Polish-American friendship and to commemorate two hundred years of our independence.

In the beginning the Parkway was an architect's and a planner's dream—something breathtakingly bold for the staid old city. Then it became a cultural oasis—the center for museums and educational institutions—linking the commercial city with stretches of Fairmount Park. As the 20th century wanes, it is a thrust to the future. As the 21st century approaches, this once quiet avenue will house untold Philadelphians as the towers rise skyward.

🌷🌷🌷
🟧🟧🟧

Past and Present
Meet in Fairmount Park

Every city touts its own beauties, but few cities anywhere can lay claim to the sylvan beauty on both banks of the Schuylkill River that are known as Fairmount Park. We can walk, bicycle or drive along the East or West River Drives today and imagine ourselves deep in the country. In the depths of the Wissahickon Ravine and at other points in the park the city's tall buildings are not visible over the treetops, and, if it were not for the hum of traffic on the drives, we could be in the pastoral world Thomas Eakins painted. It was Eakins who immortalized the scullers on the Schuylkill—some of these paintings such as "The Biglen Brothers Practicing" are exhibited today at the Philadelphia Museum of Art. The "Mount" for which the park was named is the rise on which the museum stands.

There was an amusing remark going the rounds in 1956 when Grace Kelly married Prince Rainier of Monaco that her father's domain (John B. Kelly, Sr., was president of the Fairmount Park Commission) was larger than her husband's. Indeed, the Principality of Monaco covers only .6 square miles, but the 4,077.59 acres of Fairmount Park extend over 6 square miles.

The Philadelphia park was the site of the Centennial Exposition of 1876, and several buildings from that earlier fair still stand, notably Memorial Hall and the Ohio House. Tivoli in Copenhagen isn't a patch on Fairmount Park—nor are the Tuileries or the Vienna Woods. One of the world's largest municipal parks, Fairmount contains more than two-and-a-half million trees; the Zoo, the oldest in the United States; Boathouse Row, the homes of the various rowing clubs and the headquarters of the Schuylkill Navy; cherry blossoms to rival those along the Potomac Basin in the spring; Robin Hood Dell, the Philadelphia Orchestra's (and others') summer amphitheatre for music; an olympic-sized pool; picnic areas; tennis courts; miles of bicycle paths; bridle paths; ball fields, a rock garden; an azalea garden; reservoirs; restaurants; the Playhouse-in-the-Park; hundreds of statues and monuments; and two dozen or so 18th and 19th century buildings, which comprise an unusual historical patrimony. A few of these are open to the public, and we shall visit some of them, especially the historic homes maintained by the Philadelphia Museum of Art. Most of the houses were built here originally —in the countryside. Only Hatfield House, the Letitia Street House,

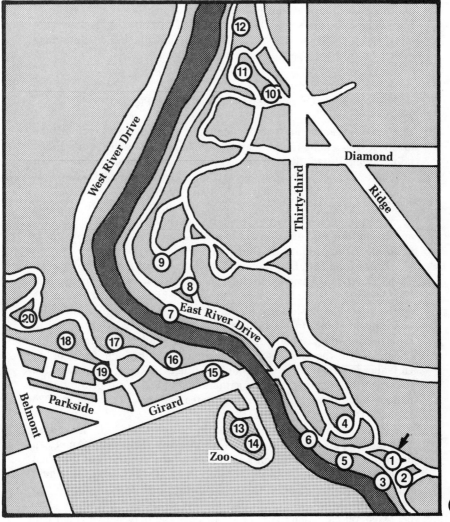

Cedar Grove and the Japanese House have been moved here from other sites.

There are various ways to reach these historic houses. In the summer months the Cultural Loop bus goes as far as the Zoo, and we can walk from there to Sweetbriar, Cedar Grove and the Japanese House. City buses stop within walking distance of three more, Lemon Hill, Woodford and Strawberry Mansion. Mount Pleasant is a little off the beaten track for walkers, but it can be reached on foot, too.

The Philadelphia Museum of Art, which is also reached by the Cultural Loop bus, conducts tours of the houses several days a week and a call to the museum (PO 3-8100) will provide the schedule of tours. The tours are scheduled various days of the week, and are subject to change. It is wise to call the museum number to determine which houses are open on a particular day.

· *The East River Drive, Lemon Hill and Mount Pleasant*

The walk in Fairmount Park along the river basin is one of the loveliest walks to be found in an American city. Take the *A* bus at any point along Broad Street—Locust, Walnut or Chestnut Street—or at John F. Kennedy Plaza, between 15th and 16th Streets on Kennedy Boulevard—and get off at 25th Street and Pennsylvania Avenue.

This is the point to decide about lunch, for there are a dining room and a luncheonette in the apartment building at 2601 Parkway; and, except for a concession at the beginning of Boathouse Row, there is no other opportunity on the walk.

Cross from 25th Street over to the Museum of Art and follow the East River Drive beside the museum to the first turning to the left.
1 This leads to the *Azalea Garden,* directly behind the museum. In the spring when the bushes are blooming, the garden is a blaze of color and a place of pilgrimage for flower lovers. The large fountain set in the center of the circular drive nearby is the *Italian Fountain,* or the "Fountain of the Sea Horses," a replica of the one Christopher Untenberger created in the Borghese Gardens in Rome. The travertine fountain (the reason it hasn't weathered well) was a gift of the Italian nation to the people of the United States and was presented in 1926 to mark the Sesquicentennial.

Nearby is a formal approach to the museum which is flanked on
2 both sides by handsome *statues* of six men who helped the American cause during the Revolution: Major-General Friedrich von Steuben (1730–94); John Paul Jones (1747–92), hero of the American navy; General Casimir Pulaski (1748–79), who died in the attack on Savannah; General Richard Montgomery (1738–75), killed at Quebec; General Nathanael Greene (1742–86)—the only native American in the group—who helped feed and clothe the Continental army; and the Marquis de Lafayette (1757–1834). They are heroically cast revolu-

Fairmount Water Works

tionaries, but are sometimes overlooked in this quiet spot. The prevalence of sculpture in the park is due to the vision of the Fairmount Park Art Association (1871), which sought to beautify the park.

At the river edge is the *Fairmount Water Works,* designed by **3** Frederick Graff. One of the most romantic collections of buildings in Philadelphia, it is an architectural achievement. Built between 1819 and 1822, the waterworks comprise a dam, pumphouse and reservoir. Classical in feeling, the superintendent's house, the pavilions on each side and the balustrades along the river make an unforgettable picture at night when viewed from the other side of the river. There is a small summerhouse on a promontory overlooking the Schuylkill falls and from here the boathouses and the scullers' shells can be seen to great advantage.

Circle the Italian Fountain and take the road nearest the water. This leads back to the East River Drive and a large bronze *statue of Lincoln the Emancipator* by Randolph Rogers (1825–92), erected by the Lincoln Monument Association. To reach one of the most beautiful Federal houses in Philadelphia, cross over to the Lincoln Monument, take the road leading up the hill and turn left at the first road cutting in. A two-or-three-minute walk brings you to *Lemon* **4** *Hill.* (Thursday, April-October, 11:00-4:00; November-March, 11:00-3:30. Second and fourth Sundays, June-September, 1:00-5:00. $.50; children $.25. Arrangements for groups by calling PO 3-8100.) The knoll on which the house stands was originally called Springettsbury, named for William Penn's first wife, Gulielma Springett. The estate was known in 1770 as Vineyard Hill or The Hills and from that year until 1799 it was the home of Robert Morris, Signer of the Declaration of Independence and one of the financiers of the Revolution. He was later bankrupt due to his land speculations, and Henry Pratt, a Philadelphia merchant and philanthropist, purchased the main part of the property at a sheriff's sale in 1799. The present house was built in that year and the next. Pratt died in 1838 and the city purchased the estate in 1844, the first of the Fairmount Park houses to be acquired. When Lemon Hill was added to the 24 acres which had been purchased in 1828, the park began to take shape.

The house itself is rectangular, with a central bay on the river side that rises three stories. The unique feature of the house is the oval rooms, with slightly concave doors, which have superb proportions and are strikingly beautiful. The furnishings are as delightful as the rooms. The dining room, with its rose-colored draperies, Sully portraits, mirror circa 1730, Empire sofa and chairs and its adjoining veranda, isn't too large, too grand or too overpowering. The oval parlor on the first floor has the same intimate quality, with its 17th century floral paintings, pianoforte (New York, 1815–18), harp, Portuguese crystal chandeliers and grandfather's clock which belonged to Ebenezer Hazard, first Postmaster General of the United States. The first floor has few rooms for a house of this size and proportions: an entrance hall, a library and a tiny tearoom or lady's withdrawing room in addition to the oval parlor and dining room. The second floor is a duplicate of the first as to plan and here the Palladian window to the floor confirms the elegance of the hall. The bedroom— Sheraton bed and bureau, oriental rugs and blue chintz draperies— has a veranda similar to the one off the dining room directly below. All of these porches have a view of the river.

Lemon Hill

Many visitors say Lemon Hill is their favorite among the houses in the park because of its elegance and simplicity. These qualities are honed to a fine point here and were probably the reason Fiske Kimball, the first director of the Philadelphia Museum of Art, selected it for his home. It is now maintained by the Colonial Dames of America.

If we descend the hill at the left as we leave, we'll be once more on East River Drive opposite *Boathouse Row*. Crossing over, walk by **5** the boathouses, which provide a somewhat late Victorian aspect to the river front. They are simple, roomy and functional. The Undine Barge Club, erected 1882–83, was designed by Frank Furness whose buildings are encountered throughout the city. The last of these clubs —the Sedgeley Club—is not a rowing club. Its small tower was once a lighthouse on the river, warning that falls were just ahead. Now it is a women's club and used for social functions.

Boathouse Row

*Part of the
Schuylkill Navy*

At the Sedgeley Club is the statue of the Viking, "Thorfinn Karlsefni," who is believed to have come to America in 1004, by the Icelandic sculptor Einar Jonsson. It is the first of many pieces of sculpture we'll see along the embankment and the beginning of the

6 *Ellen Phillips Samuel Memorial* of America's history. Mrs. Samuel, who died in 1913, left a sum of money for the memorial, but before that could be accomplished, her husband had contributed the statue of Karlsefni, which was erected here in 1920. Just beyond it is the Italianate urn, with its bas relief of cupids, which leads quite naturally to the three plazas of the Samuel sculpture complex, which was begun in 1932.

The first plaza's motif is the founding of the nation. Quotations from the Declaration of Independence, Washington's First Inaugural Address and the Book of Common Prayer are incised into the granite which forms a backdrop for the bold, larger-than-lifesize statues of "The Revolutionary Soldier," "The Statesman," "The Quaker" and "The Puritan." But it is the words of William Penn to the Indians, cut into the stone, which linger:

> *I have great love*
> *and regard towards*
> *you and desire to win*
> *and gain your love and*
> *friendship by a kind just*
> *and peaceable life and*
> *the people I send are of*
> *the same mind and shall*
> *in all things behave*
> *themselves accordingly.*

Here by the slow-flowing Schuylkill, in the city he founded, with the hum of traffic passing, his words have renewed meaning almost three hundred years later.

The next plaza concerns the second stage in our development as a nation. The symbolic figures are "The Ploughman" and "The Miner" flanking Robert Laurent's massive statue of a pioneer couple, their shoulders to the wheel and an axe in her hand. The words in stone behind them are those of Stephen Vincent Benét and Archibald MacLeish.

Facing them are "The Slave" and "The Immigrant" and Maurice Sterne's heroic statues combining both these elements. Our eyes fasten on the words of William Cullen Bryant and Lincoln as we gaze from the statues to the stone behind them.

Across the drive beneath the rock palisade is the bronze portrait bust of the martyred James A. Garfield by Augustus Saint-Gaudens, erected in 1896. It is strangely dated in concept when seen in juxtaposition to these groups of later sculpture.

Mount Pleasant

The north plaza attracts most attention today because of the "Spirit of Enterprise," the vigorous and gigantic sculpture by Jacques Lipchitz. Other sculptures by Waldemar Raemisch, José de Creeft, Koren der Harootian and Ahron Ben-Shmuel surround the Lipchitz and are intended to express his concept. The whole is exciting when contemplated in this unusual setting—the natural rock formations above the drive itself, the stone used for the sculpture, the river eternally flowing and the ancient trees surrounding it all.

Leaving the Samuel Memorial, walk north along the river for about a quarter of a mile. Here the park becomes wider—meadow-like in its expanse—and offers two landmarks to guide us. Near the river's edge are three pole-like plinths holding Carl Milles' three "*Playing Angels*" aloft. They are piping, cavorting angels, dancing **7** in time to their music. They, like the Samuel Memorial and the Fairmount Water Works, are striking when seen from the West River Drive opposite.

At this point on the East River Drive is the second landmark, a *monument to Ulysses S. Grant.* Cross over and pass the monument, **8** follow the road up the hill, and take the first turning to the left. Here, at the foot of an avenue lined with trees, stands *Mount Pleasant,* **9** the 18th century Georgian home Benedict Arnold purchased for Peggy Shippen. (Daily 10:00–5:00, except Monday and holidays. $1.00.)

The house, now in its third century, was built by Captain John Macpherson in 1761–62. Symmetrical in every detail, balanced, harmonious, elegant, Mount Pleasant dreams of the past in all its majesty. It stands as a monument to an enlightened time.

Macpherson, a privateer who had had "an arm twice shot off" according to John Adams, lived well as did many privateers, noted for their taste in fine houses, excellent wines, superb furnishings and fine clothes. He called the house "Clunie" after the seat of his ancient clan in Scotland.

Arnold bought the house (1779) as a wedding gift for his bride,

Peggy Shippen, but because of the charge of treason against him they never lived in it and eventually fled to England. A later owner was Jonathan Williams, a great-nephew of Benjamin Franklin and first superintendent of West Point. Fairmount Park incorporated it into its holdings in 1868.

The woodwork alone is worth a visit and intense scrutiny for Macpherson employed the finest craftsmen available in Philadelphia at the time. In its Philadelphia fashion the woodwork is equal to that of Samuel McIntire in Salem, Massachusetts. The grey woodwork in the hallway is the same design as in the center hall of the State House and there are the acanthus and the Greek key designs in other rooms. Some of the furnishings are especially noteworthy: the Nanking china in the dining room; a portrait of Macpherson's son, Major John Macpherson, who was the first Philadelphian of note killed in the Revolution (he was aide-de-camp to General Montgomery, whose statue is behind the museum; both were killed at Quebec in 1775); a charming portrait by Benjamin West of Mary Keen holding an orange; a magnificent breakfront by John Folwell, the man who carved the "rising not a setting sun" chair in Independence Hall; a portrait of the second Mrs. Macpherson by Charles Willson Peale; and an embroidered terrestrial globe—a rarity not seen elsewhere in Philadelphia.

Mount Pleasant is roomy and spacious, but it doesn't appear to be a large house. It is large, but hardly overpowering. A garden in the back and the West front look to the river (both fronts are identical except for the fanlights and a wrought iron railing on the East front steps). In the 18th century when the trees weren't so thick, more of the river would have been visible. At the foot of the garden is a pagoda, and there are flanking dependencies that are reminiscent of those seen in Tidewater Virginia.

Return the way we came back to the East River Drive. It is possible to continue to the Falls Bridge, cross over and return by the West River Drive, but that walk will take more time than the walk so far. If time is no object, it is a beautiful, leisurely walk, and the view of the city as it unfolds before us is one of the most unusual in Philadelphia. Or we can retrace our steps and return to the Philadelphia Museum of Art. Just beyond the Grant Monument, high against the rock is Frederic Remington's "Cowboy." It is the only large-scale work he did and, ironically, his last as well. Remington (1861–1909) selected the spot for "Cowboy" himself. By standing near the gilt statue of Joan of Arc, you can catch an A bus on Pennsylvania Avenue and be in Center City within ten or fifteen minutes.

· *Woodford, Strawberry Mansion and Laurel Hill Cemetery*

To reach Woodford and Strawberry Mansion, two other park houses open to the public, take the 32 bus from any point along Broad Street from Spruce Street to City Hall or from Kennedy Boulevard between 15th and 16th Streets. To combine this walk with the one along East River Drive, get the A bus at 25th and Pennsylvania Avenue, across from the Museum of Art and directly behind the Joan of Arc monument.

If *Lemon Hill* was not visited on the walk along the river, it can be seen now; get off the bus at 30th and Poplar Streets, cross over the railroad bridge and ascend the hill in the park by the first path. On the crest of the hill is a playground, and the path to the left leads directly to Lemon Hill, described on page 151.

Leaving Lemon Hill, return to 30th and Poplar and the bus on the northeast corner. Ride to 33rd and York Streets. Directly opposite in the park is *Woodford*. (Daily 10:00–4:00. Closed Monday. Adults, **10** $1.00; children, $.50.) Woodford has been owned by a succession of prominent Philadelphians, notably William Coleman, a member of the Junto, scholar, jurist and a man who stood high in Franklin's regard, and David Franks, one of the signers of the Non-Importation Agreement of 1765 (signers would not buy goods from Great Britain until the Stamp Act was repealed). His daughter Rebecca was one of the belles fêted at the "Meschianza," and her letters are evocative recreations of the time. Rebecca, however, married General Sir Henry Johnson, spending her declining years in Bath, England. She often remarked how she missed Philadelphia and its ways. Her father's property was confiscated because of his Loyalist leanings.

Once the scene of Tory gaiety during the British occupation of Philadelphia, Woodford now stands as a living monument to the past. Its appeal today is greater for it displays to great advantage in its Georgian rooms the remarkable Naomi Wood collection of American

Woodford

antiques. The house was remodeled in 1756 by William Coleman from an earlier, smaller house built about 1735. Franks, George III's Controller of Customs, made further improvements including the addition of the second floor with its elegant Palladian window. These are not stuffy, stilted rooms, museumlike in their formality, for a little imagination can people them with both the 18th and 19th century owners.

11   Just back of Woodford, closer to the river, situated in a small park all its own and approached by a graceful drive, is *Strawberry Mansion*. (Daily 11:00-5:00. Closed Monday. $.50; children, $.25.) The largest of the houses in the park, Strawberry was originally called Somerton; the first house here was erected about 1750. Later, however, because Somerton was owned by Charles Thomson (1729–1824), secretary of the Continental Congress, Sir William Howe ordered or permitted it to be sacked and burned.

In 1798 Wiliam Lewis, President-Judge of the United States District Court of Pennsylvania, built the center section as Summerville and the wings were added in the mid-1820s by a subsequent owner. The present name stems from the time—after 1842—when a Mrs. Grimes lived here and sold strawberries and cream to visitors.

The furnishings of Strawberry Mansion are Federal, Regency and Empire, and one of the most charming pieces is a circular "chatting couch," or *causeuse*. The 1790 Clementi spinet, the Tucker china manufactured in Philadelphia, the 18th century Philadelphia pianoforte and a splendid old kitchen can't fail to captivate the visitor.

Strawberry's entrance hall is unusual in that four doors, with identical fanlights, open from it, two to the outside, two to other rooms. One bedroom is Empire—almost right out of one of Napoleon's palaces—with a rich canopied bed, ornate French over-valance at the window. Another has a "Beau Brummell" with handsome brasses, best described as the ultimate in a man's bureau for traveling, especially on a sea voyage.

The attic is unbelievable, It is the attic dreamed of, but seldom seen, containing everything—a 1775 baby carriage, ice skates circa 1700 and 1800, a metal hip tub, a doll house, toys, kitchen untensils, everything!

Standing outside in view of the majestic white façade of Strawberry, it isn't at all difficult to imagine the carriages coming up in the great days—or even when it had begun to fade and was only visited for its strawberries and cream.

12   Abutting Fairmount Park at this point, and a geographical extension of it, is *Laurel Hill Cemetery*, whose slopes can be seen from the East River Drive, and its tombstones, monuments and mausoleums. Laurel Hill is only for those who enjoy cemetery walks; many don't. However, a walk along its paths will enable us to see a vanishing piece of Americana—the Gothic, cluttered cemetery which is fast

Strawberry Mansion

Laurel Hill Cemetery

disappearing. Take the lefthand concrete walk, pass the colonnade and proceed to the entrance of Robin Hood Dell, where summer concerts under the stars have become a Philadelphia custom. Just behind this outdoor amphitheatre is the beginning of Laurel Hill Cemetery laid out by John Notman. Planned as early as 1835, the site was once the country seat of Joseph Sims, called "Laurel." The first interment took place in 1837 when Mrs. Mercy Carlisle, who had chosen her last resting place only months before was interred. Later two estates, Harleigh and Fairy Hill, were added.

Laurel Hill is truly a *necropolis*, a city of the dead, and is situated in one of the most romantic spots in Philadelphia, overlooking the East River Drive and the Schuylkill, seeming to meet them. There is a brooding air about it, probably caused by the crowded stones—it appears to be nearly filled—and its situation of almost hanging over the river. One of its most spectacular monuments is "Old Mortality and Sir Walter Scott" in red sandstone by James Thom, a Scots sculptor, with a pony added for good measure. The monuments are distinctive at best, each one meant to outdo its neighbor in originality. In the last century Laurel Hill Cemetery was a place to promenade on a Sunday afternoon or a holiday. Strollers found it a favorite place for a ramble. Today strollers are the exception.

When the cemetery was opened, Charles Thomson, the secretary of the Continental Congress, had been resting quietly for fourteen years in the cemetery at Harriton, his wife's old home in what is now Bryn Mawr. The story is told that the promoters of Laurel Hill approached his heirs and asked to remove this distinguished American's body and his wife's to the new cemetery. They, except for one nephew, refused. When grave robbers were surprised at their task, they threw the bodies in a cart and beat a hasty retreat. However, these unfortunate bones were reinterred in Laurel Hill and a splendid monument was erected over them. There is disagreement as to whether the bodies were those of Thomson and his wife, but the bones have remained undisturbed since in a tomb under a handsome obelisk.

Laurel Hill may be only for cemetery walkers, but for them fascination will be complete, while wandering at will up one hill and down another. There is much to see. Here lie the Philadelphians who made the 19th century city what it was and Thomas Godfrey, who invented the mariner's quadrant, Thomas McKean (1734–1817), Signer of the Declaration of Independence, and our old friend David Rittenhouse, who seems to turn up everywhere in Philadelphia.

On leaving Laurel Hill, walk back to Woodford and on to 33rd and Dauphin Streets, where the 32 bus will return you to Center City.

· *The Zoo, Sweetbriar, Cedar Grove and the Japanese House*

On the last walk in Fairmount Park, we shall visit the Letitia Street House, the Zoo, Sweetbriar, Cedar Grove, with a longer walk to Memorial Hall and a still longer one to the Japanese House.

The Cultural Loop bus stops at the Zoo, or take the 38 bus from Kennedy Boulevard, near the Tourist Center on the northwest side of City Hall. The ride takes about ten minutes, and the route follows the scenic Schuylkill Expressway. Get off at Girard Avenue opposite the entrance to the Zoo.

The *entrance pavilions* are still further examples of the work of Frank Furness and George W. Hewitt; erected between 1873 and 1875, they form a Victorian entrance to a thoroughly modern zoo. (Monday through Friday, 9:00–4:30; Saturday, Sunday and holidays, 9:30–5:00. Adults, $3.50; children, $2.50. Special group rates.) **13** The *Philadelphia Zoological Garden* covers 42 acres and now houses more than 1,600 kinds of mammals, birds and reptiles. There is a special hummingbird house where the birds live in a lush tropical setting, a children's zoo and a monorail for aerial tours.

Situated in the Zoo grounds is *The Solitude*, home of John Penn **14** (1760–1834), grandson of the Founder. He is not to be confused with John Penn (1729–95), another grandson who was a son of Richard Penn. In 1785 the bachelor son of Thomas Penn, and grandson, too, of the Earl of Pomfret, built this small house and named it for a lodge belonging to the Duke of Württemberg. Called "the poet," Penn left America in 1788, and after his death his brother Granville and nephew, Granville John Penn, were the owners until Fairmount Park acquired it in 1867. It was the last holding in this country of the family that once "owned" the state, and even parts of Delaware. It is now used as offices for the Zoo.

Leaving the Zoo, cross Girard Avenue again and walk toward the river. A small set of concrete steps near the railroad bridge leads to the *Letitia Street House*, certainly one of the oldest houses in Phila- **15** delphia. At one time it stood on Letitia Street, a small street between

Letitia Street House

Front and Second Streets in the city, but it was moved to Fairmount Park in 1883, which helped save it from destruction. It was popularly believed that Penn had built it in 1682 and that he lived there during his first visit to the Colony. Inquiry and investigation of old ground lots and deeds indicate it wasn't built that early, but rather sometime between 1703 and 1715—which still qualifies it as one of the earliest houses remaining within the city limits. The house will be reopened for the Bicentennial celebration, repainted and refurnished, and the garden replanted.

There are two ways to get to Sweetbriar and Cedar Grove from here, the two historic houses in this part of the park that are open to the public. The longer way is the more scenic.

Return to 34th Street, which is the road near the river, cross over it and go under the railroad bridge and begin to walk along the wide green verge away from the Zoo, with the Schuylkill River always on the right. A short distance from this is the Sweetbriar Cut-off, and on the right can be seen the West River Drive and the river beyond. Cross the cut-off and continue under two more bridges (rather close together), which frame a deep ravine to the right. Beyond the second bridge as the hill begins to rise, a statue of an Indian woman defending her children against attack can be seen. Called "Stone Age in America," it was commissioned by the Fairmount Park Art Association in 1887. John J. Boyle (1851–1917) was the sculptor. It has poignancy standing alone on the hill. Before it is Sweetbriar itself.

An easier and less scenic way to reach Sweetbriar is to walk along Girard Avenue from the Zoo, staying on the Zoo side of the street. Because of the heavy traffic it is best to walk to 38th Street and cross to the Zoo parking lot opposite. Walk through the center of the parking lot. A path down the hill and up the one opposite leads **16** to *Sweetbriar*. (Daily 10:00–5:00. Closed Tuesdays and holidays. Adults, $1.00; children, $.50.) It is maintained by the Modern Club.

Samuel Breck, who built Sweetbriar in 1797 on the west bank of the Schuylkill, was thus living two miles from the western end of the city. Today the Schuylkill Expressway is just below the east windows and the towers of the city can be seen in the distance. Breck (1771–1862) was Boston-born, educated there and in France. In 1792 his father, unhappy about Boston taxation, removed his family to Philadelphia. After Samuel's marriage to Jean Ross on Christmas Eve, 1795, he began to build Sweetbriar. The grounds and planting were beautiful and lawns stretched to the river. Breck even owned an island in the Schuylkill which he could see from his window.

A wealthy merchant, Breck was very public spirited and his benefactions included gifts to the Library Company and the Athenaeum. He was a member of the Pennsylvania legislature and sat in the State House from 1817 to 1821. He introduced a bill for the emancipation of slaves in Pennsylvania and was elected in 1823 to the 18th Congress,

Sweetbriar

Cedar Grove

but was not re-elected the following term. In 1824 he sat in the State Senate again.

In 1838 Breck sold Sweetbriar and moved into town, where he lived until his death. In 1867 the house and grounds were incorporated into the park.

The elegant Federal-style house fortunately escaped any Victorian improvements and retains the sheer elegance of the late 18th century when it was one of the showplaces of the nation's capital. The south drawing room, whose windows look across the river toward the waterworks beneath the Philadelphia Museum of Art, is a superb example of the French influence at its best. Breck was a friend of the Vicomte de Noailles, Lafayette, Louis Philippe and his brothers, and the Prince de Talleyrand. The carved frieze on the mantels is a fine example of early Adam style decoration. The room is airy and light. Long windows to the floor contribute to this feeling as do the delicate chairs and sofa, the long, graceful draperies and valances, the French clock and candelabra, and the opulent chandelier (bought from a palace owned by the Aga Khan).

The opposite parlor, which might have been used as a dining room, although not so successfully furnished as the south one does have a companion chandelier to the one in the opposing room and a girandole above the fireplace, a Sully portrait and a collection of Birch prints that show Philadelphia in its Golden Age, the classical period of about 1800.

In the center hall are interesting murals of Boston, Charleston and Philadelphia done for the Sesquicentennial in 1926, and there is an unusual musicians gallery over the staircase. Breck's office-study is small but contains a fine Philadelphia desk of tulip and poplar with mahogany inlay and the beehive design on the brasses. A sketch of Talleyrand by Breck, dated 1834, shows the former Bishop of Autun as Breck saw him in old age. That wily schemer wasn't far from death at that point and the ravages of age and dissipation show in Breck's likeness.

There is a sidewalk of sorts leading from Sweetbriar for part of the way to Cedar Grove, which is only an easy ten-minute walk from here. Follow the sidewalk until it ends and then continue along the road. To the left are the tall plinths of the Smith Civil War Memorial and ahead is the John B. Kelly Pool. To the right is a glenlike ravine, larger than the one below Sweetbriar. This sylvan glade, for it is exactly that, is typical of those found in the park. Where the road turns right, there are stone steps descending on the right into the ravine. Just around from that at the crest of a small incline stands

17 Cedar Grove. (Daily 10:00-5:00, except Monday and legal holidays.)

Sweetbriar is the ultimate in sophistication, symmetry and classical feeling. Cedar Grove, on the other hand, began as a country house and it retains the style, charm, warmth and comfort of country living. A white fence, with roses climbing over it, encloses the garden and old trees embower the house. Cedar Grove sits peacefully and quietly in the park, but once it was the center of the life of a large, bustling family.

Since 1927 the house has been part of the park, but in 1748 Elizabeth Coates Paschall built the oldest part of it in the Northern Liberties. The early house consists of the present dining room, the room behind it which was the old kitchen, the bedroom above and the small attic room. Gradually through the years the house grew. In 1752 Elizabeth enlarged it, and it was extended again in 1795, when her granddaughter Sarah Paschall Morris inherited it. The front of the house is of regular stone, the sides of irregular stone, the back of brick. There is a wide sloping roof on the front and one side which covers what could be called a flagstone porch. This gives it even more of a farmhouse look. It also makes the house seem more welcoming.

At first the house had been a country retreat—Elizabeth used to drive out for the day from town to her farm—but by 1795 the Morris family used it the year round. The farm was situated at Harrowgate in the Northern Liberties, which then became part of Frankford and, of course, was no longer country. In 1927 the house was dismantled stone by stone and re-erected at its present location. Miss Lydia Thompson Morris, the last of her direct line and another farseeing Philadelphian, gave the entire contents of the house, so we see it as generations of Paschalls and Morrises lived in it and accumulated the possessions which they had cared for so devotedly.

Philadelphia from Belmont

The earliest furniture is William and Mary; there is also Queen Anne, Chippendale, Sheraton and Hepplewhite, and an unusual Philadelphia cherry chest-on-chest-on-chest (1714).

The great kitchen is perhaps the house's most interesting room, as often happens in these old houses. In addition to the giant fireplace, replete with all the utensils—grill, stewpot, toaster and even the ancient counterpart of a rotisserie, there is a built-in oven and next to it a built-in unit for heating water. The large brass cauldron gives us an idea of how much water was heated at one time. And there are pegs on the walls for hanging chairs when the floors were scrubbed or the kitchen crowded.

Upstairs a green, bottled light filters into the bedroom windows through the trees which screen the house. On one of these small panes of old glass, scratched by a diamond, is the legend "charming and accomplished Sally Apthorp from Boston Born 1760." The date has been scratched through and what looks like "1780" written over it. Could Sally have returned years later to "correct" her birthdate, always a woman's prerogative! And who was George Ross who scratched his name next to hers?

Cedar Grove typifies the home a Quaker family of the 18th century lived in, and the porch roof is similar to those on Quaker meeting houses. The Schuylkill Expressway is just below, but this country house in a quiet corner of the park takes us back two hundred-odd years with no difficulty at all.

Leaving Cedar Grove, we return the way we came until we reach the stone steps again, which are now on the left. Take the road leading to the Smith Memorial at the entrance to the North

18 Concourse, a broad avenue which is now dominated by *Memorial Hall*. The hall was one of the chief buildings of the Centennial Exposition of 1876 and was dedicated by President Grant. Until the 1950s Horticultural Hall stood next to it. Memorial Hall was the city's art gallery before the Philadelphia Museum of Art was opened. It is closed to the public today, but is used for dances and receptions from time to time. The basement holds a complete scale model of the entire Centennial Exposition.

19 The *Smith Civil War Memorial* was erected between 1897 and 1912 under a bequest of Richard Smith and designed by James H. and John T. Windrim. Among the military and naval men immortalized here are Generals Hancock, McClellan, Meade, Reynolds, Hartranft, Crawford and Beaver and Admirals Porter and Dahlgren. Surprisingly enough a statue of Richard Smith himself, in his typefounder's apron, is placed high on the memorial among the military and naval great!

Descend to Lansdowne Drive at the foot of the memorial, turn left and walk along it, keeping to the back of Memorial Hall, which should be on the left. A fifteen-minute walk brings us to the

20 *Japanese House* (Wednesday through Sunday, 10:00–5:00, from late April to mid-October. Adults, $1.00; children under 12, $.50.)

Japanese House

This charming house, serenely situated, was first on display in the garden of the Museum of Modern Art in New York. Later it was transferred to the park and given its proper setting. It is enhanced by a garden, pool and waterfall. The house is authentically patterned after a 17th century Japanese dwelling. It is a quiet spot in the park, ideal for reflection.

The easiest way to return is to ramble back along the way we came. Walk along Lansdowne Drive to the Smith Memorial, continue over to Girard Avenue, and at 38th Street, opposite the Zoo parking lot, the number 38 bus to Center City stops.

Upper Germantown from Cliveden to Vernon Park

The name of Germantown is the clue to the town's history. Here, some three centuries ago, a small band of thirteen families—thirty-three persons in all—having fled from the Old World established German Town. They came because of economic and religious unrest that was fermenting everywhere in Europe—from the Rhineland towns of Krefeld and Krisheim, the latter a part of the Principality of Orange-Nassau while Krefeld was subject to the Elector Palatine. The first settlers were Netherlanders and German-speaking Swiss, but they were followed within a quarter of a century by Germans from what we know as Germany today. Some of them were members of the Society of Friends and some were Mennonites.

The first stop was London. There on July 24, 1683, they boarded the small sailing ship *Concord*. They reached Philadelphia on October 6, and were met by Francis Daniel Pastorius (1651–1719), the agent for the Frankfort Company. Later that month, in Pastorius' cave on Front Street near the banks of the Delaware, which was noted in Walk 4, a surveyor having laid out the land, thirteen men met with Pastorius and drew lots for their tracts to the north. Germantown was founded in this relatively simple manner a year after the establishment of Philadelphia as a city.

In 1690 there were 44 families here and the population was 175. Harry M. and Margaret B. Tinkcom in *Historic Germantown* say: "This question of the 'national' origins of the initial settlers in Germantown is greatly complicated by the ethnic diversity common to the Holy Roman Empire, the inclusiveness of the word 'German' and the frequent wanderings of such persecuted religious groups as the Mennonites and the Quakers." After 1709 a great influx of Germans gave the town the German character it retained for many years, and the Dutch aspect of it was all but obliterated. In 1689 a charter had been obtained from William Penn, and Germantown became the first borough chartered in Pennsylvania. This borough charter was nullified in 1707, and Germantown assumed township status, which it retained until 1854 when it was absorbed into the city of Philadelphia.

Here in Thones Kunders' house on Main Street was signed the first protest against slavery in America. Four Germantown men, Garret Hendricks, Francis Daniel Pastorius, Derick up de Graeff and Abraham up Den Graef, affixed their signatures to this historic document on April 18, 1688.

During the 18th century, when many of the houses we shall examine were built, Germantown was country—real country. Germantown Avenue (or Main Street), now a busy, bustling thoroughfare in the city, was a dirt road. It wasn't paved until 1801, when the turnpike company was formed. Indians were still seen frequently—although they had begun to move slowly westward to central and western Pennsylvania—and small game was very much in evidence.

There were modest houses and farms, orchards and gardens, and a greater German migration, which began in earnest about 1730 and continued until the Revolution, reached its height from 1749 to 1754. Hence the town grew from approximately 100 houses in 1745 to 350 in 1758. The Germans themselves made up about one-third of the Colonial population of Pennsylvania as a whole, and until 1763 Germantown was predominantly German in culture, population and language. There were Dunkers, Schwenkfelders and Lutherans as well as Friends and Mennonites. Gradually assimilation took place and little by little the European character of the community lessened.

Germantown was a community of business and crafts and has had an industrial character from the beginning. It was here that the first paper mill in America was built by William Rittenhouse in 1690; textile manufacture and tanneries abounded. The first printers' type —in German—was cast successfully here, and German-language publishing flourished until the time of the Revolution.

Into this center of activity the outlanders and non-Germans began to infiltrate before the Revolution, but the terror of the yellow fever in the final decade of the 18th century brought many English-speaking citizens here as well. Moreover, as affluence came to Philadelphia, the prosperous came seeking cooler homes on higher ground to escape the humid summers that have always been the bane of Philadelphia.

The 17th, 18th, 19th and 20th centuries meet in Germantown. True, there are few physical traces of the 17th; in the seventeen years of that century the German Towners could not build for permanence. But Wyck remains and the oldest part of that beautiful house dates from 1690. We shall see fine examples of 18th and 19th century domestic architecture and, unfortunately, some 20th century ugliness in littered streets and graffiti-marred buildings. However, if we can overlook the encroachments of our own age here and there, we shall find a wealth of American history and beauty in Germantown. It was built to endure and it has for almost three hundred years.

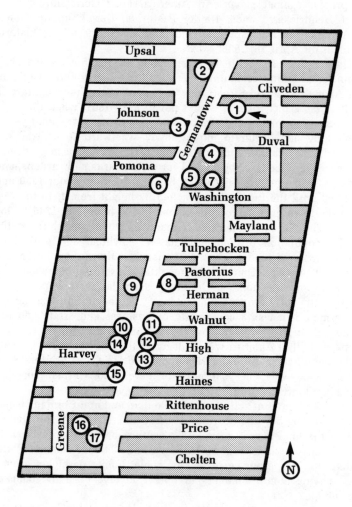

Germantown quite naturally divides into two walks, Upper and Lower Germantown. To reach Germantown from Center City for the first walk, the most direct way is the number 23 trolley going north on 11th Street. Get off at Cliveden Street. The alternative is to take the Penn-Central Railroad train from either Suburban Station at 16th and Kennedy Boulevard or from 30th Street Station at 30th and Market Streets. Taking the Chestnut Hill local, get off at Upsal Station, walk along Upsal Street to Germantown Avenue and then turn right. One block south of this turning is Cliveden Street, the starting point of our walk through Upper Germantown.

The first stop is *Cliveden,* at 6401 Germantown Avenue, a **1** monument to our history and to its preservation also. It is now owned by the National Trust for Historic Preservation. (Open daily 10:00–4:00. Adults, $2.00; senior citizens, $1.50; children, $1.00.)

The small marker, or milestone, at the corner of Cliveden Street and Germantown Avenue reads *"6 to P."* With today's transportation six miles to Philadelphia doesn't seem like a long way, but, when Cliveden was built over two hundred years ago, Germantown Avenue was a dirt road following an older Indian trail through fields, forest and stream.

Today the walk through the gates up the long, graceful, curving drive is a pleasure to be savored slowly. The lawns spread out on each side, with artfully placed clumps of trees and bushes at just the right spots, so that it is difficult to believe that we are only a few steps from one of Philadelphia's busiest streets.

Benjamin Chew, who built Cliveden between 1763 and 1767, had bought eleven acres and increased them to sixty for his country seat. Now Cliveden occupies only six acres, which is still a goodly piece of ground.

Before entering, observe the balance and symmetry of the mid-Georgian façade. The guides, who are extremely well informed on all aspects of Cliveden's history as well as that of Germantown and Philadelphia, will tell us about it later, but the tone is set by contemplating it quietly before crossing the threshold. The Palladian elegance of the 18th century with the five evenly spaced bays and the five urns on the roof undoubtedly contribute to making this one of the outstanding houses in America.

The farsighted builder of Cliveden, Benjamin Chew (1722–1810), was born in Maryland to Quaker parents. His father, Samuel, a physician, was later Chief Justice of what is now Delaware, but was then called the "Lower Counties" by the Proprietors—the members of William Penn's family. Benjamin read law with Andrew Hamilton, a distinguished Philadelphia lawyer whose name appears again and again in the records of the period. Chew later studied in the Middle Temple in London and, on returning to Philadelphia, was admitted to the bar of the Supreme Court of Pennsylvania. Because of his friendship with the Penn family and his position on the Governor's

Cliveden

Council, he was often in opposition to Benjamin Franklin. Chew was one of the commissioners who supervised the survey of the Mason-Dixon Line and was later appointed Register General, Attorney General and, finally, in 1774, Chief Justice of Pennsylvania.

Although all of Cliveden is beautiful to behold, nothing quite matches the elegance of the entrance hall with its pedimented door frames and the screen of four columns with its fully developed entablature that marks the entrance hall off from the stair hall. This hall and the façade are two of the most photographed aspects of all the 18th century houses in Philadelphia.

There are musket burns in the floor of the entrance hall, where muskets were stacked around the columns, and it must be remembered that the British occupied the house as a fortress, as a garrison, while Benjamin Chew and Governor John Penn were held in New Jersey by the Colonials during the British occupation of Philadelphia. Cliveden also heard the sound of musket fire on that foggy morning of October 4, 1777, when the British and Continental troops deployed in the Battle of Germantown. (There is an interesting diorama of the battle in the Atwater Kent Museum, which was visited on Walk 1.) The boards in these halls are white pine and have withstood the onslaught of soldier's boots, British and American spurs and the spiked heels of the 20th century.

In the parlor, which must be seen and not read about, are looking glasses that were used at the *"Meschianza,"* the fabled ball that Loyalist Philadelphians gave in honor of General Sir William Howe during the British occupation. Major John André, who was shot for abetting Benedict Arnold, planned much of it, and the other great houses such as Cliveden lent spectacular treasures to enhance the occasion. Today these glasses reflect the 20th century visitor to Cliveden as they did the dancers of two hundred years ago in Walnut Grove, the site of the *Meschianza.* There are unusual Waterford oil lamps in this room, too, and the sofa is by Thomas Affleck, one of America's great furniture makers of the 18th century. Some of the furniture displayed now was bought at an auction of the household effects of the Penn family, and we are intrigued with the window panes, which have been signed with a diamond by generations of Chews.

The dining room, with its original china, a school room (added on by 1867) and a paperpress from Benjamin Chew's office in town— a rarity today—an exceptional tall case clock, and upstairs a collection of clothes, fans and spectacles are some of the fascinating objects Cliveden holds. There is an original grid map of Philadelphia as Thomas Holme first laid it out for William Penn, which was found among the thousands of Chew papers which are still being catalogued and sorted. One of the joys of visiting Cliveden more than once is that new "finds" are being added each year, and no matter how often one comes here, new discoveries can be made. The family adds things from time to time, by gift, and Chew belongings which come on the market are purchased for the house.

Wander about in back to inspect the dependencies, the barn (a restoration with a new roof) and the statuary, which was a wedding gift to Benjamin and his second wife. Unfortunately, all the handsome carriages used by Washington, Chew and other worthies have not survived into the present.

As we make our way back to Germantown Avenue, note two rather important facets of Cliveden. One is that the stone for the house itself was quarried right on the property and that it was constructed by local labor under the supervision of John Hesser, a local mason, and Jacob Knorr, a Germantown carpenter. The front wall is made of "dressed stone," the gables and the backs of pointed field-stone. Also, Benjamin Chew was forced to sell his home when he returned from New Jersey to find it "an absolute wreck, and materials not to be had to keep out the weather." He repurchased it in 1797, and the house remained in the hands of the Chews until 1972, when the family presented it to the National Trust for Historic Preservation.

Leaving Cliveden is like leaving an old friend, for an hour within its walls enchants anyone. Now return down the sweeping driveway to Germantown Avenue.

2   Facing us on the opposite side of the street is *Upsala*, 6430 Germantown Avenue, certainly one of the finest examples of Federal architecture in Germantown. (Tuesday and Thursday, 1:00–4:00. Adults, $1.00; children under twelve, $.50.) The dates are not absolute, but old records indicate that Dirck Jansen, one of the early settlers, owned the land before 1755 and the back part of the house—

Upsala

the oldest section—is thought to date from 1740. John Johnson, Sr. (1708–94) is also said to have bought the land in 1766, so there is some speculation as to whether father or son owned it first. John 3rd inherited the property in 1797 and built the front section of the house between that year and 1801. Although the grounds are not so spacious as those at Cliveden, there is a considerable garden. One reason for the lack of encroachment is that the Johnson family owned the property almost continuously until 1941, and the Upsala Foundation purchased it in 1944. This group of citizens saved the house from destruction and undertook the restoration work.

The name itself comes from the Swedish university city, Uppsala. Tradition has it that one Mrs. Johnson was an admirer of Frederika Bremer, the 19th century Swedish writer, and named the house Upsala in her honor. Miss Bremer visited Upsala during her tour of the United States in 1849.

The house has been partially restored inside. The staircase to the third floor is spectacularly graceful—seemingly unsupported— and sweeping upward with airy grace. The wooden mantels—similar but not exactly alike—are splendid. They are delicately carved— showing a master hand like that of Samuel McIntire in Salem, Massachusetts— and the facings are of Pennsylvania marble.

Each of the three floors and cellar has four rooms off a central hall or passageway. A few pieces of the furniture were originally in Upsala, but more—of the period—has been added by interested individuals or trustees. There is Sheraton, Hepplewhite, Philadelphia and English furniture, but, most of all, there is a sense of the past.

As we leave, note that cannon stood on these grounds and bombarded Cliveden in the Battle of Germantown. Twenty-four Colonials lost their lives during the engagement.

We now continue along Germantown Avenue on the Upsala side, passing the *Sproegell House* at 6358. The black picket fence and the **3** shutters with hearts cut out of them, and the garden in front and to the rear give it a charming, lived-in appearance. It is a private residence and not open to the public. We do know that the house was built early in the 18th century and sometime around 1710 it was owned by John Henry Sproegell and later by Anthony Gilbert and William Keyser. It is typical of the houses that were here soon after the beginning of the 18th century, and, of course, it predates both Cliveden and Upsala.

We continue down the Avenue and cross to the Cliveden side when we reach Pomona Street. Here is the *Upper Burying Ground,* **4** where fifty-two known and five unknown soldiers of the Revolution are buried. Also sleeping here are eleven soldiers who served in the War of 1812 and one from the Mexican War.

The high front wall of the burying ground—completed in 1724— intrigues us and through the gate can be seen some of the tombstones, the earliest of which is that of Cornelius Teisen (Tyson), who arrived in Germantown in 1684 and died in 1716 at the age of sixty-three. We shall see variations in the spellings of the Germantown names on monuments and on tombstones. This is a common occurrence in Pennsylvania where German names went through many spellings from the beginning to the present. The cemetery is only open on special occasions.

The history of the Upper Burying Ground is a history of old Germantown itself. Both the Upper and Lower Burial Ground (which is included in Walk 12) were created in 1692, nine years after the founding of the town, by a deed from Paul Wulff. Each had its own trustees and kept its own records. Although the oldest stone dates from 1716, the trustees did not officially open their record book until 1761, when the records were gathered together under one cover from a series of fugitive papers which recorded earlier transactions. In 1760 the rest of the burying ground was enclosed by extending the wall around the sides and the back. This record book chronicled the burials from 1756, although there had been many before that time. Only those early ones, before 1756, with tombstones are now recorded. We do know that more than 1300 burials in all took place.

Here lie many of the men and women who founded Germantown and helped make it the important place it was in the early days of the Colony. William Dewees, sheriff of Germantown's independent government of 1705–6, and Zachariah Poulson, who died in 1844 after having published *The American Daily Advertiser*, Philadelphia's principal daily newspaper, for many years, are both interred here. There are Indians buried here and also Germantown's "Methuselah," Adam Shisler, who died in 1777 and whose tombstone was inscribed incorrectly to read "*age 969 years*"!

Just adjacent to the burying ground—we can see the belfry from

5 where we stand peering at the stones—is the *Concord School*, built on the eve of the Revolution in 1775. (There are no regular visiting hours, but if you ring the bell the custodian will show you through.) Many of us have heard of the one-room schoolhouse: a school with no running water but a pump outside, no toilet facilities but the "necessary" in the yard behind, no electricity, only candles, and no heat except the fireplace, which was later supplanted by a pot-bellied stove. We read about such places, but here is one in actuality, the Concord School as it was well into the 19th century. Many Philadelphians who have visited the great houses of Germantown still do not know of this unique school.

Tradition has it that because of their concern for the education of their children the residents of Upper Germantown arranged in the 1760's to have a corner of the burying ground set aside for a schoolhouse. The building, two-and-a-half stories high, completed in 1775, was constructed by local craftsmen. In October of that year the first classes were held under the schoolmaster John Grimes. The tuition charges may amuse us today. We know it was $1.50 in 1797 for the three-months quarter, and by 1815 it was $2.00 for the same period. Occasionally a night class was held for which each scholar brought his own candle. It is also interesting to realize that education at that time was considered a great privilege and one not to be abused, so, by order of the trustees, the unruly were not permitted to attend.

The schoolroom is a treasure-trove of fascinating articles for young and old alike. Here are the hard wooden benches where the calico-clad girls and the boys in linsey-woolsey sat huddled over their slates. There are a small saluting cannon to be fired on July 4th and other national occasions, the equally small fireplace (how much warmth could reach those sitting on the other side of the room?), the dunce cap for the ten o'clock scholar and a patchwork quilt on the teacher's chair to be used as a shawl on cold days. The idols of yesteryear's schoolchild, Washington and Franklin, are represented by handsome lithographs. The worn schoolbooks, frayed maps and other teaching aids are scattered about the room. This is no lifeless museum. All we need here is a grain of imagination to make the past leap to life.

Just opposite the school on the corner of Washington Lane, at 6306 Germantown Avenue, is the *Johnson House,* now the home of **6** the Women's Club of Germantown. Although the house is not open to the public, it is interesting to contemplate its history. It was built between 1765 and 1768 by the same Dirck Jansen who owned the ground on which Upsala was built. He built it for his son John Johnson, Sr. (by now the Dutch as well as the Germans were beginning to Anglicize their names), who lived there after his marriage to Rachel Livesey. The Johnsons were tanners, and the site of their largish tannery is worth going around on Washington Lane to view from the rear. Like so many in Germantown, the Johnson House was involved in the Battle (what house or citizen could avoid it?) and bullet and cannonball left their mark there, especially on three doors and the northwest wall. The house is said to have been a station on the Underground Railroad in later years.

As on all these walks, we must pause occasionally and look over our shoulder. Do so in front of the Johnson House and see the belfry of the Concord School with its weathervane—the quill pen of the scholar. It is the most unusual weathervane to be seen in Germantown.

Before we leave Washington Lane behind us, there is an historical note of a later era to recall. At *529 East Washington Lane,* now **7** occupied by the Cliveden Presbyterian Church, lived Charles Brewster Ross, his parents and his brother Walter. Charley was four and Walter six when, on July 1, 1874, they were abducted from their home by two men in a buggy. Walter was let out in another section of the city, on a street in Kensington, but Charley Ross never returned. He was the first child in the history of the United States to be kidnapped and held for ransom. For sixty years—until the Lindbergh kidnapping—children were warned not to talk to strangers, "for you know what happened to Charley Ross!"

We now walk down the Avenue and pass some rather unsightly stores and shops. However, in between these are an antique shop, a secondhand furniture store with an amazing collection of odds and ends in the window and, during the spring and summer, roses everywhere. Old roses that have survived in Germantown, like the tree that grew in Brooklyn, asserted themselves and showed their toughness through the years. No matter that there have been changes on the Avenue, the roses remain. And here and there, if we will look up above the store fronts, we can see what was once a handsome 18th century dwelling, the roofs and dormers of the past which is never far from the present in Germantown.

8 Just below Pastorius Street at 6119 we come to the tiny and historic *Germantown Mennonite Church*, built in 1770. Like so many buildings here, it was built while Pennsylvania was still a Proprietary colony. The Mennonites who have had such an impact on Pennsylvania trace their sources to the Swiss Brethren, who emerged in Zurich as the third wing of the Reformation. They arrived in Germantown in 1683 and established their first permanent settlement in America. Later they were to move westward to Lancaster, York, Harrisburg and beyond. But this was their first home and here, in 1708, they founded their first church in the New World. The minister at that time, William Rittenhouse, built a "little log church," which was what most of the early churches were, as was Old Swedes' on Walk 4. In 1702 Rittenhouse had donated part of the lot and later the present church lot and burial ground. Rittenhouse, who died in 1708 at the age of sixty-four, built the first paper mill in America. The house where his great-grandson David, the famous astronomer and clockmaker for whom Rittenhouse Square is named, was born is in Fairmount Park between Paper Mill Run and the Lincoln Drive at Morris Street. The original paper mill was on this property.

Today the congregation of the Germantown Mennonite Church has dwindled, but the church has endured here for almost three hundred years now and the building itself for over two hundred. There is no regular schedule of hours when the church is open except for Sunday services. In the tiny burying ground can be found the stones of some of Germantown's and Philadelphia's oldest families— Nice, Rittenhouse, Kulp. There is a minuscule slate stone (slate lasts longer than limestone) pathetically recording Susannah Cunyad's death in 1751, "Ag. 2 year & ten mo." And another to Daniel A. Nixon, who died June 17, 1868, at the age of eighty-three, and his wife, Susana [sic] Rittenhouse. We know that President Nixon's forebears came from Pennsylvania and these may be two of them.

9 Before crossing the street, observe a marvelous *Victorian stone house*, an extravagant example of the period. It is now the home of

Wyck

the Settlement Music School, Germantown branch, and at one time many years ago served briefly as an annex to Girls High School. The iron balustrade around the roof, its webbed tracery against the sky, provides an example of the decoration used on 19th century Germantown dwellings of the well-to-do.

Crossing the street from the Mennonite Church—the buildings we are most interested in lie on both sides of the Avenue—we walk south until we come to Wyck, 6026 Germantown Avenue, one of the most delightful of the Germantown houses. (By appointment. Call VI 8-1690. Adults, $1.00; children, $.50.) **10**

Wyck is known as the oldest house in Germantown, the western end built about 1690 by Hans Milan, who emigrated from Krefeld. He later built another house alongside for his daughter Margaret and her husband, Dirck Jansen—a settler from Dalem, Holland, who came to Germantown in 1684.

A brass plate informs us that Wyck was used as a British field hospital after the Battle of Germantown. We also learn that Lafayette was entertained here on July 20, 1825, in the course of his second visit to America. Throughout Philadelphia we find houses where Lafayette visited and was fêted. He was probably under as many roofs as George Washington because he was an inveterate traveler and guest in America.

After the second house was built, the two houses were joined, leaving between the two a large paved wagon way, roofed overhead.

Later the sides of this wagon way were enclosed and today this is a large, spacious hall or conservatory, looking into a garden on either side. The gable end of the house is to the street, so that instead of facing the street as most other houses do, Wyck faces the garden on each side of the house. In the conservatory there are double glass doors from floor to ceiling that can be opened on either side and double wooden doors that, in cold weather, can be folded over the glass ones.

Wyck has a feature that is unique among all the old houses we visit in Philadelphia. The entrance hall and stairway to the second floor bisect the conservatory and the parlor. The doors to both the parlor and the conservatory fold back, covering the stairway and also hiding the entry way to the front door, so that the two rooms virtually become one—an ideal arrangement for large receptions. The house, incidentally, was remodeled in 1824 by William Strickland (the last time any major changes were made), whose buildings were seen on Walk 1.

This large, spacious, unusual house remained in one family for nine generations, although it passed down in the female line at times and the names of the owners have changed from Jansen to Wistar to Haines. Because the owners were Quakers there is no ostentation in the furnishings, but they are fine and rich in their simplicity.

A charming story of that visit of Lafayette has been passed on in the Haines family for years. Reuben Haines—whose portrait by Rembrandt Peale hangs in the house today—was then the owner (his grandmother was Margaret Wistar, the daughter of Caspar Wistar, the New Jersey glassmaker). To give his three-year-old daughter Hannah her moment of greatness, he held her up for the great man to fondle or kiss. Young Hannah would have none of that and she slapped the elderly marquis!

Wyck

The *gardens* are old fashioned, but were planted by plant "explorers" who knew their botany. There are azaleas, holly, wistaria, crepe myrtle, boxwood, an original magnolia, and spectacular old roses here that were planted before the Revolution. There is a Spanish chestnut grown from a seedling of a tree that Washington planted for Judge Peters at Belmont in Fairmount Park.

One should wander in the gardens, see the old pump, the leafy arbors, the barn, smoke house, spring house and carriage house (once a granary)—all here on two-and-a-half acres on Germantown Avenue. And we should examine the hole for the latchstring on the door leading from the kitchen to the dining room (which had once been the kitchen). Here the latchstring hung out for the Indians. There was always milk on the table for them and they would enter silently, drink the milk and sit quietly, warming themselves by the fire. The Jansen, Wistar and Haines families followed the precepts of William Penn in a practical way. It is with this memory that we open the garden gate and enter the hurly-burly of Germantown Avenue once more.

Opposite Wyck at 6043, on the southeast corner of Walnut Lane, is *The Laurens*. This house, with its front unfortunately altered some- **11** what in our time, was bought by Dr. William Shippen as a summer home. (We saw his city home, the Shippen-Wistar House, on Walk 3.) It is said to be the first three-story house built in Germantown, and it was center of a skirmish during the Battle. Lord Cornwallis was said to have told Mrs. Shippen he had saved a sofa for her by sleeping on it—at a time when so much pillaging was occurring. In 1851 it was owned by Charlotte Cushman, the great American actress. The doorway—particularly beautiful and distinctive—was formerly in a house at the corner of Germantown Avenue and School House Lane. The front has been refaced and the four first-floor windows, two on each side of the door, have been made into two rather large ones. The rough stone on the side, however, gives us an idea of what the house looked like at the height of its glory. It is a private home and not open to the public.

Just below The Laurens at 6023 is the *Green Tree Tavern*. One **12** of the most historic and interesting houses in the town, it was built in 1748 as a tavern by Daniel Pastorius, grandson of the founder of Germantown. High in the side wall near the roof is a stone lettered "*DPS 1748.*" The initials identify Daniel and his wife, Sarah, as the owners and builders. Known variously as "The Green Tree," the "Saddler's Arms," "The Hornet's Nest," it was called "Mackinett's Tavern," when citizens gathered there on December 6, 1759. They met with a purpose, and the founding of the Union School of Germantown resulted. From this school the present-day Germantown Academy, one of the oldest schools of its kind in the nation, grew. The building is now owned by the First United Methodist Church and is not generally open to the public, but is used for church offices. The church moved it 100 feet up Germantown Avenue in 1930, so that the Memorial Chapel could be added to the church.

This meeting in the tavern reminds us that in the 18th century— and earlier—the tavern played a different role in the life of the community. The tavern was the common man's club (although the wealthy patronized them, too), it was the center of news and community activity as well as a lodging house. Horses were changed or watered and fed there, the stage deposited its passengers, letters and messages were entrusted to the owner's care, and the recruiting officer signed up the local lads for the regiment. Often trials and hearings were conducted within and, occasionally, a hanging without. Each hamlet had a tavern, even if it had no town hall or meeting house. Thomas Jefferson, then our first Secretary of State, wrote from Germantown in 1793: "According to present appearances, this place cannot lodge a single person more. As a great favor I got a bed in the corner of the public room of a tavern." Later he wrote to James Madison that he had found lodging for him and for James Monroe in a private home. "They will breakfast you," he wrote, "but you must mess in a tavern; there is a good one across the street."

On the corner of High Street we should stop and read the marker **13** on the site of *one of the first botanical gardens* in America. It was planted by Dr. Christopher Witt (1675–1765), a botanist, mystic and physician, who lived until he was almost ninety. His portrait (painted about 1705) of Johannes Kelpius, leader of the religious group known as the Hermits of the Wissahickon, is "one of the earliest, if not the earliest oil portrait extant which originated in Pennsylvania." Later, two remarkable sisters, who were scientifically active when it wasn't fashionable for women to be so, lived on the spot. The house has long since gone. Elizabeth Carrington Morris was a botanist. Her sister Margaretta Hare Morris investigated and discovered the life habits of the seventeen-year locust and was also an active woman member of the Academy of Natural Sciences of Philadelphia. Only a plaque marks the spot, now part of the grounds of Germantown High School.

While standing here and meditating on these women who were so far ahead of their time, we can see a house opposite that they saw when they lived and botanized here. On the corner of Harvey Street **14** is *6000 Germantown Avenue*, the lower floor now occupied by stores. It is typical of the houses that lined both sides of the Avenue before the 20th century changed the character of Germantown Avenue and its architecture. Even the uninitiated can spot the house as an old one. It was once owned by Joseph Johnson—the Johnsons owned a great many properties as we have seen—and remained in that family until 1822.

Although the house is no longer there, Henry van Dyke, author of *The Other Wise Man* (1896), a diplomat as well as a distinguished essayist of another era, was born at *5909 Germantown Avenue* on November 10, 1852. Van Dyke was one of America's most popular

Vernon

authors—an inspirational writer. The site of his birthplace is now part of the grounds of the high school.

We continue on the school side and opposite us on the corner of Haines Street is the *Germantown Municipal Building*, built in 1923. **15** (It is not open to the public.) Like so many of its kind, it has a tower; this one is the highest in Germantown. It replaced the Germantown Town Hall, which had been a hospital during the Civil War. The old town hall once held the bell and clock from the tower of Independence Hall. The clock was made by Isaiah Lukens, and the bell was the second one in the history of the State House. They were in place at Independence Hall from 1829 until 1877, when they were installed in the Germantown Town Hall. The clock was started and the bell rung on October 4 of that year, the centenary of the Battle. Although the Battle of Germantown took place almost two hundred years ago, it is marked everywhere and remembered by everyone. No other event in Germantown's history has quite the same general appeal.

16   At the end of the walk through Upper Germantown is *Vernon Park,* a charming park that has fallen on evil days. The park contains a variety of buildings and monuments, chief among the latter one to the colonists, who arrived on October 6, 1683. Their names are all here—Franz Daniel Pastorius, Dirk Herman, Abraham op Den Graeff, Tuenes Kunders, Lenert Arens, Reinert Tisen, Wilhelm Strepers, Jan Lensen, Peter Keurlis, Jan Siemens, Johann Bleikers, Abraham Tuenes, Jan Lueken and their families. Almost three hundred years ago this little band came to Germantown and amazingly enough their lands, houses and memory remain.

17   The park also contains *Vernon,* a delightful building. A sign tells us it was built in 1803, purchased by John Wister from James Matthews in 1812 and is now used as the headquarters of the Germantown Community Council, but the lovely lines of the house and its stately quality can't be disguised even if it is used for other purposes. The earliest part of the building, dating from the middle of the 18th century, is the southeastern portion of the rear wing. There is an interesting architectural feature, too—a fanlight in the pediment.

A *statue of John Wister* (1776–1862), which was erected by his grandson, Jones Wister, stands in front. At one time part of the park was owned by Melchior Meng, a horticulturist whose gardens were noted for their rare trees and shrubs. Some of these remain here today, notably several large holly trees. There is also a monument to the Battle and the Germantown Branch of the Free Library of Philadelphia is located in Vernon Park.

If lunch or dinner is desired after this long walk, there are two excellent restaurants nearby. Walk directly through Vernon Park to Greene Street, which borders the west side of the park, and at 5920 Greene is the Boswell House. Lunches are served from 11:30 until 2:00 and dinners from 4:30 until 8:00 (Sunday, 12:00–8:00) in an old-fashioned house that is comfortable and airy. The prices are reasonable and the atmosphere informal.

Farther along the street at 6020 is the Greene Hedges, which is also in an old house and equally informal. Cocktails are a feature here, and lunch can be had Tuesday through Friday, 11:30 until 2:30, with dinner from 5:30 to 9:30, except Friday and Saturday, when it is served until 10:30. There is a Sunday brunch from 11:00 to 2:30, and dinner that evening is from 5:00 to 9:00. It is closed on Monday.

Lower Germantown from Market Square to Stenton

Chelten Avenue, the busy thoroughfare that crosses Germantown, is the natural boundary between the upper and lower portions of the town. The same number 23 trolley that took us to Cliveden will serve here, but get off two blocks south of Chelten Avenue at School House Lane. An alternative is the Reading Railroad's Chestnut Hill local to the Chelten Avenue station. Then walk west to Germantown Avenue, turn left and walk two blocks. We are now at *Market Square*, one of **1** the most charming open spaces in Germantown.

As in all old towns, the market was the center of the com-

Market Square

munity's activity. The Market House was here until recently and also the engine house of the Fellowship Fire Engine Company, one of three Germantown volunteer groups. What is now a formal park was once a place of great activity. The prison and, consequently, the stocks were located here; Indian delegations on their way to Philadelphia broke their journeys here, and linen sellers and weavers used to offer their wares for sale in the square. Now only an occasional walker stops and rests on one of the benches. The greatest activity occurs on Sundays when the congregation from the Presbyterian church spills out onto it.

The "Union Soldier" at solitary rest atop the monument, so reminiscent of the Civil War memorials in most Pennsylvania and Virginia

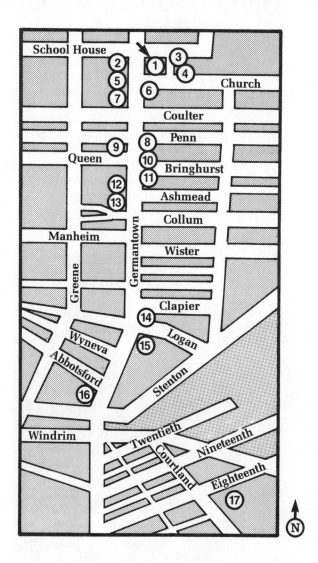

towns, has stood there since 1883, and the block on which he stands is a piece of granite from Devil's Den at Gettysburg. The cannon on the north side was from the British frigate *Augusta* (probably named for George III's mother, Princess Augusta of Wales), sunk by the Americans during the Revolution.

Our first stop is one of the most historic houses in Germantown, the *Deshler-Morris House,* facing the square at 5442 Germantown **2** Avenue. (Daily except Monday, 1:00–4:00. Admission $.50.) George Washington occupied the house on two occasions, and one might say it was the seat of government in the new Republic during two different periods in Washington's administration.

The house was built in 1772 by David Deshler, a West Indian merchant and amateur pharmacist—he was the inventor of a salve which was quite popular at the time. Five years later the Deshler-Morris House was very much in the thick of the Battle of Germantown on October 4, as the action ranged from Cliveden in Upper Germantown right down to Market Square. After the Battle, General Sir William Howe—he was very popular in Philadelphia as commander of the British forces in North America—occupied the house.

The next owner, Colonel Isaac Franks, after taking careful inventory of the furnishings and livestock, leased it to Washington during the yellow fever epidemic. The president lived there for several weeks in November, 1793, and, in spite of some difference between him and Franks about the rent and costs, he returned with Martha and her two grandchildren, Eleanor Parke Custis and George Washington Parke Custis, in July, 1794. We also know that members of Washington's cabinet—Edmund Randolph, Thomas Jefferson, Alexander Hamilton and Henry Knox—met here with the president.

Later the house was sold to Elliston and John Perot, and in 1834 to Elliston's son-in-law, Samuel B. Morris, hence the present name. A handsome portrait of the earlier Samuel Morris (1734–1812) by Meyer Dantzig after St. Mémin hangs above the stairs, and his discharge, dated January 23, 1777, is prominently displayed. It was signed by Washington when Captain Morris released the Philadelphia Troop of Light Horse (First City Troop) after its first tour of duty. We saw the home of his son, Luke Wistar Morris, on Walk 5.

The house is filled with beautiful furniture of the period, with portraits of Jonathan Trumbull, Robert Livingston and Thomas Paine, and a charming still life by James Peale (Peales are coveted in Philadelphia and many are still in private hands). Washington and his cabinet dined in the elegant dining room, and the bedrooms and the playroom on the second floor are particularly appealing. Lovely old grandfather's clocks (one made of persimmon wood with a rare cockerel finial) mark the hours. There is a life mask of George Washington and a wooden mantel from the White House. Like so many Germantown homes which were built flush with the sidewalk, this one has a magnificent side and back garden, a quiet haven for the summer months.

DESHLER-
MORRIS
HOUSE

Where yellow fever threatened
Philadelphia in 1793 and 1794
President Washington
and his family
came here as refuge here.

Open 1:00–4:00 p.m. daily
except Monday and holidays
Admission 25 cents

Operated by
THE GERMANTOWN HISTORICAL
SOCIETY
In cooperation with
NATIONAL PARK SERVICE
UNITED STATES
DEPARTMENT OF THE INTERIOR

Now walk left to the corner of School House Lane and cross over to Market Square. On the corner at 5521-23 Germantown Avenue, the building housing the Fidelity Bank is a reconstruction of the *Delaplaine House.* Walk past the bank and around the square to the *Market Square Presbyterian Church.* The structure, the third church, **3** was built in 1888, but Washington walked across the square and worshiped at an earlier one (German Reformed) erected in 1733, when he lived at the Deshler-Morris House. Services are at 11:00 on Sunday. There are cases of historic relics in the church and the Tiffany windows are particularly worth noting as is the semicircular church proper.

Just to the left on leaving the church is the handsome *From-* **4** *berger House,* which is now occupied by the Germantown Insurance Company. The First Bank of the United States is traditionally supposed to have had its offices here during the yellow fever epidemics of 1793 and 1798. Actually, the bank occupied one of the Bensell Houses which stood at 5504 Germantown Avenue. Built by John Fromberger about 1795, the house is said to have been the first brick house in Germantown—the older ones are all made of stone. From 1805 to 1811 it did house the First Bank, when that institution owned the building. The original vaults are in the cellar. It is doubtless one of the most beautiful insurance buildings in the country for the rooms

Market Square

are furnished as they appeared in the 18th century. The board room where the directors hold their meetings is furnished with the actual furniture of the time, and the formal parlor has an 18th century desk and silver inkstand worthy of any museum, in addition to the mirrors, rugs, the Waterford chandelier, tables, chairs and lowboys. The house is not open to visitors at all times, because it is a business office, but a call for an appointment (GErmantown 8-4800) usually makes it possible to see the house. Be sure also to look out the back door at the cottage near the foot of the garden—it is worthy of old England.

5   Back on Germantown Avenue again, at 5430 is the *Ashmead House*. In fact, both this property and that at 5434 were purchased in 1796 by John Ashmead, a famous Germantown carriage maker. The land at 5430 was once owned by Christopher Meng, father of John Meng (1734–54), considered by art historians to have been a fine Colonial painter who died before his promise could be fulfilled. The house at 5430 is a private residence, and that at 5434 an office.

    Most people rightly associate Louisa May Alcott with New England, her spiritual home. However, few realize that she was born at **6** *Pine Place,* 5425 Germantown Avenue, now the site of the Masonic Hall. Amos Bronson Alcott (1799–1888) was teaching at a Boston school when an invitation came in December, 1830, to teach in Germantown. It came about through the efforts of Reuben Haines, the owner of Wyck. Alcott and his bride, the former Abigail May, opened Alcott's School, and Mrs. Alcott wrote her father, "the grounds and the gardens standing back and including an acre or more all beautifully laid out." Anna, their eldest child, the Meg of *Little Women,* was born here on March 19, 1831, and on November 29, 1832, Jo herself in the person of Louisa May was born—on her father's thirty-third birthday. It is interesting to note that she only survived her father by a few weeks. When the school failed after Haines' death, the Alcotts returned to Boston in 1834, and in 1868–69 Louisa May published *Little Women,* which was to enshrine her forever in Germantown annals.

7   Opposite we find the *Friends Free Library of Germantown* at 5418, one of the earliest (1848) free libraries in the country. Three meeting houses had stood here before the present building was built in 1869. It contains more than 40,000 volumes, but no fiction. A school nearby, on the other side of the small Quaker cemetery, does have a collection of fiction, so there is a fair exchange back and forth. The library has charm and the rooms are spacious, airy and sunfilled. Dr. Samuel Longfellow, the poet's brother, called it "the best selected library in the United States." (Monday through Thursday, 9:00–4:00; Friday, 9:00–3:00; Saturday, 9:00–12:00. During the summer months, from the second Monday in June to the second Monday in September, it is open Monday and Wednesday, 2:00–6:00; Tuesday, Thursday and Friday, 9:00–1:00.)

Again we cross the Avenue to the *Clarkson-Watson House* at **8**
5275. This property now houses the costume museum of the Germantown Historical Society. (By appointment. For current hours, telephone
844-0514.) Like any costume museum, this collection is appealing to
the 20th century visitor and reflects the changes in Germantown
through almost three hundred years. It must always be borne in mind
that Germantown is only one year younger than Philadelphia; hence,
it is not only one of the oldest towns in Pennsylvania, but in the
nation. It is said that Edmund Randolph, Attorney-General in
Washington's cabinet, and Thomas Jefferson, who was Secretary of
State, lived in this house at one time. It was a common practice then
to board with families or live in a tavern and when Washington was
in residence at the Deshler-Morris House his cabinet had reason to
be in Germantown. Many of our founding fathers lived in this historic
town, along this fabled street. John Fanning Watson (1779–1860),
author of the *Annals of Philadelphia,* also lived here. His *Annals* have
proven to be invaluable to historians in later years.

Opposite us, on a diagonal, are the gates leading to *Trinity
Lutheran Church,* which was established in 1836 as an offshoot of **9**
St. Michael's. The long, narrow walk, with graves on either side
provides an outdoor aisle leading to the entrance. These are really
an extension of the peaceful and well-kept graveyard behind the
church. The building at the corner of the church property at Germantown Avenue and Queen Lane, numbered 5300, is now the *Trinity
Lutheran Church House.* (It is not open to the public.) The oldest
portion (1723) was later joined by that part built on Germantown
Avenue between 1755 and 1760 by Christopher Sower II (first spelled
Saur). Sower was the son of Germantown's first printer who produced America's first Bible in 1743 in German—years before a Bible
was printed in English in what is now the United States! Today these
Bibles are rare and highly prized by collectors and libraries. In the
basement of this house, in 1773, the first printing type of American
manufacture was cast successfully. Unfortunately, during the Revolution, when Philadelphia was occupied by the British, Sower the
Younger had published an English newspaper for them. After the
British withdrew, he was termed a collaborator and his property and
goods confiscated and sold. He died a ruined man. Trinity Lutheran
Church has a copy of the first edition (August 20, 1739) of the first
successful German-language newspaper in America. It is one of
three copies known to exist.

Diagonally opposite the Church House at 5267 Germantown
Avenue stands *Grumblethorpe,* the home of the Wister family. (By **10**
appointment: 843-4820 or 925-2251.) Built in 1744 by John Wister
a Philadelphia merchant, it has long been one of the favorite houses
of history-loving Philadelphians. Originally built as a summer home,
as Cliveden was, it eventually became Wister's year-round residence
as Cliveden did for Justice Chew. The stones for Grumbelthorpe were

quarried on the property, as were those for Cliveden, and the joists were hewn from oaks in Wister Woods, another property owned by the family.

The charm of Grumblethorpe is immediate. Its rooms are lower-ceilinged than those at Cliveden, Loudoun or Stenton and have a "cosier" appearance. In the parlor we see the "Wedding Band Ceiling," which is only a quite simple molding from which came its name. The same room has a "Courting Door" from the parlor to the street, as distinct from the front door in the entrance hall. This was used to admit the swains who came to pay court to the Wister ladies and also was used at the time of funerals!

Grumblethorpe

Grumblethorpe

The dining room is intimate and has a rusticity that the later houses of the 18th century eliminated with the grander furniture of the Philadelphia or English cabinetmakers. This room also has an amazing journeyman's bench—an intricate chest, almost like a blanket chest in size but a tool chest in complexity. The journeyman, once he had learned his trade, constructed his chest, and into it went all the skills he had learned: planing, dovetailing, doweling, decorating, the placement of hinges and locks. Anyone who could make such a chest had indeed learned his trade well. And the summer kitchen, looking out on the lovely old garden (the Wisters were interested in botany and horticulture of all kinds), reminds us that kitchens are sometimes the most inviting rooms in these old houses. One distinct museum piece in the house is a chair by Solomon Fussel, who made the chairs in Independence Hall. Grumblethorpe is one of the most appealing houses we shall visit, and it has been maintained by the Philadelphia Society for the Preservation of Landmarks, which also maintains the Powel House and the Hill-Physick-Keith House seen on Walk 3.

When the British entered Germantown for that fateful Battle which was to immortalize the village, General James Agnew occupied the house; the Wisters had withdrawn to another home to escape annoyance from British troops. Agnew was wounded during the Battle and died on the floor of the front parlor—the one with the "Courting Door." His bloodstains are still to be seen there!

After leaving Grumblethorpe to continue down the Avenue, first cross the Avenue and walk about a half-block down Queen Lane, along the side of the cemetery in back of Trinity Lutheran Church. From here, with the perspective that distance gives, we get an entirely different view of the front of Grumblethorpe with its small balcony, which was restored in recent times.

11 Just below Queen Lane, on the Grumblethorpe side of the street, at 5203 and 5205 Germantown Avenue, are the *Wister Houses* that were occupied by Dr. Owen Wister and his wife, Sarah Butler. Mrs. Wister was the daughter of Pierce Butler and the beautiful Fanny Kemble, the English actress who was a niece of Mrs. Siddons. In this house their son Owen Wister was born in 1860. He later achieved fame in his own right as the author of the perennial classic, *The Virginian* (1902), which turned many Americans into readers of the western novel. Fanny Kemble's portraits by Thomas Sully are in The Pennsylvania Academy of the Fine Arts. The desk that Owen Wister used, when writing *The Virginian*, is in Grumblethorpe.

12 Opposite the Wister houses on a diagonal, at 5208–5226, is the complex now owned by the Germantown Historical Society, one of the most active such groups in the nation. (For hours, phone 844-0514.) The buildings which make up this group are the Colonial "Squire" *Baynton House*, which contains the Society's library; the *Conyngham-Hacker House*, the main museum of furniture, china and folk art; the *Howell House*, a toy and quilt museum; the *Endt House*, the scene of the First Unity Conference of German Protestant Sects in 1743 and now used as a residence; and the *Bechtel House*, used for residential and storage purposes. All of these buildings date from between 1740 and 1772, and one can spend as much time as one likes looking over the exhibits.

13 Two sites known only to the real historian are just a memory. *Gilbert Stuart's studio*, which was located at 5140 and no longer stands, and the *Barron House* at 5106. During the summers from 1796 to 1799 Stuart painted in a small stone building at the rear of 5140. Here he painted the portrait of Washington now in the Boston Athenaeum and the Lansdowne portrait on display at The Pennsylvania Academy of the Fine Arts. His full-length portrait of "Cornplanter," the Indian chief, was done here as well. The Barron House was owned by Commodore James Barron from 1839 to 1845. It was Barron who killed Stephen Decatur in a duel at Bladensburg, Maryland, in March, 1820. We saw Decatur's grave in St. Peter's churchyard on Walk 3 and also saw the silver pitcher Barron gave to Dr. Physick, in the Hill-Physick-Keith House.

We shall walk south about eight blocks through a rather run-down part of the Avenue and, while we won't see any historic buildings en route, we shall find some at the end of this trek.

In Walk 11 we saw the Upper Burying Ground, next to the Concord School; here some eight blocks below the Wister House is the *Lower Burial Ground* at the corner of Logan Street. A walk **14** through this old cemetery is a step into the past. In 1692 Leonard Arets set aside by deed a half-acre of ground for burial purposes for Lower Germantown. By 1750 this cemetery was becoming crowded, so the trustees limited burials to citizens of Lower Germantown, and, as in so many cemeteries of the time, a space was designated as "Strangers' Ground."

Here among the old trees, rose bushes and weathered stones lie 41 soldiers who fought in the Revolution and soldiers from the War of 1812, the Seminole, Mexican and Civil wars. One of the graves of interest is that of Sergeant Charles S. Bringhurst, who three times climbed to the rampart atop Fort Sumter to replace the flag when it was shot down by the Confederates during the opening engagement of the Civil War. The earliest tombstone is of Samuel Coulson who died at the age of nine weeks on October 18, 1707.

William Hood, a Germantown resident, gave the money for the front wall and gate in exchange for being allowed to select his own burial spot near the entrance. Hood died in Paris in 1850 and was buried in the grave he had chosen on the very day the work was completed on the entrance gate and wall. The cemetery isn't usually open except Saturdays in late spring, summer and early autumn.

Before descending the hill, note the *Mehl House* at 4821 and the **15** *Ottinger House* at 4825. Both houses, now private residences, were built before the middle of the 18th century and served as barracks for Hessian troops during the Battle. When the driveways were being paved recently, the remains of several soldiers were found (probably buried in the garden which was not uncommon in those days). The barn at the rear of the Mehl House was built, in part, in 1742 and now serves as the theatre for the Germantown Theatre Guild. There are tunnels in the cellar of the Mehl House, but no adequate explanation has ever been given for their origin. The Ottinger House was first acquired in 1785 by a coachmaker, Christopher Ottinger, and remained in the family's hands until 1929. Many of the homes of Germantown remained in family hands for well over a century.

We are now on *Neglee's Hill,* a section of the most historic areas. Descending, cross over the Avenue from the Mehl and Ottinger Houses, and below Wyneva Street at the corner of Abbotsford Road, find *Loudoun,* one of the glories of Germantown and of Philadelphia. **16** (By appointment: 248-0235. $1.50.) Built about 1801 by Thomas Armat, it commands a promontory and creates an illusion that we are back two centuries in time.

The original house or the east end was built in 1801, the west end in 1810, and the Greek portico in 1830 at the height of the Greek Revival, and as late as 1888 a two-story loft was added. The house, incidentally, was named after Loudoun County, Virginia, where Thomas Armat first settled when he came to America from Cumberland, England. This imposing Federal house stands 30 feet above the

Avenue and some 100 feet back from it, lending it an aspect of grace and serenity. Inside are furniture and paintings of the 18th, early 19th, the later Victorian period, and the 20th centuries. Over the course of five generations of one family are reflected changing styles and fashions in the decorative arts.

There are many reasons for seeing Loudoun—but it is worthy of a visit solely to see the splendid brick-floored kitchen in the basement. The old dressers for dishes, the worn and richly-hewn table, the generous fireplace, the pots and utensils that made up the culinary kingdom of the great house are all here to see. It has the richness of an English or early American tavern.

In 1819 Jane Caroline, daughter of Thomas Wright Armat (son of the builder), married her cousin William Armatt, of Baltimore, and the spelling of the name changed. Their daughter Anna in turn married Gustavus G. Logan, great-great-grandson of James Logan, William Penn's secretary who was the builder of Stenton. Gustavus was also the grandson of John Dickinson, author of the *Letters from a Farmer in Pennsylvania*, for whom Dickinson College, Carlisle, Pennsylvania, was named. Dickinson refused to sign the Declaration of Independence on principle, but in spite of his Quaker beliefs he served in the Continental Army. The nation was small, and prominent families knew each other in those days, so it was not unusual for someone like Gustavus to have two famous forebears. Unfortunately, despite them, he was a bounder and abandoned his wife and children abroad. Maria Dickinson Logan, the daughter of Anna and Gustavus, lived in the house until her death in 1939 when she, like so many foresighted Philadelphians before her, bequeathed Loudoun and its treasures to her native city. Among Maria Dickinson Logan's papers

Loudoun

after her death was also found evidence that, had Philadelphia remained the nation's capital, the capitol itself was to have been built where Loudoun now stands.

We must also pay tribute to James Skerett, the second husband of Jane Caroline Armatt (1798–1856). A man of taste and discernment, it was he who had the vision and the money to furnish Loudoun as we see it today.

And best of all, Loudoun has a ghost! He is referred to familiarly as "Little Willie," but he is (or was) William Armat Logan (1852–60), a son of Gustavus and Anna. "Little Willie," it is thought, was backward, but backward or not, he is still active and things happen at Loudoun to indicate that he is about—such as finding the books in the library out of order from time to time.

The tour of Lower Germantown began with the Deshler-Morris House, one of the finest examples of its kind but a simpler house than, say, Loudoun or Stenton, the one we are about to see. The four finest examples of domestic architecture in Lower Germantown are the three mentioned and, of course, Grumblethorpe.

Finding Stenton is a bit more difficult than locating any of the others. Walk down the hill from Loudoun to the Wayne Junction Station of the Reading Railroad. Then cross over and walk down Windrim Avenue four blocks to 18th Street, keeping the railroad tracks on the left. Stenton is situated in the confines of Stenton Park, a striking 18th century jewel in the midst of 20th century industrialism and bad housing. When Logan lived here, however, this was country, and all the land about Stenton looked much as Stenton Park does today.

Stenton (Tuesday–Saturday, 1:00–5:00; $1.50) was once the home of **17** one of Philadelphia's greatest citizens, James Logan (1674–1751), but today he is eclipsed in the public mind by William Penn and Benjamin Franklin and the Signers of the Declaration of Independence. He came to Pennsylvania in 1699 as secretary to Penn and, when Penn returned to England in 1701, Logan was appointed attorney for the Proprietors (the Penns). He remained in this office of confidential secretary for half a century as well as holding public offices in the Colonies.

Logan made many contributions to the city (Logan Circle was named for him), but we probably remember him today for only two. One is his magnificent library of over 2,000 volumes, which was the basis of the Loganian Library, now housed in the Library Company of Philadelphia, 1314 Locust Street, visited on Walk 6.

Our other memory is a visual one—the splendid 18th century manor, Stenton, and its various buildings and gardens which were contained on a plantation of 511 acres acquired between 1723 and 1730. The house itself was finished by 1730. And what is more, this "compleat" 18th century man designed it himself and named it for his father's birthplace in East Lothian, Scotland.

Stenton

The generous entrance hall, the expansive stairway and the ample dining room and library invite the visitor to linger. The dining room has a "whispering closet," where a servant could be stationed to listen to visitors before the Logans joined their guests. The closet had an opening into the hall, screened by slats, and a door folded back over this part of the wall, so the visitor couldn't know he was being overheard. The 18th century's version of wire tapping!

The parlor is completely paneled and has handsome Delft tiles around the fireplace. The firebacks were made at Durham Furnace, in which Logan had an interest. The boats developed and owned by the furnace were used by Washington and his troops to cross the Delaware, not the small ones depicted in the well-known painting.

Logan, who was in general merchandising, was also a farmer, one of the larger fur traders, and he owned part of a ship with Robert Trent for whom Trenton, New Jersey, is named. He was a good businessman, invested his money well and prospered in the New World. In addition he corresponded with some of the finest minds of his age and he knew many languages, possibly some Arabic. When he read in Latin, he made his notations in the margins of the book in Latin and, when he read in Greek, he did the same in that language.

The library off the entrance hall, or at least the one which is thought to have been his reading room, had window seats. He, like others of his time, would begin reading at one window seat and as the sun changed would move to another and another, always benefitting by the sun over his shoulder.

One charming aspect of Stenton today is the absence of electrical fixtures, although there are some outlets hidden from view, so we see it in the light that Logan and his family did. When the light begins to lower and fade toward late afternoon, the shadowy aspects of the rooms add a sombre note.

General Sir William Howe chose Stenton as his headquarters from which to direct the Battle of Germantown and Washington had the good sense to occupy it on August 23, 1777, on his way to oppose Howe at the Brandywine. It is the only house in Germantown to have been used by both commanders as headquarters. Washington dined here later, on July 8, 1787, with Dr. George Logan, when he was in Philadelphia to attend the Constitutional Convention.

James Logan was succeeded by worthy descendants—except Gustavus who deserted his family in Europe. His eldest son William (1718–76) succeeded him as attorney for the Penn family and William's son Dr. George L. (1753–1821) received his medical degree from the University of Edinburgh (the Logans returned to the land of their forefathers for their education). George's wife, Deborah Norris, the first woman member of the Historical Society of Pennsylvania, preserved the correspondence between Penn and Logan and history will forever be in her debt for this. It is interesting that Deborah wasn't very fond of Thomas Jefferson—his liberal views were probably too much for her. The family continued to live on this gracious estate in this sixteen-room house for six generations until it became the property of the City in 1900. It is maintained by the National Society of The Colonial Dames of America in the Commonwealth of Pennsylvania.

Before leaving Stenton we should look at the *log house*, which was built about 1790 as a barn. It stood for many years at 16th and

Race Streets on the grounds of the Friends Select School until, in 1969, it was moved to its present location to preserve it. With some alterations to the interior, it now serves as a home for Stenton's custodians. When it stood in the shadow of City Hall, it served as a home for the caretakers of the Friends Buiying Ground, then a home for faculty members and a classroom facility for the Friends Select School.

After the walk through Lower Germantown we can return along Windrim Avenue to the Wayne Junction Station of the railroad. The trains stop here with great frequency, so by checking the posted schedules we can get a train into the Reading Station, 12th and Market Streets, in ten minutes. Or we can return to Center City by way of the southbound number 23 trolley.

Suggested Readings

Still one of the most delightful books on Philadelphia, although long out-of-print, is Agnes Repplier's *Philadelphia, the Place and the People* (Macmillan, 1898). It is witty, astringent and written in a lively manner. No wonder those who remember Miss Repplier recall her as the doyenne of Philadelphia letters.

In another and more contemporary vein, and equally enjoyable, is Nathaniel Burt's *The Perennial Philadelphians* (Little, Brown, 1963). There is no aspect of Philadelphia and Philadelphians that the author hasn't uncovered, dissected and examined with warmth, compassion and a certain detachment.

Anonymous, but vastly entertaining and gossipy is *Philadelphia Scrapple* (Dietz Press, 1956). It set the city humming when it was published. Obviously the work of more than one author, the book is written with authority even though its tone is light and ever so mocking.

No perusal of Philadelphia history would be complete without consulting Carl and Jessica Bridenbaugh's *Rebels and Gentlemen* (Reynal and Hichcock, 1942). The book has stood the test of time well—forty-odd years now—and the reader is always aware of the authority behind it.

Unfortunately Christopher Morley's *Travels in Philadelphia* (McKay, 1920) is dated for the reader of the present day who knows little or nothing about Philadelphia of 50 or 60 years ago. Originally written as a series of newspaper essays, the book is filled with city lore and written with a love which shines through. However, much which Morley wrote about is gone, so the essays should be read as period pieces of a time past, written by a gentle spirit imbued with a rich sense of humor.

In a different vein, and a delight for layman and scholar alike, is *Miracle at Philadelphia, The Story of the Constitutional Convention, May to September 1787,* by Catherine Drinker Bowen (Atlantic-Little, Brown, 1960). This distinguished biographer brings alive the men and the events of this crucial period and gives the reader a new awareness of our heritage.

Unlike all the others mentioned is *The Worlds of Chippy Patterson* by Arthur H. Lewis (Harcourt, Brace, 1960). C. Stuart Patterson, Jr., was a Philadelphia aristocrat born to privilege. He devoted his life to defending the lowly, the criminals, the denizens of Skid Row in the courts of law. Although he died over 40 years ago, there are many Philadelphians who remember this brilliant Philadelphia gentleman with a great heart and a passion for the downtrodden.

No source could be of greater value than Scharf and Westcott's *History of Philadelphia* (1884). It is a mine of information and need not be read from beginning to end. A chance turning of a page, or a look into a random chapter, can prove a delight to historian and layman alike.

ABOUT THE AUTHOR

John Francis Marion is a Philadelphia historian whose books cover a wide range of subjects. His *Famous and Curious Cemeteries* was honored by the Athenaeum of Philadelphia with a citation naming it the "outstanding work of nonfiction" by a Philadelphian during 1978.

Mr. Marion was born in Norfolk, Virginia, and was educated at the Pennsylvania State University. He entered book publishing in 1953 as Promotion Director of the J. B. Lippincott Company. Following that he was for ten years Editor-in-Chief of the Chilton Book Company. Since 1972 he has devoted himself exclusively to writing and lecturing. His articles have appeared in the *New York Times,* the *Christian Science Monitor,* the *Philadelphia Inquirer,* the Philadelphia *Bulletin* and *Smithsonian* magazine.

Mr. Marion's books include *Bicentennial City: Walking Tours of Historic Philadelphia, Lucrezia Bori of the Metropolitan Opera, The Charleston Story* and *Philadelphia Medica,* a tribute to the city's distinguished history in medicine. In 1980 he published *The Fine Old House,* a history of the SmithKline Corporation. His latest work is *Within These Walls,* the story of Philadelphia's Academy of Music.

Index

203

CREDITS

Credits and sources are given in the order in which illustrations appear in the text. Abbreviations have been used in some cases: AKM, Atwater Kent Museum; CP/OCR, City of Philadelphia, Office of the City Representative; FLP, Free Library of Philadelphia; INHP, Independence National Historical Park; PAFA, Pennsylvania Academy of the Fine Arts; PCPC, Philadelphia City Planning Commission; PCVB, Philadelphia Convention and Visitors Bureau; PHC, Pennsylvania Historical Commission; PMA, Philadelphia Museum of Art; PPD/FLP, Print and Picture Department, Free Library of Philadelphia; UP, University of Pennsylvania.

Frontmatter, P. v, INHP. P. vi, Rare Book Department, FLP. P. viii, copyright Bernie Cleff, photographer. P. x, Alois K. Strobl, PCPC. P. xiv, PCVB.

Walk 1. P. 2, FLP. P. 5, CP/OCR. P. 6, The Carpenters' Company of the City and County of Philadelphia. P. 9, Alois K. Strobl, PCPC. Pp. 11-12, INHP. P. 15, AKM; AKM, Robert C. Grant, photographer.

Walk 2. Pp. 21-22, Christ Church, Jules Schick, photographer. P. 23, INHP. P. 24, The National Archives. P. 28, PPD/FLP; PCVB. P. 33, Christ Church, Jules Schick, photographer. P. 34, Alois K. Strobl, PCPC; CP/OCR.

Walk 3. P. 41, Alois K. Strobl, PCPC. Pp. 42 and 46, Cortlandt V.D. Hubbard. P. 51, Philadelphia Redevelopment Authority; CP/OCR. P. 52, Alois K. Strobl, PCPC. P. 57, Cortlandt V.D. Hubbard.

Walk 4. P. 59, Alois K. Strobl, PCPC. P. 62, PHC. P. 65, Cortlandt V.D. Hubbard; INHP. Pp. 66-67, PHC.

Walk 5. P. 72, PCVB. P. 75, private collection. P. 76, Cortlandt V.D. Hubbard. P. 78, drawing by George Gerba, courtesy of Walnut Street Theatre. Pp. 81 and 83, Pennsylvania Hospital.

Walk 6. P. 85, PPD/FLP. P. 89, PAFA, Harris & Davis, photographers; PAFA. P. 90, Alois K. Strobl, PCPC. P. 94, collection of the author. P. 95, PCVB. P. 97, St. Luke and the Epiphany Church. P. 98, The Historical Society of Pennsylvania; INHP. P. 100, Library Company of Philadelphia.

Walk 7. P. 104, PCVB. P. 105, Jules Schick. P. 108, detail from an etching by Pravoslav Sovak, commissioned by and courtesy of the Print Club. P. 111, Frederick F. Willis. P. 113, The Rosenbach Foundation, Charles P. Mills & Son, photography.

Walk 8. P. 123, Cortlandt V.D. Hubbard; UP, Lawrence S. Williams, Inc., photography. P. 124, UP. P. 126, UP, Frank Ross, photographer. P. 129, UP. P. 120, Drexel University, Eugene H. Mapsik, photographer.

Walk 9. Pp. 133-135, Alois K. Strobl, PCPC. P. 137, PPD/FLP. P. 139; (Swann Fountain photographs) CP/OCR; (Elkins Library) Rare Book Department, FLP. P. 140, PMA; John Francis Marion. P. 142, PMA. P. 143, PMA, A.J. Wyatt, staff photographer. P. 145, PCVB, J.J. Barton, photographer. P. 146, PCVB.

Walk 10. P. 151, Cortlandt V.D. Hubbard. P. 152, PMA. P. 153, PCVB; CP/OCR. Pp. 155 and 157, PMA. P. 159, PMA; PPD/FLP. Pp. 161 and 163, PMA. P. 165, PPD/FLP. P. 167, PCVB.

Walk 11. P. 172, Historic American Buildings Survey, Jack E. Boucher, photographer. P. 174, CP/OCR. P. 179, Cortlandt V.D. Hubbard. P. 180, John Francis Marion. P. 183, CP/OCR.

Walk 12. Pp. 185, 188, 189, CP/OCR. Pp. 192-193, Cortlandt V.D. Hubbard. P. 196, John Francis Marion. P. 198, Cortlandt V.D. Hubbard. P. 202, INHP.